THE WILDERNESS WORLD of CAMERON McNEISH

ESSAYS FROM BEYOND THE BLACK STUMP

www.theinpinn.co.uk

The In Pinn is an imprint of
Neil Wilson Publishing
303a The Pentagon Centre
36 Washington Street
GLASGOW
G3 8AZ
Tel: 0141-221-1117
Fax: 0141-221-5363
E-mail: info@nwp.sol.co.uk
www.theinpinn.co.uk

A catalogue record for this book is available from the British
Library.
ISBN 1-903238-30-7
Typset in Aldine

Printed in China
by RDC Group Ltd

CONTENTS

FOREWORD

The ridge from A'Chioch to Ben More on the island of Mull is a steep, rocky and immensely enjoyable route to the summit of one of Scotland's finest mountains. You clamber round and over rock outcrops; you catch your breath as a bird of prey efffortlessly soars overhead; you stride along a ridge with sweeping slopes and corries beside you; and you arrive at the summit with the sea glinting in the sunlight and the whole of Scotland's western seaboard spread out across the horizon. It was a few years ago that I last made this journey, together with Cameron McNeish. We were filming a walk across Mull for the *Wilderness Walks* series; and our walk ran the whole range of sun, rain, mist and snow, whilst we covered steep hillsides, long and empty glens, and some of the wildest and most desolate moorland you will find anywhere. We crossed one single-track road in the entire journey.

Experiencing the wilderness of mountain and corrie, of moorland and wide empty spaces, is an essential part of discovering both our humanity and our spirituality. In this book Cameron McNeish takes us by the hand and leads us through a series of such experiences. Rooted firmly in an abiding love for his homeland of Scotland, he ranges with us across the world too. We learn what it is to feel small, to be humble, to sense the proper perspective of our place in a vast world, to experience fear. And we also learn what it is to be enchanted and uplifted and to feel through the physical encounter with wild nature to something much deeper.

There could be no better guide than Cameron. He is passionate about the wilderness. He knows the hills better than anyone. His journey takes us to some familiar places, like the quartzite ridges of Beinn Eighe or the great sweeping dome of Beinn Macdui or the plunging waterfall of the Grey Mare's Tail in the Border hills. He surprises us with the unfamiliar, too, in the rock-strewn jumble of hills that makes up the heart of Knoydart or the sunshine mountains of southern Spain. This is a book for savouring memories, for culling ideas, for stopping for a moment to think.

To stand on a high mountain with corries and ridges and far horizons all around you; to listen to the distant roaring of water; to see the sea glistening in the west; to perceive the world in a tiny delicate flower or a crag-lined peak rearing out of the mist: this is the stuff of wilderness. This book helps us to touch it and to treasure it. What is more, it helps us to understand it.

Rt Hon Chris Smith, MP

April 2001

ACKNOWLEDGEMENTS

My name might grace this book's title but there is a huge supporting cast. A wilderness world might suggest a pretty solitary existence, a place lacking in human company, but even as someone who more often than not walks alone, backpacks alone and scribbles alone I'm very aware that over the years I have grasped, with varying degrees of gratitude, the ideas, philosophies and advice of many individuals. Without their input my wilderness world would have been a harsher, poorer place.

First of all warmest thanks go to Peter Lumley and Roger Smith who, all those years ago, had enough confidence to allow a wet-behind-the-ears but enthusiastic young mountain writer access to the pages of their outdoor magazines. Both are firm friends to this day. In the broadcast media I owe thanks to the late Murdoch MacPherson, Christopher Lowell and Neil Fraser of the BBC and to Richard Else of Triple Echo Productions, my producer and director on the BBC2 *Wilderness Walks* television series.

Even in such solitary activities as backpacking, mountaineering and wilderness travel we are rarely removed from the inspiration of those who pounded the trails and climbed the hills before us. Such inspiration, and much encouragement, has come from my peers too, fellow hill-goers, colleagues and co-protagonists in the ongoing battles for the protection of our wild places.

Individuals like Tom Weir, the late Bill Murray, Hamish Brown, Jim Perrin, Chris Townsend, Chris Brasher, Jim Crumley, Dick Balhary and Dave Morris here in the UK, and Ray and Jenny Jardine and Annie and Dave Getchell in the US, have all given freely of their knowledge and experience to make this writer's time in the wild places so much more meaningful. Tim Greening, Glen Rowley and Rex Munro of KE Adventure Travel have helped expand my horizons to some of the more remote corners of the planet.

For permission to plunder and re-work various features I have written for their newspapers over the past few years I'm indebted to Ken Smith of the *Strathspey and Badenoch Herald* and Andrew Jaspan of the *Sunday Herald* and to the authors of all those books mentioned in the bibliography who have, to a greater or lesser degree, inspired, motivated, enthralled and challenged me. My friend and colleague John Manning has given the tremendous benefit of his copy-editing skills and once again Neil Wilson has shown a confidence in my ability to produce a book that I'm not sure I've ever really warranted. May his faith be rewarded…

Sincere thanks go to Chris Smith, who escapes from the smoke-filled corridors of power whenever he can to enjoy the delights of highland hills, for taking time from a particularly hectic schedule to write the foreword to this book. I am indedted to him. To my good friend and neighbour John Hood I want to give a special thanks for his enduring patience when my writing projects have largely determined the destination of so many of our mountain trips together, and I'm so aware that the mountain-bum lifestyle I enjoy so much could never have been possible if it hadn't been for the forbearance and serenity of my wife Gina who, I'm delighted to say, has enthusiastically embraced the mountain-bum lifestyle herself in recent years.

Cameron McNeish

A SONG WORTH SINGING

It was cold and crisp this morning, with a vibrant freshness that suggested winter had well and truly arrived. A pall of smoke hung above the village, suggesting a stirring of life in these early wintry hours. A limp haze hung over the river valley and softened the harshness of the frosty scene. The river itself was unusually pensive, subdued, its higher tributaries probably frozen and choked with ice and snow.

But on the middle ground, on the high moors, the streams and burns still sang their songs and I wanted to march to their tune. Here was a light-hearted mood, a light classical gaiety, and I would match my stride to their whim. I was, as always on this daily walk, expectant, and I wasn't to be disappointed. The sense of elevation, the rhythms, the infinite variety of natural colours combined to create a very special melody. Whatever the rest of the morning brought I knew I would march to the greatest rhythm on Earth, the heartbeat of the land.

Music is a gift that the native cultures of Australia suggest we owe our very existence to and it's intriguing that the aborigines believe their ancestors *sang* the world into being. The songs their ancestors sang created the land itself – and the animals, the birds and plants. Even today native Australians go walkabout in the outback to experience what they call the 'songlines', singing the old songs and tunes and thereby continuing the very essence of creation.

Similarly, the North American native culture gave importance to the chants and rhythms of their tribal songs, singing to the plants and the beasts before harvesting or hunting. In the 7th century, Caedmon, who is remembered in Poets' Corner in Westminster Abbey as the first poet of Anglo-Saxon England, once had a dream when he was a young man working in the stables and gardens of the Abbess Hilda of Whitby. In this dream he was told by an angel to lift his voice and sing, and when he meekly enquired what he should sing he was commanded to sing of the glories of creation! In a sense that's what this book is all about.

For the past 25 years I've had the privilege of being able to sing of the glories of creation through articles and books I've written, through television and radio programmes I've made and through the magazines I've edited. It's been an evangelical work, spreading the good news of the joys of mountains and wild places, a work that has taken me to some of the most beautiful places on Earth. The *raison d'etre* of such evangelism is to encourage people to explore mountains and wild places for themselves, in the belief that as folk get to know these areas they might begin to love them and be prepared to fight for them when developments come along that threaten their beauty and sanctity.

"Where would the world be," wrote the poet Gerard Manley Hopkins, "once bereft of wet and of wildness? Let them be left. O let them be left, wildness and wet; Long live the weeds and the wilderness yet."

For an increasing number of people the word 'wilderness' is symbolic of a landscape that is wild, remote, spiritually uplifting and mercifully free of the excesses of mankind. Unfortunately my dictionary defines the word as: "tract of land uncultivated and uninhabited by human beings; waste; desert; wild; state of confusion."

As someone who is frequently introduced as Scotland's Mister Wilderness you'll understand why this particular definition fails to enthral me!

Now and again I become faintly irritated by those who suggest that there is no such thing as wilderness in the UK. Because man has touched all our wild areas in some way or form doesn't necessarily mean that such landscape has lost its ability to excite us, to refresh us, to help teach us our place in a larger, more cosmic scale of things. Perhaps we should consider this word 'wilderness' as an adjective rather than a noun, an adjective that essentially defines a quality that produces a particular mood or emotion in us when faced with wild land.

In the definition of the word as producer Richard Else and I recognised it for our television programmes *Wilderness Walks*, we brought together two popular conceptions of 'wilderness' – a landscape that is beautiful and spiritually uplifting, and at the same time a landscape that appears to be inhospitable and threatening. By bringing together these two emotions we discovered a definition that was infinitely more satisfactory than the negative quality most dictionaries suggest. We were attracted by the notion of wilderness as a landscape that brings those sensations of mystery and tacit threat together with the more acceptable appearance of beauty and sanctity.

While such a definition fulfils the landscape value of wilderness it also suggests challenge, risk and uncertainty, perhaps even adventure. As someone who is essentially a mountaineer, in the widest sense of the word, I'm attracted to that concept but wilderness has a function way beyond that of an adventure arena.

Thousands of people are discovering that wilderness offers them a sanctuary, a haven, somewhere they can escape the growing pressures of burgeoning urbanisation.

It's even been written that the greatest value wilderness has to mankind is the healing of psychological wounds, and mountain, lakes and forests could well become our psychiatrists. Can you imagine it? Stress therapy will be solitude and silence scheduled at regular intervals. And all on the NHS!

But even by the above definition we have relatively few wilderness areas left in the UK and certainly nothing of the uncultivated and untouched landscapes that can be found in other countries of the world. We have little land that is unaffected by agriculture, forestry, hydro or urban growth but, even so, a rising swell of opinion suggests that our remaining wild areas are well-worth preserving. Indeed, given the political will and the necessary funding, our countryside, and in particular our mountain areas, could well return to something of their former glory and in future years be recognised not as the opposite of civilisation, but as an essential part of it.

What we desperately need is a more measured and sustainable management of our mountain environment in a way that not only recognises the needs and aspirations of the human communities who live there but a management process that recognises mountain walking and climbing as a genuine land use. We can forever discuss and debate subjects like sustainable management of mountains and the conservation and preservation of mountain landscapes but we have to ask ourselves some very fundamental questions, the most notable being: "What are our mountains for?"

Not long before he died, Bill Murray, Scotland's most articulate mountaineer, answered that very question in a little booklet called *Scotland's Mountains: An Agenda for Sustainable Development*. This is what he wrote:

"Walking and mountaineering can certainly teach how vital wild land is to our physical and spiritual health. It teaches values, gives purpose and enjoyment. But wild land is not there simply to minister to our needs of recreation. Beware the exploiters who blindly assert that 'mountains exist for public enjoyment' and then proceed, for expedient motives or money, to destroy the very qualities that most make the mountains worth knowing – their natural beauty and quiet. Land and wildlife have their own being in their own right. Our recreation is an incidental gain, not an end in itself to be profitably pursued by exploiting land where that means degrading it. The human privilege is to take decisions for more than our own good; our reward, that it turns out to be best for us too."

I hope this book of essays is in line with Bill Murray's thinking; I hope its spirit is one of reverence for and celebration of wild places, not in the normal anthropocentric view of man being dominant, or even as man having stewardship of the Earth, but offering instead an ecocentric perspective that suggests the Earth does not belong to man but, conversely, man belongs to the Earth.

Increasingly I'm aware of wilderness as something else, not as an arena for conquering nature, nor as a racetrack, nor as a playground in which I can try to sharpen my personal spirit of achievement, but as a place of worship. Through the spirit of wilderness and through the grace that spirit offers us, the achievement we gain is measured more in terms of fulfilment and depth-of-being rather than how many mountains we can climb over a long weekend.

For more than 35 years I've frequently hitched my pack on to my back and eased myself into these wilderness areas. I've climbed the Munros and the Corbetts. I've backpacked the trails and climbed the crags. I've trekked the distant ranges and even climbed some big mountains. I've loved it all and learned from it and my life has been enriched by exposure to wilderness. But the experience of the years has taught me something far more fundamental, far more discerning.

I've realised that wilderness and wild landscapes have allowed me to discover realms of my own life that I was previously unaware of. That some curious healing process takes place every time I rediscover wilderness as a world filled with adventure and alive with spirit, a world in which I've been able to transcend the limits of my own human-centred thinking.

As Bill Murray so eloquently wrote, wild land teaches values, gives purpose and enjoyment and we are fortunate that the capacity to experience such benefits is our birthright.

The ability to understand such things as sacred is our choice.

Bill Murray once told me that the publishers of his first book, *Mountaineering in Scotland*, told him they thought it had too much 'spiritual' content and asked him to tone it down. He refused and many thousands of inspired readers have appreciated the benefits of that decision. I don't believe it is possible to separate the mountains from the mystic – take the sacred out of wilderness and you're left with the cold, dead relics of the Earth's bones.

Mountains and wilderness areas are universally recognised as symbols of religious aspiration and I think the Psalmist had it right when he wrote: "I will lift up my eyes unto the hills, from whence cometh my help?"

But note the question mark at the end of that plea! Popular usage of the quote has missed out the fact that the Psalmist wasn't making a declaration, he was asking a question.

His help wasn't the hills but, as he goes on to declare: "my help cometh from the Lord who maketh Heaven and Earth."

His help came from the god who had created the hills, the god who had infused the earth with life and spirit.

It's in this spirituality, this sacredness, that we can begin to gain full measure of the worth of the mountains. It's in this aspect of the mountain's character that saints, sinners, philosophers, writers and artists have sought refuge, not to escape from something but to discover it! It's this aspect of wilderness that gave our aboriginal forefathers a meaning in life, a purpose, a belief system that supported them and gave them a reverence for the land, a reverence that has been absent since our western Judaeo-Christian culture first saw wilderness as something without soul, the dwelling-place of the Antichrist, a landscape to be tamed, robbed and ravished.

Our ancestors' reverence for wild landscape might have been absent from western culture in recent decades but I don't believe it is ever fully lost. It is, as wilderness poet Gary Snyder suggests: "... perennially within us, dormant as a hard-shelled seed, awaiting the fire or flood that awakes it again."

The Wilderness World of Cameron McNeish breaks down into various strands – some philosophical observations, some feisty arguments, several environmental pleas and much idealistic speculation. All of it is laid against the bedrock from where much of it grew – the mountains and wild areas of Scotland.

It's my hope that something in it might spark off the fire that awakens a reverence for the land in the reader, and that which was dormant may rise from the flames into a new and fresh awareness of the wonder of those parts of our landscape we can truly call wild.

Rise, lift your voice and sing to the glories of creation – it's a song worth singing.

CHAPTER ONE

WILDERNESS
CONNECTIONS

It's often been said that modern man has lost touch with the landscape and that the only way to get back in touch with the organic, living world in which we live is to return to the wild places as often as possible. To try to re-connect. This connection is the Holy Grail of the wilderness traveller, a self-transcendence that allows us to push forward the boundaries of our own being...

The trailhead is a North American term for that place where the tarmac stops and the dusty trail begins. Australians refer to it as the black stump. Sometimes this road-end is no more than a parking space at the edge of a forest. It might be a muddy, churned up turning area at the end of a single track road or it might be a proper car park. However it appears in reality the trailhead is heavy in symbolism. This 'black stump' is a portal, our gateway to dreams, a physical and at the same time a psychological cross-over between leaving what we would call civilisation and what lies beyond.

The more urban the trailhead is, the greater is the mental impact when leaving it.

Some American National Parks assign specific backpacker campgrounds at the trailhead. Such a campground isolates the tiny backpacker tents from the recreational vehicles (RVs) and the trailers, the lightweight nuts from the mobile condominium freaks who no doubt enjoy their own brand of wilderness experience once they can break free from wrestling 30-foot-long motor-homes around mountain roads.

One man's wilderness, after all, is another man's roadside picnic…

The designated backpacker campground in California's Yosemite Valley is a friendly place where the camaraderie of a shared passion brings folk together over a simmering stove or around a dusk campfire. National Park rangers invariably appear at some stage to ostensibly check up on wilderness permits but, I suspect, more because they identify with those who are seeking the wilderness and all its joys.

"Hi, how you doing? Where you from?"

"Scotland," I reply, "Here to enjoy the sun and the warmth of Yosemite."

"What brings you over here?"

"Oh, the mountains, the forests, the wilderness (you can talk about wilderness in America, refer to it as such in your conversations and people don't think you're being fanciful), just chilling out for a few days."

"Well you have yourself a great time, and mind those bears, they're getting kinda active these days."

"Thanks, and I will… got my bear-proof food container. I'll be fine."

She wanders off to the next tent, resplendent in her green National Park uniform, full of *bonhomie* and cheeriness. I get back to packing my gear, eager to be off and curiously nervy about the 4,000ft climb into the Yosemite high country, the rolling pine-covered hills that lie beyond the black stump.

This nervousness invariably appears right out of the blue, a tension that can't be put down to any single cause. I know I'm capable of climbing 4,000ft with a 40lb pack and I know that if I find it tough going all I have to do is slow down a bit, become a tortoise for a while instead of a hare. I'm also aware that time is not at a premium – seven days lie before me, seven days to wander the trails in a desultory stravaig, merely following my fancies. Seven days to enjoy the rare luxury of doing what I want, when I want to do it, in one of the most remarkable landscapes in the world.

But there's a danger in portraying such luxury as some kind of wilderness idyll. It's rarely that, even if the sudden and dramatic change of lifestyle is more often than not mentally and spiritually rewarding.

Often it's a case of trading one set of fears and anxieties for another, little problems that in their own way can create shadows which threaten all prospect of recreation, problems that might be simply annoying in everyday urban life but take on almost epic proportions in the less certain environment of wilderness. A rubbed heel isn't a major catastrophe if you're enjoying a day walk and, while it doesn't necessarily have to cause a lot of grief in the wilderness, it nevertheless does demand some sort of quick, remedial action. Likewise, while we are rarely far from a water source in our everyday urban environment, wilderness travel calls for regular top-ups of liquid to sustain us and such sources of liquid might well be few and far between.

We can babble on about bears, snakes, rockfall, steep ground and thousands of other objective dangers but the really pernicious fears and anxieties are less easily defined. I guess you could bracket them all under the general and largely unsatisfactory heading of 'a fear of the unknown'. Fortunately, most of these anxieties can be laid to rest through experience, and years of solo backpacking can make you pretty immune to much of it. But the shadows can still lurk in the back of the mind, haunting those first hours, or even days, of any wilderness sortie.

I've examined this curious paradox more fully in the chapter on the Chamonix to Zermatt Haute Route but, suffice to say for the moment, once you've managed to work through the anxieties or ignore them there comes that remarkable moment in any wilderness trip when you connect, a vital moment when you no longer feel as though you're a stranger visiting the wild places but a citizen of the land community you're walking through, a kinship that in its own way is deeper and more personal even than direct ownership.

This notion of connection is essentially about shrugging off our Western anthropocentrism, casting aside the urban notion that man is dominant and that everything else in nature has been created for man's welfare or pleasure. Paradoxically, connection often comes in a sudden revelation of man's insignificance when compared with the more lasting reality of mountains, forests and star-studded skies. A bear encounter can have a curiously humbling effect on us and an Alpine electrical storm can portray a force and a power that is way beyond humankind's ability to reproduce.

Oregon-based adventurer and lightweight gear guru Ray Jardine defines connection more in terms of style, suggesting that our wilderness outings should be just more than physical walks along trails.

"More important is our presence in the wilds," he claims. "How we carry ourselves, how softly we move upon the landscape, how aware we are of the patterns of life around us and how we interact with them. This 'earth philosophy' is a bridging of the gap between human and nature, a bringing together for a greater awareness and deeper understanding of the natural world around us in all its glory, of our relationship with that world, and of our own inner nature."

I discussed this phenomenon with Ray at some length when we made a *Wilderness Walks* television programme in his home state of Oregon. As we hiked along the Pacific Crest Trail through the Three Sisters Wilderness I was aware of his well-being, his oneness with the landscape we passed through. He later told me he sensed the tensions I was carrying – the concerns and anxieties that go jowl-in-cheek with making a television programme.

"I was aware of a great eagle walking along behind me," he told me, "an eagle whose wings were tied and who so desperately wanted to cut loose and soar."

Ray suggests that the reason why 'connection' is so vitally important is that it's like a stepping-stone in the middle of a wide creek we could never jump across.

"We might remember that despite our almost overwhelming technology, we are still flesh and bone," he says. "Our bodies are an integral part of Mother Earth. The air we breathe is her breath, rippling the grasses in the meadow. The water we drink is her life-blood, tumbling from the snowy heights. Our flesh comes from the soft, rich earth, our bone from the sun-baked rocks. Every molecule in us is not our own, but a part of Mother Earth. We are borrowing that molecule from her, and will have to give it back when we leave.

"This is one problem with city life, where we tend to hide from all that. But in fact the more richly we connect with Mother Earth, the higher and farther we can walk our Paths. With this in mind, each footstep blesses the earth and the journey itself becomes sacred. I think everyone experiences this."

I like this concept of sacredness, for when connection does occur it is often a hallowed experience, as though a divine intervention has separated us from our former self into something new, refreshed and re-created – a born-again experience! The moment of connection, this new relationship, sometimes becomes evident within a few hours, at other times it can take a few days. Occasionally, just occasionally, it doesn't happen at all…

I leave the trailhead and for three hours climb the steep trail below a soaring ocean of vertical granite. Spray from cascading waterfalls keeps me cool and despite the weight of my pack there is a reassuring familiarity in the creak of the harness as it hugs me around the waist. Part of me wants to rush, to push on with emphasised strides in an effort to reach the top but the sensible side of my brain tells me to cool it, that there's no rush, no timetable, no strict schedule to keep. Once again I have to relearn the luxury of freedom.

There are more than 135 switchbacks to be negotiated before the angle of the trail eases off near the top of Yosemite Falls but, despite the steep gradient and the heat of the morning, it's a delightful ascent beneath shady gold-cup oaks and the occasional Douglas fir. Every so often I get a glimpse down into the valley below and it's like watching a movie. The cars, the buses and the tourist attractions of Yosemite Valley are not part of my world any more, they've been left behind for a softer, gentler world, a world in which time has very little meaning.

Eventually the trail climbs up through a long, steep trough in the cliffs to emerge into an open forest of Jeffrey pines and white firs. The scent of sun-warmed resin fills my nostrils and I stop for a drink from the creek. The water is clear and refreshingly cold. Some day hikers pass by, out on a climb from the valley. Invariably there is a pleasant but brief chat. The brevity invariably comes from me. Never rude or intentionally unpleasant, I just want to reach the point where I can connect and sustained conversations with others can create a barrier to that connection. Most folk understand and are usually too breathless to get into a conversation anyway but a German lady is keen to chat, recognising my accent. She wants to tell me the full and unexpurgated account of her family holiday a few years back when she went to Loch Ness to try to see the legendary monster. Fortunately her daughter senses my mild impatience so I take the opportunity to remove myself as naturally and as quickly as possible.

The trail climbs briefly again, out of the creek's gully to follow a crest which parallels the edge of the cliffs. Soon, it slowly drops down to the clear waters of Yosemite Creek where white granite slabs slope down to the lip of Upper Yosemite Falls. The stream flows gently over the smooth slabs before suddenly gathering itself to plunge over the lip of this sheer cliff to become the 1,430ft Yosemite Falls, one of the longest waterfalls in the world.

Incredibly it was here, in 1869, that John Muir, the wilderness prophet and the father of National Parks 'connected' with this Yosemite landscape in such a transcendent fashion that "one's body seems to go where it likes with a will over which we seem to have scarce any control".

There is a fascinating study to be done on John Muir's apparent fearlessness. Generally recognised as the finest mountaineer of his time he appeared, again and again, to take unnecessary risks and yet, as writer and Muir enthusiast Terry Gifford has pointed out, "Through a discipline of tuning in to wildness, Muir could take risks and trust his judgement of the conditions".

This ability to 'tune in to wildness' was a vital constituent in Muir's character and, while he was not unfamiliar with fear, he did write: "I think that most of the antipathies which haunt and terrify us are morbid productions of ignorance and weakness."

It seems that John Muir had developed the ability to overcome fear and harness the energies of what most of us recognise as a negative sensation and turn them into something positive, just as an athlete will recognise nervousness as a positive flow of adrenaline. Here, on the very lip of Yosemite Falls, Muir overcame his terror to perform an act that can only be described by sane and rational people as suicidal madness.

Intoxicated by his first views of Yosemite Valley from above, he decided what he really wanted to experience was a view of the falls as they tumbled over the edge. "I approached Yosemite Creek," he later wrote, "admiring its easy, graceful, confident gestures as it comes bravely forward in its narrow channel, singing the last of its mountain songs on its way to its fate." He wanted to "lean out far enough to see the forms and behaviour of the fall all the way down to the bottom".

Suspecting all he had to do was peer over the edge where the sloping granite apron would meet with the perpendicular wall of the valley, he discovered that below what appeared to be the edge there was another small brow over which he could not see. Undeterred, he examined the brow and noticed a narrow ledge, about three inches wide, on the very brink, "just wide enough for a rest for one's heels".

Nervously, he tried to reach it, making use of the edge of a rock flake for support but to reach the rock flake he had to shuffle down a smooth and steep slope close beside the torrent. He decided not to venture any further, but then changed his mind. Finding tufts of artemisia growing in a crevice he stuffed the bitter leaves in his mouth, "hoping they might prevent giddiness".

Then, with uncharacteristic but not wholly surprising caution, he crept down to the tiny ledge and managed to shuffle along it for some 20 or 30 feet until he was close to the out-plunging cataract.

"Here I obtained a perfectly free view down into the heart of the snowy, chanting throng of comet-like streamers, into which the body of the fall soon separates. While perched on that narrow niche I was not distinctly conscious of danger. The tremendous grandeur of the fall in form and sound and motion, acting at close range, smothered the sense of fear, and in such places one's body takes keen care for safety on its own account. How long I remained down there, or how I returned, I can hardly tell… My first view of the High Sierra, first view looking down into Yosemite, the death song of Yosemite Creek, and its flight over the vast cliff, each one of these is of itself for a great lifelong landscape fortune – a most memorable day of days – enjoyment enough to kill if that were possible."

As I stand and watch the swirling waters of Yosemite Creek prepare to launch themselves into the abyss below I am horrified at the thought of trying to emulate Muir's actions. But even as I recognise my own fears and extreme reluctance to follow in Muir's footsteps, I detect in his excitement something of the inexorable urge to explore such danger, to infuse one's senses with the sensations of exposure to such risk and come out of it triumphant and richer for the experience.

My own little gamble into such risk was yet some days away.

Returning to my pack I eat some lunch before climbing up into the shady woods that cover this Yosemite backcountry. The boulders of a terminal moraine remind me of the glacial origins of this land of natural wonders and soon I leave the Jeffrey pines and white firs behind for more stunted red firs and lodgepole pines. Still enthralled by Muir's achievement I enjoy the climb through the woods but, as I sit beside some open meadows, the haunt of voracious mosquitoes, I go into a lull of mild homesickness, as though a cloud was obscuring the sun.

As the afternoon wears on I meet some folk who suggest I might like to camp with them – they've found a beautiful spot with fresh water and few biting insects. I'm tempted, for the shadow of the homesickness is still lingering, but eventually decide to move on for another hour or so, ostensibly to be by myself and I'm glad I do. I find a lovely little sandy shelf surrounded by white granite boulders, juniper bushes and tall pines. A cascading stream pours over glaringly white rocks just a few yards away and there is just enough breeze to deter the mosquitoes.

I spend a couple of hours organising myself, washing socks and washing myself before lying back against my pack for half an hour to enjoy the last flamboyant gestures of the dying sun. Experience has taught me that when homesickness strikes I can either allow my mind to fester on it or busy myself with other things. As usual the little chores of camp-life keep me occupied and after supper I'm in bed and asleep long before my watch strikes nine.

These little bouts of homesickness are not unusual and I guess most people prefer company on trips like this and, by every reasonable standard of thought, they are being very sensible. Author and backpacker Colin Fletcher once wrote that for efficiency and comfort and the rewards of sharing, and above all for safety, a walking party, like a political party, should consist of at least two or three members. But there are times when I like, indeed I prefer, to be alone: when trying to regulate thoughts, when I feel the need to contemplate my feeble input into this great universe they call Creation or when I simply want to contemplate that Creation itself. Or, as is often the case, when I'm simply fed up, bored, disgusted, disappointed or feel rejected by people. Solo backpacking then becomes a therapy rather than a test and that therapy, like much remedial treatment, is deeply personal and is best sought alone.

I've often stood at the edge of a vast, uncaring wilderness and hesitated, just a little, in some degree because my childhood bogeys are not quite dead in me but knowing that out there, somewhere in that wildness, is an environment where my own concept of self can slip below the threshold of awareness. By relying on the skills and experiences hard-won over many years, I can grasp the opportunity to interact with something else, something bigger and more essential than mere me. Loss of that self-consciousness can lead to self-transcendence, to an awareness that the boundaries of my being can be pushed forward, even just a little bit.

The first time I experienced such a thing was on a youthful visit to the Skye Cuillin. Here, having reached the jagged crest of our toughest hills, I experienced such a combination of ecstasy and relief that I could exalt in the wild surroundings in a way that could only be described as euphoric. And in that heightened state it became clear to me that for the first time in my life I felt at one with the mountain. I wasn't simply a visitor casually climbing some scree and rock, I was part and parcel of the whole *potpourri* of rock, air, water and light; for the first time I experienced a sense of kinship with that wild and beautiful landscape. I had connected with the mountain and transcended my own being. It was the beginning of a long and thoroughly delectable addiction to the mountains of Scotland and the wild places of the world.

The next morning is hot and it's a big climb up to Ten Lakes Pass. My pack feels heavy and awkward, as though it is wrestling with me, and I feel sluggish and just a tad sickly. I wonder if the cheese I ate for breakfast had been okay – it looked as though it had been sweating a bit in the food bag. I push on and the day becomes hotter and stickier. The mosquitoes attack remorselessly and, just as I reach the large and wet Half Moon Meadow, where the mosquitoes are at their most voracious, I lose the trail. It descends into a narrow creek, crosses a stream and on the other side, where a fallen tree bars progress, it appears to vanish into a thicket of juniper bushes.

I recross the stream several times, looking for a logical line past the bushes but the trail, at one point clear and inviting, simply disappears. Eventually, beyond the junipers I find one or two ducks, small and unobtrusive way-marking cairns, and follow them, trusting in a combination of intuition, map work and luck. After one or two false trails I come across some more ducks but they don't appear to be marking any set trail. The red firs and lodgepoles form a relatively dense thicket and the way-markers suggest a route that climbs steeply up and over some pretty rough hillside. Then, just as I experience the first little stabs of concern, a trail appears, wide and well-worn. Relieved, I follow it for a distance but sense I'm heading in the wrong direction, south instead of north-east. Checking the map it becomes evident where I am – a trail drops down from Ten Lakes Pass, traverses across the slopes and descends to an Alpine cirque that contains a tarn, Grant Lake. I've stumbled across Grant Lake Trail.

All I have to do now is turn round and walk in the other direction, ticking off the features on the map as I pass them, counting the number of streams I cross and checking my wrist altimeter from time to time. Less than 30 minutes later I reach the junction with the Ten Lakes Pass trail. I'm so delighted I let out a whoop that makes a mule deer buck lift his head in surprise before bolting off into the woods. Soon I'm even more delighted with the views from the pass, out across the amazing landscape of glacier-scoured Tuolumne towards the serrated peaks of the high Sierra Crest.

There is always this sense of achievement on reaching a high point with a view, as the world around you opens up and you can look down on it but on this occasion there was an even greater sense of satisfaction because I had lost my way and found it again. This sense of satisfaction is invariably accompanied by a sense of mild astonishment that my observations and instincts were correct. Even more incredible is that by using something as complex as a topographical map and a small bit of plastic with a magnetised needle I had the ability to not only travel through such a vast wilderness with some certainty as to where I was going but that I could find such an isolated spot as a mountain pass after losing the trail.

Successful mountain navigation never fails to delight me.

The thrill of such successful navigation is part of the feedback of the whole flow experience of such a trip as this, part of what author Mihaly Csikszentmihalyi calls 'the psychology of optimal experience'. This flow experience is the state in which individuals become so involved in an activity that nothing else seems to matter; the experience itself is so enjoyable that we will do it even at great cost, for the sheer sake of doing it.

Csikszentmihalyi suggests that the phenomenon of such enjoyment is made up of various components, one of them being the provision of clear goals and immediate feedback as you achieve those goals. The delight and satisfaction of reaching the major goal of the day, the magnificent viewpoint of Ten Lakes Pass, was the immediate feedback, a reassurance to a fragile soul like me that my skills were at least adequate to cope with the challenge at hand.

It's a steep descent to the little collection of cirques that contain the ten lakes and the evening mosquitoes are really biting now, enjoying their supper with relish now that the repellent has worn off. I drop down below the crags of Colby Mountain, named after William Colby, an early president of the Sierra Club, and into a forest of mountain hemlock and western white pine. Hoping for a breeze from one of the lakes I find a good little camp site tucked away below some crags and after supper settle in for the night behind my mosquito-netted tent door.

The blighters are still biting in the morning and I clear up camp as quickly as I can. The lakes are in a large hollow, like a huge corrie, and I have to climb for quite a distance to get out of it. There's little hardship in it though, for scenically it is superb with the lakes nestling like gems in their own individual hollows, sparkling in the sunlight and reflecting the deep blue sky, a sky that is to remain flawless for the entire day.

As I top the rise coming out of the Ten Lakes hollows I don't expect such a view. It literally takes my breath away and I have to sit down on a rock to drink it in. The whole of the Sierra Crest is laid out before me and, in the foreground, the biggest jumble and tumble of white and grey rock I've ever seen seems to pour down from the heights. Crags of shining white granite lie interspersed with white domes and dumplings, like the moraines of some astonishingly large glacier. I can clearly understand why the scientists originally thought Yosemite had been wrought by some primeval and cataclysmic force. I've certainly never seen anything like it. The map informs me I'm looking at the bare rock of the Tuolumne Canyon, forming the boundaries of the Tuolumne River as it cascades its way down towards Hetch Hetchy. If Hetch Hetchy is as impressive as this view of the Tuolumne canyon then it's no wonder John Muir's heart was broken when they dammed it and flooded it as a water catchment for San Francisco.

The fantastic views are followed by an equally superb descent down into the valley of the South Fork Cathedral River and as I follow the rocky trail down the steep switch-backs the valley floor below me looks enticing with forests of pine broken by large green meadows. The river gently cascades through it all. I can even see the trail as it makes its way up the length of the valley to where, according to the map, it will eventually turn back on itself in a huge switch-back and gently climb the far wall of the valley. From my elevated position the distant trail looks to be at an impossible angle, skirting the summit slopes of Tuolumne Peak. I reckon I'll be topping out close to 10,000ft (3,050m).

As I leave the sedge-filled meadows and the bedrock of the higher slopes behind and enter the coolness of the mature forest I'm aware yet again of the wonderful natural integration of woods and mountains in areas like this, an integration that we've generally lost in our wild areas of Britain. In Scotland I'm constantly saddened by the miles upon miles of deer fencing which separate forest plantations from hill slopes, slopes that are in themselves so often cruelly degraded by over-grazing and over-burning.

But here there is harmony, a gentle blending of forest and montane scrub, no harsh demarcation lines between that scrub and the alpine zones of bare granite, ground-hugging vegetation and the odd windblown whitebark pine. And beyond it all the peaks, majestic and dominant, rise to the heavens.

There's a oneness to it all, a wholeness that in turn gives me a feeling of well-being and an awareness that, at last, I've truly connected!

My spirit now soaring, the walk up the valley is truly memorable. I stop at one point and lie down on a slab of white granite and look up at the blue sky. It's pleasantly warm and I allow the sounds and smells full access to my senses. The scent of pine resin is almost overwhelming and from somewhere close by a squirrel scolds me for invading his territory. Small birds flirt from branch to branch in the trees above and the gentle rumbling of the nearby stream forms the bass line to the whole melody, the timeless theme music of the High Sierra. It is marvellous to lie here, fully connected and infused with the sounds and the smells and the impressions of such a wild landscape but it was an event that was to occur later in the day that would really set my mind reeling.

Once lunch is over I take stock of the situation. I can follow the trail back along its switch-back high above the South Fork Cathedral River, eventually crossing a high pass before descending to the Polly Dome Lakes area, or I can leave the security of the trail and climb high to cross a rocky and possibly snow-covered pass between Tuolumne Peak and Mount Hoffmann, a mountain that I knew from a previous visit to Yosemite. By taking the short-cut I can be down beside May Lake, a beautiful spot, by tea-time.

Spirits still soaring I decide to take the mountain route and leave the trail behind, making my way uphill, off-trail, below the spreading branches of lodgepole pines, red firs and western white pines. It doesn't take long to clear the forest and reach the open juniper-dotted slopes of Tuolumne Peak's south-west ridge. I can see the col above me, a narrow portal offering easy access through the high divide, but my attention is taken by a narrow ridge to the left that appears to lead to higher slopes and probably better views.

Feeling adventurous and abandoning thoughts of the easier col, I reach the foot of the ridge, strap my trekking poles to my pack and begin climbing the sun-kissed granite. Immediately I become absorbed in the fluidity in each move, hands and feet moving in harmony, feeling, testing and measuring each move. I can feel the warmth of the sun and can still smell the resin wafting up from the woods below and every few feet I stop and gaze around me, thrilled by the all-embracing intensity of the view.

I'm so engrossed in the thrill of movement on this steepening rock that I forget about the 40lb backpack hanging from my shoulders and it's only as I haul up over an intervening rib that I suddenly become aware that I probably couldn't climb back down the ridge, even if I wanted to. In fact there's no probability about it – I couldn't. Aware of the dragging weight of my pack now, and even more aware of the perilous nature of my predicament, I do the only thing I can – continue up.

Slower now, looking to reach holds, I'm aware that the rock is becoming steeper. I reach a small buttress in the ridge and traverse to the right of it searching for an exit from the ridge, a gully or groove that might carry me to easier ground but there isn't one, only the textured smoothness of the white granite walls. Returning to the ridge crest I move out to the left but a steep drop yawns below my feet and I scamper quickly back to the foot of the buttress.

The white rock rises above me for a good 20 feet, sheer on the right but less steep and more broken on the left. I try to visualise the moves, following wide cracks to a ledge where a shattered groove bears back to the centre of the buttress and eventually to the top. Can I climb it with a heavy pack on my shoulders? What if I become stuck? What's the rest of the ridge like beyond the buttress?

As I consider my options I become vaguely aware, as though a distant part of my mind is trying to reach me, that the flow experience that has brought me this far will see me through. The complete involvement I have with this rock, the air around me, the very totality of the experience, amounts to a heightened sense of control. I wait and allow the thought to take root, allowing this rather abstract notion to take dominance over the more logical awareness that I can't down-climb the ridge and I can't sit here and wait for someone to rescue me. In short I have little option but to climb on.

Once that decision is taken, a curious thing happens. As soon as I reach up into the crack above my head something seems to click. My fingers curl round a wonderfully reassuring rugosity within the crack and I pull up on it, my feet discovering holds of their own. Within two or three moves I'm moving calmly, confidently, climbing out above the sheer drop before reaching the groove that carries me up to the top of the buttress.

As I pull up over the lip exhilaration washes over me, an excitement that is sweetened by a sense of relief for the ridge has broadened out and it's no more than a walk to a rounded subsidiary summit. I slip the pack from my shoulders, smiling broadly to no-one in particular, and fall to the ground, consumed by a sense of well-being and intense satisfaction. It's as though my consciousness has been isolated during the previous five or ten minutes, allowing only a very limited selection of information to penetrate my awareness.

Only those processes that empowered the movement of my hands and feet, the positioning and balance of my body and the concentration of my mind on the task at hand were allowed access, and even the awareness of the exposure below me as I moved out to the left of the buttress seemed relatively insignificant.

But now awareness floods my consciousness – awareness of the vastness of the views around me, the rolling oceans of granite domes and peaks which stretch to the horizon, the greenness of the forests below, the glint of turquoise-coloured lakes deep-set in their glacial bowls. Awareness of a sense of achievement, the overcoming of fears and doubts and objective dangers and, greatest of all, the sense that not only had I been in control but had been capable of exercising control in a situation that had been potentially hazardous. And it's only when the outcome of such a situation is in doubt and when you're in a position to actually influence the outcome, that you really begin to appreciate whether you had been in control or not.

And I suppose that, in essence, is a pretty good definition of adventure.

The rest of the trip is no downturn after that event, in fact if anything it becomes better. As I drop from Tuolumne Peak yet another aspect of the Yosemite backcountry comes into view, the granite sweeps and domes of Tenaya, rising in red burnished plates to Cathedral Lakes and, towering above them Cathedral Peak itself, first climbed by John Muir.

A few days later I make my way from May Lake to Glen Aulin, then on to Tuolumne, to meet the PBS film crew I'll be working with for the next few days. During the course of our filming we follow in the footsteps of Muir, trace his route up Cathedral Peak and discuss the ideas and philosophy of this man who was to become wilderness prophet to the world.

Throughout our discussions and interviews I recalled the tall, lean, bearded Scot who stood, heels wedged on that tiny ledge above the plunging Yosemite Falls, overcoming his fears and weaknesses. In my own limited way I realised, too, that connection with wilderness is in effect a discipline of tuning-in to that wildness and so, like John Muir, we can also 'take justified risks, trusting our judgement of the conditions'.

Once we have gone through that process of connection, once we are tuned to the wildness of the land, we become less preoccupied with self. And it's only then we actually have an opportunity to expand the concept of who we really are. It's then that self-preoccupation leads to self-transcendence and a feeling that the boundaries of our being have been pushed forward, even just a little bit. It's then that we realise that occasional risk is necessary if we are to love life, life in all its glorious fullness.

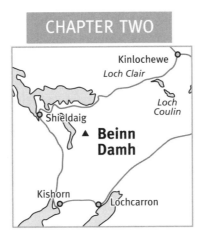

CHAPTER TWO

A RARE SOLITUDE ON
BEINN DAMH

Sometimes, just sometimes, the first glimpse of a mountain can have a profound effect on you. You could describe it as love at first sight but I sense it's something deeper than that, for it's often not only the natural beauty of the hill that grabs your attention so keenly but the circumstances in which you first experience it.

I'd been making my way through slobbery snow drifts in the Coulags pass between the head of Loch Carron and Glen Torridon in Wester Ross on one of those wet and dreary days when your heart almost convinces you that the weather couldn't be any more miserable on the high tops but your head tells you different.

In effect I was in retreat – I had had enough sleety rain for one day and my thoughts were already transfixed on the warm bar of the Ben Damh Lodge. As I crossed the Bealach na Lice and began the descent towards the grey waters of Loch an Eion I couldn't decide what I would order first – a pint of beer or a hot bowl of soup.

Suddenly, as though a magic wand had brushed across the sky, the clouds began to evaporate leaving a still, solemn and silent evening. The speed of the change, while welcome, was unnerving and distinctly eerie. Where a dark grey curtain had hidden the hills from sight long blue shadows now stretched out across the upper snow fields while a rosy glow gradually deepened and suffused every mountain top in sight. Across the loch the dark sandstone tiers of Beinn Damh gave way to flushed snow slopes, accentuating the steep flanks, beautifully scooped corries and craggy shoulders that give this 2,959ft/902m Corbett such character. Its sudden appearance took my breath away, one of those special moments, like a divine manifestation, that a Highland winter occasionally blesses you with. I've never forgotten it and Beinn Damh has become an old friend.

This little hill, the most westerly of the mountains that flank the south shore of Upper Loch Torridon, offers a rare solitude despite the fact that it shares many of the attributes of its higher neighbours – the popular magnets of Beinn Alligin, Liathach and Beinn Eighe, the Munro trio which draw the mass of hill-walkers to their steep flanks. Given Beinn Damh's position, between the other shapely hills of the Ben-Damph and Coulin deer forests and, of course, the Torridonian triplets of Alligin, Liathach and Eighe, there is also some justification in claiming it to be a better viewpoint than its more illustrious neighbours, as I discovered recently when I climbed the hill again during a brief spell of settled cold weather.

There was room to park several cars on the A896 Sheildaig to Annat road just above the Loch Torridon Hotel near the bridge over the Allt Coire Roill and 70m or so back up the road towards Shieldaig a wicker gate on the left gave access to a stalkers' path which climbed uphill through the typical Torridonian forest of pines and rhododendrons. After about half a mile the rhododendrons faded out and the trees became smaller, their heads bent to the prevailing winds and their limbs contorted and twisted. These are the senior citizens in the family of the pine forest, the patriarchs of the woods, and sadly there are few youngsters to replace them. Exposed pine roots poked through the paper-thin skin of the earth, damp and slippery after the frosts of the night.

An unforeseen slip or stumble was the last thing I wanted here – in contrast to the stillness of the woods the sound and sight of an 80ft waterfall was dramatic. Just ahead, the Allt Coire Roill takes a sudden plunge over a sandstone cliff and into a deep rocky chasm below, its spray filling the air like drifting smoke.

Beyond the tree-line the sunshine beckoned, burning the top-most peaks until they looked like islands on a great dark sea of shade, and beyond the glistening summits the sky burned almost as black. The footpath divides here – the left branch follows the Allt Coire Roill towards the Drochaid Coire Roill, and the right fork climbs into the Toll Ban, the 'white corrie' of Beinn Damh. I took the latter route and followed the path as it climbed steeply up the upper slopes of the corrie towards the broad col that separates Beinn Damh proper from its northern outlier, Sgurr na Bana Mhoraire (it's well-worth walking south-west across this broad saddle to gaze down the very steep westerly scree slopes into Loch Damh below, and you can get an even better view by making the short diversion to the summit of Sgurr na Bana Mhoraire).

This saddle top itself is pretty featureless and in the hard, granular snow the path had vanished. I crunched my way south-east, towards the first of two subsidiary tops, which is easily bypassed on its west side. Great quartzite boulders fill the dip between these two tops and from the second a narrow ridge makes an airy staircase to the main summit where the cairn sits on the very edge of the steep Coir' an Laoigh, a high eyrie with dramatic views as one would expect from a mountain which has the Torridon giants on one side and the tops of the Coulin deer forest on the other. You can't get a much better position for a mountain than this. Beyond the glistening cornice the mountains rolled on as though forever.

The north-east ridge, the Stuc Toll nam Biast makes for a steep and fairly intimidating line of descent, especially under snow conditions, down to the pass of the Drochaid Coire Roill where the left fork of my earlier ascent route runs across the foot of Coire Roill. I would think this route makes a better ascent route – its always easier scrambling uphill than down. A good scramble for another day perhaps? If you do decide to descend this way, bear in mind that most of the difficulties can be avoided on the right. Most folk will be more than happy descending the way they came.

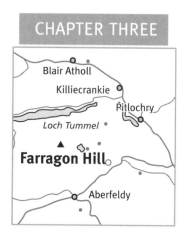

CHAPTER THREE

Blair Atholl
Killiecrankie
Pitlochry
Loch Tummel
Farragon Hill
Aberfeldy

AN ALASKAN VISION ON THE HILL OF SAINT FHEARGAIN

You can see the ragged skyline of the Farragons as you drive north on the A9 south of Pitlochry, a little-visited hill area that lies in the shadow of Perthshire's finest peak, Schiehallion. The Farragons' broad, knobbly ridges, which run from Meall Tairneachan in the west to Farragon Hill itself, make up the highest points of a huge forested area between Loch Tummel and Strath Tay. A walk linking the two hills, both of them Corbetts, the Scottish hills between 2,500ft and 2,999ft (762-914m), makes a good winter day and can be tackled in a number of different ways.

If you have two cars you can leave one on the B846 north of Loch Kinardochy, the minor road that runs between Tummel Bridge and Aberfeldy. Drive round to Edradynate on the minor road between Aberfeldy and Grandtully and follow the track that runs north from the farms of Blackhill and Lurgan to Loch Derculich and then over the ridge of the Farragons before descending to Loch Tummel. Leave this track about a kilometre beyond Loch Derculich and head west over tussocky ground to climb Farragon Hill itself by its eastern ridge. Meall

Tairneachan lies about three miles to the west, from where it's an easy descent to the B846 at Loch Kinardochy. Alternatively start from the north side of the ridge at the foot of the Frenich Burn, a long horseshoe shaped route but be warned – this route involves some pretty strenuous bog-trotting!

I chose an even easier route to the two hills. I left my car at the parking place at Tomphubil, just south of Loch Kinardochy, and followed the edge of a forestry plantation due east towards Meall Tairneachan. This gives the advantage of starting off at over 1,000ft (305m)and although the initial slopes are steep and heathery you gain height extremely quickly on a faint path which follows a dry-stone wall at the edge of the plantation. Much to my surprise I was on the summit of Meall Tairneachan within an hour, enjoying some far-flung views to the north and east towards the Dalnaspidal hills and the blue Cairngorms. Unfortunately the west looked gloomy, with the views cancelled out by grey curtains of rain hanging over Schiehallion and the Glen Lyon hills. I had little doubt the rain would reach me soon.

Just below Meall Tairneachan a great man-made corrie houses a labyrinth of baryte mines, together with their various buildings, fences, bulldozed roads and signs, but by carefully walking as far south as possible I managed to avoid the worst of the workings and maintained at least a sense of unspoiled landscape. By taking this line I was forced on to a high-level route between the two Corbetts which unfortunately fights the grain of the land; several steep-sided tops and ridges formed natural barriers which had to be crossed before I could reach the broad Lairig Laoigh, an ancient through-route between Strath Tay and Loch Tummel.

From the Lairig, complete with its own reed-fringed loch, it was a boggy tramp to the steep, west-facing slopes of Farragon Hill, named after Saint Fheargain, the fourth Abbot of Iona who once ministered in the nearby Pitlochry area. It was a steep climb to the summit but an interesting one, following grassy ramps between rocky outcrops. Soon, tucked out of the wind by the summit cairn, my hopes of a good view were ruined by a thick encroaching mist and the rain curtains I had seen earlier. Rather than return to my starting point by compass bearing, I swallowed my environmental concerns and decided to make use of the bulldozed track that skirted my inward route, the rough road that is primarily used for the extraction of baryte minerals from the nearby mines.

Earlier, as I had tried to avoid the unsightly workings of the mines, I tried to convince myself that such places were part of our industrial heritage and that mountains could never be the sole domain of hillgoers, however much we would like that to be the case. I recalled too a similar industrial heritage that is celebrated by the Chilkoot Trail in Alaska. Just over 100 years ago, gold-rush fever hit this part of North America and thousands of prospectors made their way north with dreams of untold riches. Mines were developed and new towns were created but very few of the hopefuls became rich. Today, the Chilkoot Trail stands as an epitaph to those characters and the trail itself is an open-air museum of industrial heritage. With these thoughts swirling through my mind and the Farragon mist swirling across the track in front of me I received something of a start when I heard a low rumbling and there, through the mist in front was a scene that could have come straight from Alaska's Chilkoot Trail itself.

Corrugated iron buildings, power generators and huge gaping holes in the hillsides – the baryte mines appeared through the mist like a timepiece and I half-expected to run into the likes of Dangerous Dan McGrew and his Yukon mining cronies, celebrated in verse by the redoubtable Scots exile Robert Service. Other than the whine and rumble of the generator the place was deserted, which only added to its surreal atmosphere. I wandered part-way down one of the gaping holes in the hillside, until the darkness engulfed me and sent me shivering back to the daylight. I thought of those who descend into such places every working day, deprived of light and space and the smell of living things and in more ways than one I was glad to finally follow the track down the hillside, through the pine-scented forest and back to the road.

"This is the Law of the Yukon, that only the Strong shall thrive;
That surely the Weak shall perish, and only the Fit survive.
Dissolute, damned and despairful, crippled and palsied and slain.
This is the Will of the Yukon, – Lo, how she makes it plain."

Robert Service

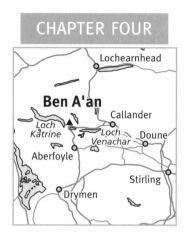

CHAPTER FOUR

BEN A'AN – LOWLY BUT LOVED

It was reading Geoff Connor's book about the late John Cunningham and his cohorts in the Creagh Dhu Mountaineering Club (*Creagh Dhu Climber*, The Ernest Press) that made me return to Ben A'an, the haunt of many a youthful sortie and by common consent one of the very best 'wee' hills in Scotland.

Protruding like an afterthought from the shoulder of Meall Gainmheich, Ben A'an presents a three-tiered face of schistose crags to the forested world of the Trossachs, small but challenging crags that have attracted generations of Scottish rock climbers, including the post-war Creagh Dhu club.

Edinburgh climber Jimmy Marshall, later to become the Creagh Dhu's first honorary member, recalls his first meeting with the Clydeside-based climbers on Ben A'an. At the time many myths surrounded the Creagh Dhu – they were seen as an introspective, aggressive bunch who didn't welcome outsiders. Paradoxically, Marshall's first recollection was of how friendly they were. A friendly bunch, but definitely wild.

"They always climbed on Ben A'an because it was handy to get to from Glasgow," Jimmy told me. "They took the bus over to Aberfoyle, then they'd hike over the Duke's Pass to the Trossachs Hotel where they had these tremendous thrashes. They had a particularly famous one when they had this huge session in the bar, stole the targes and swords off the walls and they were running around in the snow, smashing the place up and thinking, 'this landlord's a bloody great guy, he's not doing anything about this'. The truth was that the police had become stuck in the snow on the way over."

According to Connor, Ben A'an was popular with the Creagh Dhu climbers not only because of the delights of the old Trossachs Hotel but also because the numerous glades in the surrounding forest offered plenty of shelter for dossing out and plenty of fallen wood for camp fires. It's also worth remembering that the Glasgow bus stopped at Aberfoyle in those days and the climbers had to hike over the Duke's Pass on the A821. The hills we take for granted nowadays were, even a short time ago, comparatively remote.

Inevitably, there is now a Forest Enterprise car park at the very foot of Ben A'an and the 1,489ft/454m 'mini-mountain' has become one of the most popular walks in Scotland. And justifiably so, particularly when the autumn gold begins to usurp the suffocating greenery of summer and the higher grassy slopes turn blond and the leaves lighten into yellows and ochres, reds and russets. I can't think of a better autumnal viewpoint than the summit of Ben A'an, a grand eyrie perched splendidly above the waters of Loch Katrine. The loch's shoreline leads the eye to the west where, on a clear day, all the Arrochar Alps are displayed in full and impressive array. Further north the Crianlarich hills come into view, boasting the unmistakable outline of the Castor and Pollux of the Southern Highlands, Ben More and Stob Binnein, heavenly twins joined together by their common bealach.

At your feet lies the transverse glen which gives the Trossachs area its name.

The term is said to be derived from 'Trosaichen', a word now obsolete in the Gaelic language that can be loosely interpreted as a transverse glen joining two others. This well-describes the heartland of the Trossachs, a great jumble of rock and forest which separates Loch Katrine from Loch Achray. Beyond it lies the Bealach nam Bo, the pass of the cattle through which the Macgregors were said to spirit away their stolen herds and, beyond it, on the slopes of Ben Venue, the rock-strewn Coire na Uruisgean, the corrie of the urisks, or goblins. According to *Scenery of the Southern Confines of Perthshire*, published in 1806, an urisk was: "a sort of lubbery supernatural who could be gained over by kind attention to perform the drudgery of a farm. They were supposed to be spread throughout the Highlands each in his own wild recess, but the solemn meetings of the order were regularly held in this cave of Benvenew."

The route to the top of Ben A'an is straightforward. Cross the road from the car park and follow the path uphill. This initial section is steep and is often quite muddy but it does allow you to gain height quickly and directly. Enjoy the song of the chaffinches, the heady scent of pine and the opening views behind you as you climb up below the canopy of trees. After a while the steepness relents considerably and a signpost indicates a viewpoint to the left. It's well-worthwhile leaving the path and visiting this outlook as it offers the first glimpse of Ben A'an. It's a good view too – framed by spruce and larch it looks steep and exposed and for all the world like a mountain several times its height.

Return to the path now and continue uphill. Soon you'll leave the trees behind and the views begin to open up across to the crags, bluffs and corries of Ben Venue and the long stretch of Loch Katrine, the finest of all the Trossachs lochs. Continue on the path and climb again, up wet and broken ground, helped significantly by some sensible path construction work. Higher up this section of path there is a lot of loose rock and scree and after heavy rain there is always a lot of running water. Climb over this rough ground, contour round the back of the hill, where blaeberries grow in rich profusion during the summer months, cross some wet, mossy areas, then climb up the final few feet to the rocky summit.

This is a place worth lingering and, if you enjoy a challenge, try to sprint up the Ten Second Slab. This is the boiler-plate slab which leans up to the summit cairn, and it's claimed that good climbers will scale it in 10 seconds. If you're like me you'll take just a bit longer!

There is a descent route from Ben A'an which leads off to the north and west and which drops down through the forest to the north shore of Loch Katrine, but it's an ill-defined and awkward path, often very wet and slippy. Best advice is to return to the car park the way you came.

CHAPTER FIVE

THE HAUTE ROUTE –
CHAMONIX TO ZERMATT

Sometimes, just sometimes, we're tempted to believe that our wilderness trips can in some way isolate us from everyday problems, that backpacking through mountainous areas can sequester us from those things that concern us in our normal, urban routines. While there is an element of truth in that notion, it's occasionally worth reminding ourselves that the wilderness environment is rarely problem-free and even amid the freedom and fresh air of the wild places some of those concerns, in their own way, can appear as awful as a tax investigation, or even worse...

We'd had a tense night. All the previous day the weather had been foul – incessant rain and low cloud – and we'd climbed out of the steep-sided Val d'Herens to try to gain as much height as possible before crossing the next big pass on our route, the 2,900m (9312 ft) Col de Torrent. I knew that these high slopes above the Val d'Herens were used as cattle pastures but we'd been trying to camp as discreetly as possible. We were all too aware that the Swiss discourage wild camping (although paradoxically, they appear happy enough to rip up most of their mountain slopes in the name of ski development).

We had found a little niche between a couple of large, protective rocks, well away from the footpath, and well away from prying eyes. Exhibiting the skills of a contortionist we'd managed to get ourselves dried off and into fresh clothes, never an easy task when two people are sharing a small, lightweight tent. We cooked supper in the bell end of the tent to the pitter-patter accompaniment of rain on the flysheet.

My wife Gina and I were backpacking between Chamonix and Zermatt. We were following the Walkers' Haute Route, a convoluted line that runs against the grain of a corrugated mountain landscape between the Rhone Valley and those high peaks that form the great icy walls of the Mont Blanc massif and the Pennine Alps. The better-known skiers' Haute Route more or less follows the crest of the high mountains, with relatively little altitude gain and loss but the walker's route doesn't get off so lightly. Rising and falling like a roller coaster, the Walkers' Haute Route crosses the long, north-projecting ridges of the Pennine Alps, a total of 11 high passes with a height accumulation of more than 36,000ft/11,000m. Descending into deep valleys fragrant with the scent of pine and hay, visiting timeless villages and hamlets, the route inevitably climbs again to rocky passes and cols, the haunt of marmots, ibex and chamois, a backpacking trip spiced with views of the most stunning and majestic mountains in Europe.

Earlier in the day we had left the tiny village of Arolla, set below the great glaciers that tumble down from Pigne d'Arolla and Mont Collon. In low cloud and drizzle, wrapped in our protective cocoons of Gore-Tex, we had tramped down-valley to the village of La Sage where we had cheered ourselves up for an hour in the comfort of a small village café. The afternoon had been spent climbing through the mist on switch-backed roads and footpaths, a silent and surreal ascent. Chalets and timber buildings occasionally loomed out of the smirry mist, amorphous grey shapes turned out to be a copse of trees, occasionally upstanding rocks. One time it was a bull, flat-faced, ring through its nose, its breath condensing in the cold air. At no time could we could see much more than 20m ahead of us. Only my altimeter watch suggested we had gained any real height.

Despite trying to camp discreetly, our tent was spotted by a passing cowherd. The mist had risen slightly and the cowherd had stopped on the opposite hillside and watched us for a while. Feeling slightly guilty about camping without asking permission I waved but he ignored my greeting and, for much of the evening we lay in our sleeping bags listening to the increasing clamour of cowbells. It sounded as though the beasts were being driven towards us. Would we have to endure an entire night driven to distraction by this bovine tintinnabulation? Could this be the cowherd's idea of a bad joke? My depression, initiated by the foul weather of the day, had obviously fed such a conspiracy theory and we were more than relieved when the bells eventually faded into the drizzly night as the cattle, bound for the sweeter pastures of the lower valley, passed us by. By the time we slipped into sleep silence had wrapped itself around our tent. I dreamed of backpacking in places where cows didn't have bells and sheep graze quietly…

Aware of the Swiss' disapproval of wild camping we had adopted the 'stealth camping' approach, a term coined by my American friend Ray Jardine. Ray has taken the word stealth as a derivation of steal, in the sense of moving or behaving inconspicuously, trying to avoid being noticed. Stealth camping avoids the established campsites and company of others and brings you closer to nature but in fact our definition was closer to Ray's derivation of 'steal'.

With an long standing abhorrence of mountain huts, which tend to be over-heated and inevitably overpopulated with snorers, coupled with our traditional Scots reluctance to spend money on hotels, we simply wanted to borrow, or steal, a patch of turf each night to pitch our tent, a little out-of-the-way green spot where we would have a view, preferably with a water supply close at hand. Unfortunately, finding a suitable combination of these three elements proved more difficult than we had imagined.

It astonished me how little wild land there is in the Alps below the snowline. High slopes that haven't been scarred by the ski industry are used as pasture land by cattle farmers. Herds of cattle, all with great bells hanging from their necks, graze these high alpine pastures, up to

10,000ft (3,000m) in some areas and cattle have an alarming aptitude for leaning against backpacking tents, more often than not with disastrous results for the occupants. Indeed, on the French side of our very first pass, the Col de Balme, a notice board had warned against camping for that very reason. Our reluctance to camp within a mile of a cow was understandable.

The next morning was spectacular. Like our tensions, the rain had evaporated during the night and left a clear, and cold, sky. There was a frost on the tent, slivers of ice in our water bottles and we packed up with cold-nipped fingers, eager to reach the high col above us where the sun could rid us of the cold dampness and warm our bones.

Exactly on cue we reached the pass at the same time as the sun. The views were outstanding. All thoughts of the night's tensions were forgotten as we sat in the newly-found warmth and identified the mountains arrayed before us. The Weisshorn dominated everything; close by lay the multi-topped Zinal Rothorn and its neighbour, the Ober Gabelhorn. Mont Collon, Pigne d'Arolla and Mont Blanc de Cheilon choked the head of the Arolla valley we had left the day before. We even caught a glimpse of an old friend – the Grand Combin, that incredible snow-clad peak that had dominated our days earlier in the week between Valle de Bagnes and Arolla. And away beyond them all, its great snow dome lifted majestically above the intervening ridges, was Mont Blanc itself, in whose shadow we had started our Alpine trek just a few days previously.

This is what the guidebooks had promised, this is what we had promised ourselves – early mornings in the mountains, blue skies, sunshine, tumbling glaciers, twisted ridges, shapely snow-covered peaks and green alps, and the promise of at least one good mountain day ahead of us. This morning the Alps breathed in visual perfection and were not to be found wanting.

It was a happy and content duo who wandered down the winding path from the Col de Torrent, past the azure Lac des Autannes to Lac de Moiry. Marmots whistled their alarm calls and small birds darted from hummock to hummock in front of us, leading our dance in the sun. Snow-clad peaks shimmered before us and our next pass, the Col de

Sorebois, offered a comparatively easy ascent. We were on holiday in one of the most spectacular countries in the world and the days stretched before us with the rich promise of fresh adventure.

But even through this elation I found myself contemplating how curious it was that even on a long walk like this, a two week holiday in the Alps, doing what I do and love best of all, I should be inflicted by doubts and fears. Little tensions and anxieties appeared to grow out of all proportion to their seriousness. Even in the perfection of this outstanding day, my joy was shadowed by concerns. They hung there like little webs in my consciousness, tenaciously, like dark clouds on a summer's day: concerns about the weather, about route-finding, about finding drinkable water and about where to camp – silly frustrations that took the edge off the joy of the moment.

It was as though I'd traded one bunch of worries and concerns, the usual conflicts about work and domestic matters, for another set of problems, albeit concerns of a simpler and less complex nature. I knew of course, deep in my knower, that these new concerns were all conquerable. They weren't particularly life-threatening and didn't endanger our comfort and plans to any unreasonably level, and I knew that with a minimum of effort I could solve them.

That of course was the critical factor.

I didn't have to rely on others to ease the stress; I didn't have to work my way through a time-consuming consultation process to come up with an answer; I didn't have to look up timetables, schedules or almanacs, and I didn't have to make appointments with lawyers or doctors to solve the problems. These were the simple day-to-day domestic concerns man has faced since time immemorial – finding a place to stay that is dry and warm, finding water to drink and food to eat and avoiding danger – what the writer Colin Fletcher refers to as grappling with the tangible instead of wrestling with the abstract.

But such simple problems, such age-old problems, are made no less complex by the knowledge that you can cope with them. They still exist, they still niggle away in the dark compartments of your mind and tend to be exacerbated when you have responsibility for others. My wife, who is also my closest friend, was walking with me. She is less experienced in the ways of the wild, less confident in her ability to cope with bad weather, steep ground and exposed slopes. In many ways we consolidate each others' skills for she has infinitely more common sense than I have and a let's-get-on-with-it attitude that more often than not compensates for my more airy-fairy, romantic notions of wilderness.

I had been concerned for her earlier in the week. It had been a long and difficult day. Early in the morning we had climbed from the tiny hamlet of Clambin, above the village of La Chamble, to the Cabane du Mont Fort, a height gain of some 2,300ft/700m made more difficult by the fact I lost the footpath amid the scars of bulldozed tracks newly-created to serve the nearby ski temple of Verbier. From the mountain hut we had three passes to cross, and a glacier, and a traverse of one of the most God-forsaken landscapes I've ever seen: the aptly-named Grand Desert, a great cirque of angry rock and scree, grey and desolate, an empty quarter of decay and destruction.

The traverse was particularly difficult for Gina as she finds boulder-hopping and negotiating rough scree slopes quite difficult, but it wasn't all bad. In fact it was a day of contrasts – a magnificent belvedere path, the Sentier de Chamois, led to the first pass, edging its way below steep crags, round sheer corners and up and down rocky buttresses. Across the valley, giving the impression we could reach out and touch it, rose the snowy splendour of the multi-topped Grand Combin, its snow wreaths dripping like cream, feeding the tumbling glaciers that poured from its flanks. And, as a bonus, as we neared the first of our day's passes, the Col Termin, a small herd of ibex clambered up the rocks in front of us, completely unconcerned by our presence.

One of them, a large and muscular buck with great swept back antlers, made his way up the steep crag beside us, stopped, turned round and gazed back across the col. His positioning was perfect. I managed to take a photograph across the Cirque de Louvie below us, with the ibex's head, shoulders and antlers silhouetted against a backdrop of the snow-tipped peaks of Rosablanche.

From the (8,787ft/2,679m) Col Termin, another good path traversed the steep slopes below the Bec Termin to our second pass, the broad Col de Louvie at 9,515ft/2,901m. From there the terrain became notably unfriendly, an angry landscape of boulder screes, stony chutes, snow patches and the lower reaches of the Grand Desert Glacier. Gina had never crossed a glacier before so I had to gently encourage her over the ice and running rivers of freezing cold water. There was no real objective danger but I could sense her tension. By this time she was tired and had to look with care to each step. Once across the glacier we thought we could see the final pass of the day just ahead of us but we were wrong. We still had to cross a rubble-strewn plateau before dropping again, this time to a silted glacial lake, from where the red-painted waymarks pointed to a steep and scree-covered slope, a tortuous sting in the tail.

Even the final descent from the col felt longer than it should and, by the time we had descended to the Cabane de Prafleuri, we decided against camping and booked in at the hut. In fact there were few places to camp anyway – the whole upper cirque of the Prafleuri was derelict, a miserable place, grey and gloomy and chilled by the running waters from the glaciers above. Quarriers had used the natural devastation of these glaciers to their advantage and their work had wrought its own destruction to the coombe. Vehicle tracks, muddy and rutted, criss-crossed the area and long-abandoned buildings hung from the slopes in various stages of decay. We were happy enough not to camp amid the gloom.

It had been a day of ups and downs, not only on the ground but in our spirits. We'd been uplifted by close sightings of marmots and ibex and the views to the wonderful Grand Combin but there was a real downside to it all. The horrendous damage that man inflicts on mountains in the name of ski development, almost as depressingly grim as the mining and quarrying in the great but sad cirque of Prafleuri, is surely too high a price to pay for a sport that claims to be environmentally friendly and sustainable. It was one of my favourite mountain authors, the late Bill Murray, who wrote shortly before he died: "Land and wildlife have their own being in their own right. Our recreation is an incidental gain, not an end in itself to be profitably pursued by exploiting land where that means degrading it.

Next morning the weather matched the surroundings – grey and gloomy. There's a lot of truth in the notion that our spirits go up and down in direct correlation to the barometer. It's probably a British thing – we see so little of the sun and blue skies that when we are finally exposed to such conditions our spirits naturally soar. When it's dull, grey and wet we respond with a depressed spirit, indeed many people can become so depressed that they become ill, victims of sunshine deprivation. The clinical condition known as Seasonal Affective Disorder is no myth – my own son suffers from it and has to resort to wearing a light visor for an hour or so ever day during the dark months of December and January. Psychologists in northern latitude countries like Norway and Iceland claim that SAD is a prime cause of stress, depression and even suicide. The condition has never affected me to the extent that I suffer clinical depression but it certainly wears me down. That's probably why I long for trips to mountain areas like California's Sierra Nevada, a range of mountains with the sunniest and mildest climate of any mountain range in the world.

I like the guarantee of good weather. To be fair, we'd enjoyed a fair amount of blue sky and sunshine but for much of this trip I found myself barometer-watching, eagerly anticipating a slow rise in the atmospheric pressure which would normally signal the advent of good weather and, paradoxically, dreading the inevitable drops.

The weather is also a great topic of conversation in the mountains, a topic we Brits are well practised in. We met an old lady one morning, an Englishwoman living in Arolla and she told us the weather would improve in the afternoon, be good the next day but it would probably snow by the weekend. I hoped she was joking but, as it happened, she wasn't. On our last two passes, the Forcletta Pass and the Augstbordpass, we experienced falling snow and when we camped in the campsite at Tasch, just below Zermatt, we woke in the morning to frozen water bottles and a tent flysheet that was stiff and thick with frost. And it was only early September, the coldest September for years according to locals.

I guess it's fortunate we have no control over the weather and because we can't control it there's little point worrying about it too much. But we do. We fret and complain, check the barometer again and become convinced the weather forecasters are wrong. Civilisation offers us all the shelter we would ever need to protect us from bad weather; indeed we could barricade ourselves away for months on end if we wanted to, safe and dry and warm, entertained by books, videos and television and provisioned by regular deliveries from the supermarket. But the wilderness exposes us to the weather and to all our innate fears. No-one wants to be trapped on a high col in a blizzard. No-one wants to be soaked through on a windswept mountainside, so we have to plan accordingly, we need the flexibility to adjust our plans to suit the weather of the moment.

Despite popular misconceptions the wilderness doesn't embrace us and hold us to its bosom in a protective clutch. The whole concept of a loving Mother Nature is nothing but a myth thought up by urban mystics. But, by the same token, neither is the wilderness hostile. In truth it's indifferent. Wilderness doesn't need us, it doesn't even notice us and because of its indifference the wilderness is a place where we can both lose ourselves and, paradoxically, find ourselves. It's a place where we find both darkness and light, joy and sorrow, hope and despair and, despite the fact that our best trips are those in which our spirits take off and soar in the heavens for days or weeks at a time, the reality is that even the bad times can offer us teachable moments in which we can grow and further equip ourselves from that great storehouse known as experience.

In Shakespeare's *Hamlet,* the hero claims: "there's a special providence in the fall of a sparrow. If it be now, 'tis not to come; if it be not to come, it will be now; if it be not now, yet it will come; the readiness is all."

So often we lack such readiness, and discover with some surprise that providence seems to lie in wait when a situation is looking at its blackest, then pounces into our lives bringing with it an unexpected ray of sunshine that disperses the gloom and leaves us richer for the experience.

Such providence can turn a potential problem into a rich blessing.

The Turtmanntal has been described as a valley lost in time, a remnant of a forgotten world. Within its forested flanks you feel you have stepped back a hundred years in time. There is no ski development, no gaudy chalets, no hotel complex. The village of Gruben-Meiden is a cluster of timber houses and a hotel, set around the tiny white chapel. Close by the Hotel Schwarzhorn is plain and clean and friendly; we decided to stay there, since there was nowhere to camp. And we made the most of it, luxuriating in the hot showers, enjoying a plain but pleasant meal and greedily quaffing a couple of bottles of local Valais wine.

When I came to pay the bill in the morning the hotel managed to live up to the valley's old-fashioned, lost-in-time, tradition. The girl wouldn't accept my credit card. "Cash only," was her stark insistence. The reputation of Switzerland as the epicentre of the world's economy had obviously never infiltrated the steep-side bastion of the Turtmanntal!

Digging deep in all my pockets I managed to find enough cash to pay the bill, right down to my last Swiss franc, leaving me completely cashless. We didn't worry unduly about it. All we had to do was cross the 9,345ft/2,849m Augstbordpass, drop down to the town of St Nicklaus and find a bank with a hole-in-the-wall cash withdrawal facility. This after all was Switzerland, the country of the gnomes of Zurich and the most modern banking systems in the world.

It was slightly inconvenient, as we'd set our hearts on staying at Jungen, a highly recommended hamlet high above the Mattertal but it was doubtful if they'd accept credit cards either. Everything appeared fairly straightforward but life on the trail isn't always like that. We dropped down from the summit of the Augstbordpass to St Nicklaus, a huge descent which left us knee-wracked and footsore. We found the bank (it was Sunday so it was closed) and its hole-in-the-wall facility but for some perverse reason it wouldn't accept my credit card.

Cashless, we had become down-and-outs for the night. There was no campsite in St Nicklaus and it looked as though we might have to climb back up the hill to try to find a stealth camp somewhere, a thought that didn't appeal to us at all. It was then that providence, in the form of the local stationmaster, turned the uncertainty of the afternoon into an evening of sheer delight.

Seeing us pass, no doubt looking rather disconsolate, he asked us, in perfect English, if there was anything he could do to help us? We

The glacial landscape of Yosemite with Half Dome standing proud.

Cathedral Peak, first climbed by John Muir.

Minimalist backpacking with hiking guru Ray Jardine.

Yosemite Falls where John Muir overcame his fears to experience the sensation of being a waterfall.

Annie Getchell of PBS Television and the author perched on the tiny summit of Cathedral Peak.

Ben A'an in the Trossachs – lowly but much loved.

On the Sentiers de Chamois between the Cabane du Mont Fort and the
Col Termin on the Walkers' Haute Route.

A chamois surveys his kingdom.

The lovely hamlet of Jungen, set high above the Matterdal.

Sgurr nan Each in the Fannichs.

Beyond the Cabrach from the summit of the Tap o' Noth.

Seana Bhraigh, a contender for Scotland's remotest Munro.

Loch Skeen and the slopes of White Coomb.

The densely forested slopes of the Kumaon Himalaya have escaped the mass deforestation of many other Himalayan regions.

explained the position and he waved his hand as though to negate the problem. "I have a friend in Gasenried, on the other side of the valley. He has a lovely hotel and it's well-used by walkers. And he takes credit cards. No problem. I'll phone him and tell him to expect you."

I hesitated, not fancying the idea of having to walk another 2,000ft up the opposite hillside, but he waved away my objection. "There is a bus leaving in a few minutes. The tickets will cost you nothing and from the bus stop it is only a ten minute walk to my friend's hotel."

That sorted out we were even more delighted when he hurried out after us as we were about to board the bus. "I've telephoned my friend again and said your little lady looked to be very tired. He said he would come and collect you from the bus stop."

And so he did. Armin Truffer-Lauber and his family ran the excellent Hotel Alpen Rosli in Gasenried, high above St Nicklaus. The views from our room were spectacular and so was the dinner we ate in the evening. We even had an *en suite* bath, which both of us made full use of. As I lay in the hot water, soap bubbles floating around my ears, I reflected on my amazement, and delight, at how complete strangers so often come up trumps and turn my normally curmudgeonly attitude to the human race upside down. The stationmaster at St Nicklaus saved our day and restored my faith in people, at least for a while.

These little experiences of our long walk in the Alps serve as a reminder that there is sometimes a danger that our expectancy of long walking holidays is rose-tinted. While there is more often than not a real and genuine release from the everyday problems that afflict us in our normal working routine we would only be fooling ourselves by pretending that life on the trail was nothing but strawberries and cream.

The problems, difficulties, concerns and tensions are as real on a mountainside as they are in a city office, in a university, or even at home, but remember this: such problems tend not to be life-threatening, they will not result in bankruptcy and, other than in the most drastic cases, divorce doesn't even come on to the agenda. Whether you like it or not the normal experience of a long mountain walk is a *potpourri* of emotional highs and lows, a cornucopia of impressions and feelings that drag your spirit into the slough of despondency one minute only to send it soaring with the eagles the next. On balance we tend to soar more often than we slough and thankfully, because of the selective nature of our memory, we tend to lean towards the happier experiences rather than fall back into the dark holes.

But there is always the risk that we allow such trivia to inflate to such an extent that it fills our complete consciousness, and once that darkness squeezes out the light we might as well call it a day and go home. Those who are new to the trail will face a host of fears and uncertainties, all of which have the potential to inflate and explode and send you scurrying for the comforts of four brick walls and a tiled roof. It's therefore vital to pin-prick those little balloons of uncertainty before they get too big.

Experience helps a lot – it doesn't always stop the problems appearing but it teaches you how to deal with them and the more trips you complete the more you realise how easily the little fears and uncertainties can grow out of proportion. Your fretting becomes less overwhelming with the years but the syndrome is still there. We just learn to control it, and control it we must, before it controls us.

I recorded my reactions to that Alpine trip in some detail in a series of daily notes and I was intrigued to discover, some weeks after our return home, that my memories of the trip were diametrically opposite to some of the fears and concerns I had written down at the time. Even the bad times were good. It's as well our memories are selective...

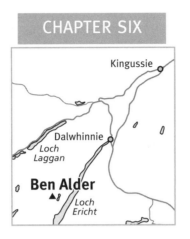

CHAPTER SIX

BEN ALDER – A HILL WORTH RAVEN ABOUT

It was dark by the time I reached Alder Bay. Earlier in the day I had left Rannoch and followed the winding 'Road to the Isles' track that skirts the eastern fringes of the Rannoch Moor. From Loch Ossian waterlogged footpaths took me east towards the open jaws of the Bealach Dubh between Geal Charn and Ben Alder before another track, a beautifully-maintained one this time, took me down towards Loch Ericht and the bay.

The shaft of white light from my headtorch pierced the darkness as I stumbled downhill and eventually the white gable end of the remote Benalder Cottage suddenly appeared in front of me. I had initially planned to spend the night in the cottage, now used as a bothy but, enveloped in the Cimmerian blackness of the night, I opted for my tent and a stretch of turf way beyond the building.

Ben Alder is a remote mountain, a big bastion of a hill that demands a long walk-in and I reckon it's all the better for that – it turns an ordinary hill-walk into an expedition and gives the mountain a distinct air of gravitas. A friend of mine was badly frost-bitten on Ben Alder a few winters ago and two others severely underestimated the remoteness of the hill and had to be helicoptered out. It's ill-advised to underestimate Ben Alder.

Situated close to the south-western reaches of Loch Ericht, Ben Alder's upper reaches make up a vast plateau that contains about 400 acres of ground above 3,500ft (1,067m). Cairngorm-like, it's surrounded by wind-scoured corries, particularly those that show their sculptured faces to the east. These great hollows often hold snow long into the summer, the melting waters of which feed the high-level Loch a'Bhealaich Bheithe, beyond which lies, like a cradling arm, the long ridge of the neighbouring Munro, Beinn Bheoil.

Ben Alder and Beinn Bheoil form two of the high points in a great tract of land between Loch Laggan and Loch Ericht. No roads and few tracks pierce this wilderness but access can be gained by the Glasgow to Fort William West Highland Railway, from the station and bunkhouse at Corrour. There's also a handy youth hostel at the western end of Loch Ossian. This is the start of a long 27 mile traverse of Ben Alder and Beinn Bheoil, eventually walking out to Dalwhinnie to return home by train, a fabulous weekend expedition. Whichever route you take, you are assured of fine hills which make the most of their central position to offer majestic views in all directions, a wild area that is rich in legend and folklore.

One of the more contemporary tales is the haunting of Benalder cottage. Many walkers have apparently heard strange noises in the night, like furniture being moved around, but I was more interested in the tale of the Witch's Stone, a great split boulder which lies close to the Allt Fuaran Mhic Bheathain which I had passed in the darkness the night before. The story behind the stone is this. Redcoats were searching for Charles Edward Stuart after Culloden when it became known that the Prince was in hiding with Cluny Macpherson somewhere on Ben Alder. Arriving near Alder Bay, the soldiers met an old woman and they offered her a bag of gold coins if she told them the whereabouts of Cluny's Cage, Macpherson's hiding place. The old woman grabbed the money bag and told the soldiers to follow her up a faint track and into the mists that rolled down from the mountain's summit.

As they approached the summit, a young corporal stumbled and fell flat on his face. Slightly dazed, he eventually managed to get to his feet and following the others through the mist he was just in time to see the old woman and the soldiers fall head-long over a cliff, and hurtle down on to the rocks a thousand feet below. But before their screams had died away, the old witch rose from the rocks in the form of a raven and, screeching in triumph, flew off in the direction of Alder Bay.

Shocked, the corporal returned downhill and saw the witch-bird perched on a rock. Creeping up quietly behind the raven he raised his sword and brought it down with all his strength, killing the bird outright. Such was the force of his blow, the rock itself was virtually cleaved in two. And if you don't believe me, go and look for yourself. The stone is still there, split in half by the fury of the corporal's sword.

From Benalder Cottage the route to the summit is fairly straightforward. Follow the burn up to the rock-splattered Bealach Breabag. Don't cross the bealach but just short of its summit climb the broken ground to the left to reach the prominent ridge that forms the rim of the impressive Garbh Choire. Follow the ridge for about a kilometre to reach a high lochan, the Lochan a' Garbh Choire, and at this point leave the corrie edge and cross the huge, flat plateau, to the summit cairn and trig point. In misty weather accurate navigation is essential.

North of the summit two slim ridges offer a choice of descent – the Short Leachas, which drops down just north of Loch a'Bhealaich Bheithe, and the Long Leachas, which forms the southern boundary of the Bealach Dubh. The Short Leachas is steeper and involves some good scrambling while the Long Leachas is technically easier. A third descent option gives the opportunity of climbing Ben Alder's Munro neighbour, Beinn Bheoil. Make your way back down to the Bealach Breabag and from a point south of the bealach summit turn north-east and climb heather and boulder slopes to the summit of Sron Coire na-h-Iolaire, a magnificently airy perch high above Loch Ericht. North, the ridge stretches out for some distance and after a short descent climbs steadily to the summit of Beinn Bheoil.

An excellent footpath runs downhill from the Lochan a'Bhealaich

Bheithe to Culra bothy where another path runs past Loch Pattack to the new Disneyesque-styled Ben Alder Lodge and the bulldozed track alongside Loch Ericht to Dalwhinnie. There has been some exceptional footpath work carried out on this estate and the bothy book at Culra contains many compliments to whoever has sweated and navvied so hard. Ben Alder Estate is one with a long reputation of kindness and welcome to walkers. It's certainly much appreciated.

CHAPTER SEVEN

BEYOND LOVELY LOCH A' BHRAOIN

It has been said that Loch a' Bhraoin in Wester Ross is pretty ordinary in terms of landscape. A sentence in an environmental report prepared for Norweb Hydro by a company called SGS Environment made the following arrogant assumption: "The area is attractive but typical of large areas of Scotland, and thus of no special value."

Whoever wrote those unseeing words had obviously never crept down from the high Fannichs on a late winter afternoon, tired but with spirits lifted by the quiet presence of the loch. They had obviously never experienced the spirit of the place as the sun sets, turning the sky purple and pink, the very same hues reflected in the water, the surrounding hills inky black as daylight gives way reluctantly to the creeping dark.

Norweb Hydro wanted to dam Loch a' Bhraoin, pipe the water from the Abhainn Cuileag to a turbine house further down the glen and string power lines across the entire area. Okay, I hear the fatcats say, but that's progress and we need sustainable power in the Highlands – and what about the local jobs that will be created? Well, let me tell you, councillors and do-gooders and developers and your like, this appalling scheme would have produced a paltry maximum power output of 3,200 kiliwatts, at a time when Britain already has surplus generating capacity and is bringing on-stream more huge gas-fired power stations. Oops, I almost forgot – operation of this plant would produce one full-time job!

The attraction for Norweb was the extra sum paid by the Government for each unit of power produced from a renewable source. In short, money-grabbing greed induced by the Government at the cost of the destruction of Scotland's greatest asset: her landscape.

In the 1980s similar schemes were proposed for the Grudie and Talladale Rivers which run into Loch Maree from the Flowerdale Forest. Following an outcry, the proposals were rejected by the Secretary of State. If this scheme at Loch a' Bhraoin went through, the floodgates could have been opened up for similar projects at Loch na Sealga and the Gruinard River, Loch Maree and the River Ewe, the Kirkaig River, Loch Assynt and the River Inver, the Traligall River at Inchnadamph, the Laxford, Loch Dionard and so on. Those who love the wild places have to constantly be on their guard, have to be prepared to write letters and lobby councillors and Members of Parliament, and should make it a duty to participate in the politics of conservation. I talk to hundreds of hill-goers every year who whinge and complain that they don't want to become involved in politics, but not to do so is a shameless act of irresponsibility. We can bury our heads in the sand, but don't be surprised if, when we eventually pull our heads out, places such as Loch a' Bhraoin have been lost forever.

Thankfully this particular planning application was turned down and thousands of hill-goers breathed a sigh of relief for they appreciate the worth of Loch a' Bhraoin. Most hill-walkers are familiar with it because it forms the prelude for forays into the western Fannichs, those big hills of Sgurr Breac and A'Chailleach, Meall a' Chrasgaidh, Sgurr nan Clach Geala and Sgurr nan Each. Mirroring the distant Craig Rainich and the northern slopes of Slioch, the waters of the loch lie beyond the skeletal ruins of an old boat house. It's a lovely scene as you cross the wooden bridge over the Abhainn Cuileag which begins its tumultuous course through a succession of ravines and gorges, all overhung with alder and rowan, towards its confluence with the River Broom just below the

Corrieshalloch Gorge.

There are nine Munros in the Fannichs and the main thrust of the group is the long ridge immediately north of Loch Fannich, a ridge that can be reached by a muddy stalkers' path from Fannich Lodge. It's a rather broad and uninspiring ridge to be honest but things improve as you head west, your eyes drawn to the north face of Sgurr nan Clach Geala, the Peak of the White Stones, at 3,586ft/1,093m without doubt the most impressive of all the Fannichs. With its near neighbours, Sgurr nan Each and Meall a' Chrasgaidh, Sgurr nan Clach Geala lies on the east side of the footpath which runs through from Loch Fannich to Loch a' Bhraoin, a stalkers' path which offers a fine exit from Sgurr nan Each after a traverse of all three Munros.

Beyond Loch a' Braoin, this stalker's path follows the Allt Breabaig south for a kilometre before crossing the burn and traversing across the big, meaty flanks of Meall a' Chrasgaidh. Leave the path here and take to the heather, a long and relentless climb to the domed summit at 3,064ft/934m. As its name, the Rounded Hill of the Crossing would perhaps suggest, Meall a' Chrasgaidh lacks the ruggedness of some of its near neighbours.

From Chrasgaidh a long slope leads to a wide bealach, crowned by a tiny lochan. I once camped up here, arriving in a dense fog. As I cooked my supper the mist began to clear to leave a temperature inversion covering everything below me. Out west, the pinnacles of An Teallach rose to its broken crest, with the sun just dipping between its twin summits of Sgurr Fiona and Bidein a' Ghlas Thuill, casting an orange-pink glow on the low clouds below it.

Beyond the bealach, rocky slopes lead to the north-east ridge of Sgurr nan Clach Geala. This is the undoubtedly the finest of the Fannichs with its high, hanging corrie and steep buttresses. Its graceful curved ridge rises to a narrow summit ridge and then widens as it descend to another bealach, the Cadha na Guite. The shapely 3,328ft/923m summit of Sgurr nan Each lies before you and it's an easy climb to the top. Return to the Cadha na Guite, drop down the slopes to the west-north-west and follow the stalkers' path back to lovely Loch a' Bhraoin.

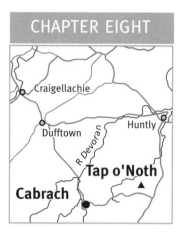

BEYOND THE CABRACH

A clutch of marvellous little hills form the highest points in the well varied stretch of countryside that lies between the Spey, the Deveron and the Don, and nowhere are they better viewed from than the craggy summit of the intriguingly named Tap o' Noth.

This majestically conical hill rises to a mere 1,851ft (564m) but it dominates the countryside around the north-east village of Rhynie. It's a fairly easy walk to the summit, despite the apparent steepness of the slopes, and the views from the rocky top are widespread, with the prominent ridge of the Buck of Cabrach (2,366ft/721m) to the south-west, Ben Rinnes (2,755ft/840m) looming over tree-clad hills to the west and the isolated swells of Knock Hill and The Bin to the north.

An ancient local rhyme proclaims, "When Tap o' Noth puts on her cap, the Rhynie folk will get a drap", so make sure you get a decent day to enjoy the far-flung views from the summit.

This is a fascinating landscape, perhaps not the currently fashionable wild land of Munros and Corbetts and certainly not in any sense a wilderness, but a worked and lived-in landscape that has been softened and mellowed by generations of gritty fairm-toon workers. The agricultural heritage of these north-eastern corners of Aberdeenshire, Buchan, Banff and Moray is a craggy, hard-nosed legacy, celebrated even today in the traditional bothy ballads. In days gone-by you had to be blessed with perseverance to be a north-east farmer as you cleared the boulder-strewn fields and cultivated the thin skin of earth that covered the bony land. Much the same determination was required to sing your way through a 46-verse north-east bothy ballad.

The legacy of all that agricultural toil is a landscape that is now tamed and controlled. Great blocks of monoculture forestry contrast harshly with the softer greens and browns of the gently rolling hills and only the distant swell of the Cairngorms give any suggestion of ruggedness. The predominant schists, diorites and limestone break down into thin but comparatively fertile soils and the cultivated fields are lush compared to the bare heather moors of the Cabrach, Glen Livet and Glen Fiddich to the west, a contrast which is marked when seen from the Tap o' Noth's summit.

This blunted top is formed by a circular wall of vitrified stone, melted and fused by the tremendous heat generated by the firing of a wooden Iron Age fort. It's likely the name Tap o' Noth comes from the Gaelic 'taip a'nochd', which roughly translates as a look-out top, but Peter Drummond, in his excellent *Scottish Hill and Mountain Names*, prefers the local folk tale. Legend has it that the hill's giant, one Jack o' Noth, having stolen the sweetheart from his neighbour, Jack o' Bennachie, was flattened on his own hilltop by a huge boulder hurled by his cuckolded neighbour.

The route to the summit is more complicated than it looks and it's a route I know well. Some years ago I learnt to parapente here, running downhill from close to the summit until the wind filled the parachute and lifted me gently from the ground. Hours were spent slowly and effortlessly descending from the summit, suspended from the multi-coloured canopy and gazing out at the surrounding landscape, taking in its features and possible landing places. The downside was the long haul from our landing spot back up the hill to take-off.

Despite that it's always good to return to the Tap o' Noth, *sans* parapente. From the car park at Scurdargue a track leads to a gate which gives access to a field of rough pasture. The track crosses the field into a stand of woodland where, at the top left corner of the wood (north-west), it passes through another gate and runs steadily uphill beside a fence, through a thicket of broom bushes. All the time you get the distinct feeling you're being carried away from the hill itself and there's a temptation to break your way through the broom to reach the lower slopes. It's worth sticking with the path though.

Another stand of forestry appears ahead, with rough pasture land on its right. Avoiding the forestry you can choose a line up over the pasture to reach a broad track which climbs up Tap o' Noth's western slopes from the north end of the plantation. This track runs all the way to the top, up the tight zig-zag on the hill's south flank and through the main eastern portals of the summit fortification.

By any standard, the size and scope of this hill-fort is extraordinary. The second highest hill fort in Scotland (the highest is Ben Griam Beg in Sutherland at 2,034ft/620m), the area enclosed by the surrounding walls is about the size of a football field. This grassy and semi-level interior is protected by these massive vitrified walls, but who lit the fires that burned this wooden Iron Age fort at such a temperature that the stones of the walls literally melted and fused together? Indeed, who built the fort in the first place? Examples of vitrified fortifications are to be found throughout Scotland but nowhere is there anything on this scale. According to Adam Watson, this fort of Tap o' Noth dates from the same Iron Age period as the fort of Dunnideer near Insch in Aberdeenshire. However, the large archway of Dunnideer Castle apparently dates from medieval times, possibly made of materials from the older fort.

It's good to lie up here, sheltered from the winds by these ancient walls, and consider the events that led to the destruction of this once-great fort. The fire must have burned for days, even weeks, and the great cloud of smoke must have covered the countryside like a dark cloak, the ominous legacy of a conquering race. The gentle fields and rolling hills that surround the Tap o' Noth could never be described as wilderness but, up here on the summit, the shimmering mists of time provide a wilderness setting that allows even the least fanciful of minds to roam widely in the impossible quest of recovering the lost fragments of our history.

CHAPTER NINE

ENCOUNTERS OF A
NATURAL KIND

O ne of the great joys in spending time in wilderness is the
opportunity to observe the comings and goings of those
birds and beasts with whom we share this planet. In
watching a squirrel scampering up a tree or wondering at the
majestic flight of an eagle we become aware of the simple magic
of the moment. In that wonder there is often a sense of beauty,
an instinctive recognition of the existence of order, a determined
pattern behind the behaviour of things, a celebration of order
and harmony. But there are some beasts living out there who
simply remind us that man is not as dominant as he thinks he is
and those lessons are probably the most valuable of all...

Backpacking alone in the high country of Yosemite National Park I
experienced one of those little wildlife encounters that makes your mind
reel. I had been in the high country for several days, easing myself into
that mood of tranquillity that the wilderness provides. As I approached
a granite boulder that lay on the side of the trail a large, pale-brown-

going-on-grey canine shape appeared, stopped in the trail and calmly gazed at me. There was no surprise in its look nor alarm, its close-set eyes looked almost kindly and its black nose twitched slightly. Astonished, I half expected to see someone come round the trail and call it to heel – for all the world it looked like a large Alsatian dog.

In my surprise I half-whispered a greeting, as you would to a dog, then a brief, very brief, shadow of alarm passed across my mind as the dog, or whatever it was, continued to stand and stare at me. I was still walking and was slowly reaching for my camera when it suddenly turned and walked back into the woods. Curiously, the little cloud of fear still lingered as I passed the rock seconds later, as though I half expected the beast to jump out at me, snarling and salivating. Was it lying in wait behind the rock? Was it perhaps hiding there? But I knew better and beyond the rock, about 30 yards away, I just glimpsed a long-legged shape with a long tail float into the bush.

At first I thought the animal might have been a wolf, the wolf of legend, the mysterious wolf that had given succour to the Roman Empire, the indigenous wolf of the North American native people, but this was surely coyote country? As far as I was aware wolves hadn't existed in Yosemite National Park for more than 100 years but when you're backpacking on your own miles from anywhere the mind can play fanciful tricks – there was something in that face, the close-set eyes, the prominent ears, the black cheek markings and in the general demeanour of the beast….

In fact it was a coyote – I checked with photographs later – but the encounter made me realise once again that man is the intruder in areas like this. I also became aware that my own basic anthropocentrism had reared its ugly head in that shadow of fear, that I was reacting to ancient alarm instincts that were buried deep within my own genetic make-up.

But there were also deeper and more ancient instincts that reared up within hours of the encounter. It seemed as though some place of mystery had been opened up and I had experienced an affinity with that particular wild animal. For most of my life I have known the precious intimacy that can be shared with pets, in my case dogs, and for a brief moment I recognised that same intimacy in a wild creature, in this case a coyote. In that brief encounter my world and the coyote's world became the same. I found myself looking back at myself through the steady gaze of the coyote's eyes – I sensed the kinship that we share with all wild animals. In that moment I was aware that there is no separation between them and us: it was the meeting of two as one that stood out prominently in my memory.

Most wildlife encounters aren't so dramatic but I've been blessed over the years with several such face-to-face meetings with wild animals and all of them have bestowed on me a sense of beauty and magic, sensations that never fail to fill me with hope and optimism, feelings that can be curiously rare in a sometimes dreary world.

Such encounters can have a lasting effect and bring a wide array of sensations and instincts into play. I've known sheer delight when watching a family of otters slipping and sliding into a river from a muddy bank. I've been stunned by the aerial speed of a peregrine falcon tearing the sky in two. I've sat, highly amused, below an ancient Caledonian pine from where a red squirrel has scolded me for invading its space and I've known downright fear when faced with the huge bulk of a Californian black bear at close quarters, even though I knew all I had to do was shout at it and it would, in all probability, run away.

In all these situations, even that of the bear, I was aware of the simple wonder of the moment and, in that wonder, always a sense of beauty, an instinctive recognition of the existence of order, a determined pattern behind the behaviour of things, a celebration of order and harmony.

The first time I realised this kind of natural harmony was a number of years ago as I walked through a forest near my home in the Cairngorms. It was early in the morning and the woods were hushed with the misty expectancy of early summer. Several roe deer bounded across the track in front of me, ethereal in the still evaporating mists, their coats a bright brownish red. As I walked quietly round a particular bend in the track, I came upon a young doe browsing at the edge of the forest above the track. I stopped and froze and slowly reached for my camera that was hanging from my rucksack strap.

Never have I seen such an attractive beast; her movements all had a winning abruptness, from the jaunty way she picked up her legs as she moved from patch to patch, to the jerky flicking of her tail. Just as I managed to focus on her she suddenly looked up at me, warned by some ancient animal instinct. In the brief moment that her dark liquid eyes met mine through the lens of the camera I was so totally and utterly bewitched by her guileless innocence that I could not press the shutter release.

Her nose was black and twitching slightly, and around it the short wax-smooth pelage was white, contrasting richly with her auburn coat. But it was her eyes that enchanted me, so dark, so impenetrable, showing no sign of the fear that her instincts so surely must have been signalling to her. As quickly as she looked up at me she was gone, vanished in a blur of total precision and perfect deportment so fast that I barely had time to take the picture. As it happened all I managed to get on record was a flashing warning tail as she turned to bound into the trees but I was left with a much more important experience than a mere photographic snapshot – an almost overwhelming wonder of the immensity of that moment as I gazed eye-to-eye into the beautiful symmetry of nature. If I had been carrying a gun rather than a camera I would have broken it over my knee and thrown the pieces away in that blinding moment, rather than attempt to take the life of something so innocent, so exquisite…

So often beauty in nature is a product of function – look at the wonderful markings and colours of so many of our common birds – and yet there is still something within our Judeo-Christian heritage psyche that reacts against the inevitability of evolution. We try to disprove evolutionary theories by creating myths, even about our wildlife.

Legend claims that our little orange breasted robin was once as drab as a city sparrow. It was when the robin tried, in vain, to wrest the crown of thorns from the head of the crucified Christ that his breast became saturated in the blood of Jesus, creating the identifying feature we know and love today.

And just as the valiant robin tried so hard to relieve Jesus of his discomfort so he was helped by another little bird who tried his best to pull the nails from Christ's hands and feet. So hard did he try that all he managed to do was get his mandibles crossed, ending up with a rather deformed-looking beak. Today, of course, we recognise the crossbill because of that feature. But the crossbill, also known as the Scottish parrot, can be seen in the pinewoods of Strathspey effectively using his 'deformity' to remove seeds from tough pine cones.

Other birds have religious connections. Take Gille Bride, the servant of Saint Bride. This is the oystercatcher which, tradition claims, sheltered Jesus with his wings as Christ was trying to avoid the dark forces of Satan. For his brave deed the oystercatcher was taken under the protection of Saint Bride, the patron saint of all birds. In some areas the skylark is supposed to have an even more exalted patronage. In Eriskay, for example, he is known as uiseag Mhuire, or Mary's lark.

According to the poet Longfellow, when Noah decided that the waters had began to subside and land must be close, he sent out a dove to search for it. A kingfisher, who at that time was apparently clad in dull grey feathers, was sent out shortly after the dove but the kingfisher had decided that life on the Ark was not particularly to his liking and had little intention of returning. Unfortunately, the mountainous land that he discovered didn't look very appealing either. Instead, he flew higher and higher until the very sky turned his back blue and the sun burned his breast bright red. He flew so high that he lost the Ark and, in a wild panic, descended back to the land in search of his erstwhile home which suddenly didn't appear so bad after all. Even today, the kingfisher spends all his time flying up and down rivers in search of his lost home.

But not all birds have Judeo-Christian connections. The scurrilous magpie is associated with evil, the preponderance of which is associated with the number seen at any one time. Magpies are certainly increasing in numbers, especially in urban areas, so this legend doesn't augur well for the future of our cities. It was the Brahan Seer who once claimed in the Gaelic: "Chunnaic mi Pioghaid is dh'eirich leam, Chunnaic mi dha's gum b'iarguinn iad, Chunnaic mi tri a's b'aihearach mi, Ach ceithir ri m'linn ch'n iarainn iad."

Translated, the Seer's words claim: "I saw a magpie, to me then luck did die, I once saw two and they troubled me, Great joy was on me when once I saw three, But four forever let me not see."

The red fox is another creature that has enjoyed mythical

connections; folk tales of Reynard the Fox, widely circulated during the Middle Ages, were enormously popular. Reynard was regarded as a lone hunter, a poacher, sly and cunning. Often thought to be half-dog and half-cat he was considered a breaker of convention, at home, both day or night, in the woods, hedgerows and, indeed, on the hills. Politically too, by using the fox as a champion of peasant aspirations, Reynard was commonly seen as a hero, using his inherent native cunning to keep one step ahead of officialdom and establishment figures.

I have to confess to a stout admiration for the red fox, although in more than 30 years of wandering hills and mountains I've only encountered a hill fox on three occasions. The first time was in Morvern where I was walking with Tom Weir. We had sailed into Loch a' Choire in a friend's boat and Tom and I climbed the hill just west of Kingairloch village. We were so engrossed in our blethering it was a surprise we saw anything but, as we sat down by some rocks to eat our lunch, some sixth sense suggested to me that we were being watched.

Responding to the intuition, I looked slowly round and was surprised to see, not 20 yards from where we sat, an old dog fox nonchalantly watching us from the top of a bluff. I quietly nudged Tom to look behind and as we took our cameras from our packs old Reynard stood up, shook himself and padded off up the hill, as relaxed and unconcerned as you like. It was the highlight of our day.

My second sighting of a hill fox was less of a formal encounter. I was walking in upper Glen Lyon when I stopped for a breather and looking back down the hill from where I had come I noticed a russet blur. It was a fox running up the hill from the roadside. As he approached me he obviously caught my scent for he drastically changed direction and ran off over an intermediary rise. I suspect he had been scavenging down near a farm, was disturbed by a car on the road and had fled up the hill.

The most recent encounter was the strangest of all. My wife Gina and I were camping by Angle Tarn below Bowfell in the Lake District. We had arrived at the tarn in the late afternoon after a cold day of blustery showers. Our plan was to cook and eat our evening meal, then walk it off by climbing Scafell Pike, England's highest mountain, in the evening. It was a grand evening wander and we arrived back at the tent about nine o'clock, had some supper and settled in for the night, a very wet one as it happened.

At three in the morning I was abruptly wakened by the sound of things falling over in the bell end of the tent, no more than ten inches from my ear. When I pulled down the zip between the inner and outer tent and shone my torch, I immediately realised that our food bag, a large white net bag with the next morning's breakfast and lunch inside, was missing. Thinking that a sheep had perhaps nosed in under the tent I jumped out of my sleeping bag and into the wet, dark night, wearing no more than my underpants. Torch in hand, with the rain teeming down, I saw that it wasn't a sheep but a fox, who sat no more than 20 yards away tearing at the bag, trying to get at the food inside.

As soon as the fox saw me, it tried to run off, dragging the bag behind it before giving it up and making good its escape. I retrieved the bag, came back to the tent and as I approached it my wife, who by this time was wondering what on earth was going on, shouted at me to turn around. There was the fox, following no more than ten yards behind. With little apparent shyness and a disconcerting lack of fear, it watched me as I threw the food bag into the tent and climbed back in to dry myself off. After a few minutes it padded off into the night, apparently unfazed by the experience.

I can only think that the fox was used to stealing from tents. Many people camp at this spot and climb Scafell Pike as we had done, leaving their tent unattended. Possibly our fox was a vixen with a family to feed, or perhaps it was a tame fox, possibly hand-reared and used to human beings. Whatever the reason, our fox encounter made it a night to remember.

More often than not our encounters with wild beasts and birds are simply accepted as part and parcel of a good day in the hills but occasionally such encounters are remembered as being particularly distinct in themselves, making an otherwise ordinary day something rather more memorable. One such occasion was on the marvellous Sgurans ridge, the western outliers of the main Cairngorms massif.

Six-thirty saw me tackle the Foxhunter's Path from Achlean, through a haze of gossamer mist, brightly lit by the sun which was obviously shining strongly above the topmost strands. Sure enough, as I topped the broad crest of Carn Ban Mor I burst clear of the mist into a world of intense brightness. In front of me, the undulating plateau of the Moine Mhor lay wreathed in a sea of cloud, only the higher tops breaking through to stand out like islands in a woolly sea.

A herd of red deer hinds shared the summit with me – as though intoxicated by the already-hot sun they lay still as I passed within 20m of them. I could smell their pungent scent, the deer mustiness, and could even hear them chewing. They were just too hot to bother with me.

In front of me the long slopes of Sgor Gaoith rose into the blue sky. A marvellous peak this, Peak of the Winds, almost leaning outwards over the great void which holds Loch Einich. The granite appears as though piled block-on-top-of-block, as though an ancient giant has tried to dam the creeping wall of the plateau to stop it collapsing into the glen below.

On wild misty days, the grim rock formation below the summit, known as A'Chailleach, can be heard hurling abuse at her lover across the glen, Am Bodach of Braeriach. Legend claims the old woman of Gaoith always out-shouts the old man of Braeriach!

No abuse today though as I sat and wondered as the mists evaporated around me – lifted as though drawn by some unseen magnet to dissipate into a blue sky and leave the hills a parched pale green and brown. For the first time all summer the hills around me looked dry – parched even. I wondered how the birds were reacting to the lack of moisture? Certainly the pipits that constantly threw themselves off the edge of the plateau seemed lively enough, and the golden plover brood of five juveniles was as good as most years.

But it was great to see a young dotterel, probably one of this year's chicks, making short test flights over the gravel on Sgoran Dubh Mor. His short and repetitive "trri-trri" sounded confident enough, though he lacked the fine blended plumage of his elders. His back was marked boldly but the white band which should have circled his pale brown chest was hard to make out. His little flights were erratic, sweeping low over the ground in that familiar curved wing action. His splendour will come, and when it does he will be among the prettiest birds of the high tops, An t-amadan Mointeach – the fool of the peat mosses, a rather unkind Gaelic name for what is possibly the tamest, and finest, of all the plovers.

Away from the peat-mosses, lower down the hill, there is a favourite hill lochan of mine where I frequently go to indulge this addiction of wildlife watching. It's a reed-fringed tarn of real character, nestled in a quiet hollow among some low lying hills.

A curlew, the very spirit of these places, sings its melancholy song, full of the soul and solitude of these hills, a marvellous, echoing sound in the still of the early summer's evening. I watch the long-billed wader climb on tremulous wings before gliding to earth again, frustrating me by constantly beginning its song, then cutting it short as though not very sure of how it's supposed to finish. Up she goes again, and the same things happens; a short spurt of song, a bubbling of music, then defeat. Undismayed she tries again, and this time she remembers it.

As she glides earthwards she releases a torrent of liquid notes, a rapturous song full of the emotion of the wilds, a song which ends with a long wailing whistle as she alights on some heathery knoll.

Compared to the curlew the sound of the red grouse is a gruff apology of a song, a guttural croak as he rises from the heather from below your feet in a crashing and flapping of short, stubby wings. His "Go-back, go-back" tells you exactly what he thinks of your intrusion. But the croaking of old man grouse alarms other residents.

Down on the lochside two old friends take to the air on quivering wings, long bills relentlessly crying their high-pitched 'tittie teetie.' Towards me they fly, before slamming on their air brakes to hover, tiny white-edged wings beating ten to the dozen, before heading back to the loch, skimming the water surface like a flat stone. On a rock on the far shore they stop, curtsying with that airy grace of theirs, dainty little sandpipers, tripping along the shore now, happy little birds who bring a lot of pleasure throughout the summer months.

Some time ago I came up here on a chilly evening and found myself glassing a couple of curious-looking divers. With black mantles and backs, chestnut red throat and breast these were certainly grebes, but it was the golden yellow 'ears' or 'horns' which grew from the sides of their heads that gave the game away: these were Slavonian grebes, rare enough birds in this part of the world.

I've visited these grebes fairly often since first seeing them and watched their courting in fascination. The male would swim around, jerking his head to the left, then to the right, stretching his neck as high as he could to show the golden tufts of his horns to best advantage. Then I watched them build their nests, each bird swimming into the reedy bay, beaks full of rotten water weeds with which to build their floating home.

The rare corncrake is another bird that has given me enormous pleasure but it's also been known to send people into frenzies of frustration. Some friends of mine were making a television programme on the Hebridean island of Pabbay and, unfortunately for them, they had camped in a field close to where a pair of corncrakes were nesting. At first the climbers were delighted to be camping so close to what has become a rare species but, after a few morning of being wakened by the corncrake's rather monotonous rasping call, they were almost ready to do the unthinkable. Chances are they'd never even have found the birds.

Corncrakes spend much of their time hidden in tall vegetation and the only real clue to their presence is their song. May and June are the best months to hear them as the birds have just newly-arrived from Africa and are eager to set up their territory, find a mate and nest. The song is easily recognised – it's a continual rasping, buzzing sound and has basically two notes, 'crake-crake' repeated frequently, sometimes for hours-on-end, especially, it seems, when you're trying to sleep!

The decline in number and range of corncrakes, as with so many species, reflects the changes in agricultural practices that have taken place in the United Kingdom. The mechanisation of grass-cutting in particular, combined with earlier cutting dates, has led to a greater mortality and loss of nesting grounds. Mowing of grass tends to take place later in the year in north and west Scotland and so this area has become, more or less, the corncrake's last stronghold in Scotland.

But as the corncrake fights for survival, one little bird appears to be flourishing in the high places of Scotland: the snow bunting. Of all the bird songs there can be few as moving and evocative as that of the male of the species. A rare breeder in Scotland, the snow bunting is a true lover of the high and lonely places, a black and white fleck of beauty to be seen against the harsh wind-scoured tundra.

Perhaps it's the gaunt nature and the solitude of the snow bunting's breeding ground that evokes such a sense of passion in the listener but I can't think of a birdsong that is more moving. I've often lain among the rocks in the high Cairngorms just as the first shafts of warm sunshine began to burn off the thin swirling mists that often shroud the plateau. In this magical atmosphere it's wonderful to simply watch and listen to this small bird of the high places:

With its jet black mantle and dazzling white wings with ebony primaries the cock snow bunting is as vivid in those surroundings as its song was intense in the early morning stillness. Rising from the tundra-like screes the bird rapidly beats his white wings until he's 50 feet or so above the ground. Then, fluttering his outstretched wings like a skylark he glides earthwards again with an explosive and intense song, continuing for all he's worth as he lands on a rock with wings upstretched.

As his wings close the outpouring of song becomes almost a cry, a moving and powerful sound in those surroundings, half the voice of some sentient creature proclaiming itself and half the voice of the arctic wastelands; weird, almost lost, but totally triumphant!

In a land where the basic elements of rock, air and water so heavily predominate it sometimes seems odd that there should be any illusion of triumph. Vast wind-scoured slopes and gashes of glens offer little in the way of comfort or ease, yet up here the untroubled waters and the ancient stones cast a spell as soothing as they are dramatic. The high lonely lochans reflect the mood of the skies which in turn dictate the future, ordained by the winds and clouds.

The experience of being up here is a special one. I've learnt through these hills the simplicity of being, uncluttered by everyday things, the ascending grace conceded by these vast lands to all who are prepared to ask for it. But, while these hills are so powerful in their own way, they are also sensitive, fragile even. Our tenuous relationship needs to be nurtured. Along with a small sparrow-like bird and massive granite mountains, we belong to a biotic community and only when we view our relationship from that stance can we begin to benefit from it. But beware! Nurturing the relationship can become addictive…

CHAPTER TEN

BIKES, SORE BUMS AND
THE OLD BRAE

number of years ago when mountain bikes were the latest transatlantic import and prats like me thought they were genuinely meant to ridden up mountains I took one to Ben Macdui in the Cairngorms. By using the ski chairlift I reached the summit of Cairn Gorm without too much sweat and toil but immediately scared myself witless by trying to ride the bike downhill towards the broad expanse of the Cairngorm plateau. By the time I reached the summit of Ben Macdui I was exhausted – I had carried the bike most of the way and had been regularly overtaken by parties of ramblers.

The descent from Macdui and back across the plateau was slightly more successful until I attempted to cycle down a great snow wreath in Coire Cas. Please don't ask me why I tried to cycle down a steep snow wreath – I've often asked myself the same question – but I suspect it had something to do with exhaustion and a hot sun beating down all day long on a bald and empty head. I had a faint idea that I might be able to use the handlebars or the pedals as some sort of ice axe in the event of a slide but no sooner had I aimed the front wheel across the snow than the studded tyres slipped from underneath me, the bike and I parted company and I slid down the rest of the slope on my backside, the fastest thing on snow outside the Cresta Run.

Fortunately for me there was a band of black Cairngorm scree separating the foot of the snow wreath from some hideously large boulders and I hit that scree backside first. With my bum looking like a pound of mince I couldn't sit down for a week, never mind sit on a bike and later it took my wife the best part of an hour to scrub the gravel from my nether parts. I still have the scars to prove it.

Nowadays my use of bikes is much more canny. Like many other hill-goers I've discovered that a mountain bike can get me closer to the hills I want to climb, especially if those hills are out-of-the-way and remote, sequestered from the nearest road by miles of interminable forest tracks. Seana Bhraigh in the North-West Highlands is a good example.

An old guidebook describes Seana Bhraigh as a 'noble mountain', lording it over the vast empty quarter between Inverlael and Strath Mulzie and in that sense it is dramatic and imposing. But it's also rather dignified, as befits its name, 'the old brae'. From the south the mountain is no more than a crest of a wave in an ocean of heather and peat but from the north the prospect is in complete contrast. The wave suddenly crashes down in an almost vertical 1,300ft (400m) precipice into the depths of the Luchd Coire which lies below the imposing peak of An Sgurr, the steep pinnacle which forms the climax to the narrow and rocky Creag an Duine ridge. The main summit, at 3,041ft (927m) above sea level, might in itself be less impressive than its subsidiary tops but it does offer the best views of the rest of the mountain.

Lying in comparative isolation to the north of the Beinn Dearg group many people concentrate on Seana Bhraigh as a solitary peak, leaving its nearest neighbour Eididh nan Clach Geala to be climbed another day. With this single objective you give yourself a wider choice of approach – from Glen Achall near Ullapool or Strath Mulzie in the north, from Gleann Beag in the south-east, or from Inverlael in the south-west. All four routes necessitate long approach marches on either unclassified roads, bulldozed tracks or forest tracks and all benefit from the use of a mountain bike.

Most folk will approach the Inverlael Forest from the south – from the A835 Dirrie More to Ullapool road – and the most straightforward route to Seana Bhraigh starts from the foot of Gleann na Squaib at Inverlael. A bike quickly covers the first couple of miles of forest tracks as far as Glensquaib where you can leave it locked up in the woods. From here a path bears north-east through the remainder of the forest and begins climbing the prominent prow of the Druim na Saobhaidhe which forms the northern wall of Gleann na Squaib. The footpath then crosses the Allt Gleann a' Mhadaidh to enter the narrow confines of Coire an Lochain Sgeirich and its little rosary-string of lochans, climbing gently on to the vast plateau north-east of Eididh nan Clach Geala.

More small lochans dimple the surface of this high, grassy plateau, what Craig Caldwell called 'a wilderness of lochans' in his book *Climb Every Mountain*. The navigation can be awkward here in misty conditions but a rough path does weave its way around more lochans towards the rim of the deep and impressive Cadha Dearg, the Red Pass. I once sat hereabouts for a good 30 or 40 minutes watching a golden eagle below me as it quartered the air space in search of food, so much at home, at ease, in this wild, atmospheric corrie with great crags forming its eastern and northern extremities. I had to drag myself away but the summit was close and the walk around the great rim is no hardship. It's then up long, grassy slopes, skirting a bump that can knock your navigation out in cloudy weather, and up final stony slopes to the summit – a breathtaking point with a windbreak cairn sitting on the very edge of nothing!

The view across the void of the Luchd Coire to Seana Bhraigh's eastern top, Creag an Duine, is one of immense spaciousness with the montane wonders of the north-west arrayed before you in all their unique splendour – the hills of Coigach and Inverpollaidh, Suilven, Canisp and Quineag.

And when you return to Glensquaib you'll find it's something of a luxury to pick up your bike at the end of this relatively long 17 mile day and virtually freewheel all the way back to Inverlael. The last time I used a bike I only had to turn the pedals twice in the whole descent. 'Mountain bike' is a misnomer – I reckon they could be more sensibly called forest bikes.

CHAPTER ELEVEN

Boreraig
Dunvegan Portree
Kyleakin
Ardvasar

BORERAIG AND THE
TEARS OF THE TIDE

It's been said that the emptied village of Boreraig has the smile of an oasis. A poignant smile perhaps. Bleached moorlands, yet to be resurrected into the pale greenery of new life after the long, wet winter, spread south between Skye's and Loch Eishort like a waterlogged mattress. Splashing across it into the narrowing glen of the peaty brown Allt na Pairte, with west coast drizzle smirring any hint of a view, I would have welcomed a smiling landscape but then, rounding a rocky bluff, I was stopped short by green, corrugated fields which pressed a bright green crescent into the cusp of brown hillside that flowed down from the moors above. And beyond the fields, spread out like a map, lay what is left of the village of Boreraig.

Curiously, despite the obvious ruins, the bracken fronds that have swallowed up the lazy beds and the scrubby sycamores that choke the burn, there is still a lushness about the place. A solitary standing stone exudes a proud but worn antiquity, and tumbled cottages, their tall gable walls still standing, surround a more imposing building: a house and byre, possibly that of the former tenant farmers. Nettles choke the doorway and close by I stumble across the bloated carcass of a long dead ewe, its eye sockets as empty as the ruins it stares at.

I was aware of a cruel sense of irony in the symbolism of that rain-soaked and matted fleece, a reminder that there is nothing as inevitable as change. The people went and the sheep took over the land. Today, with agriculture in severe decline, one wonders how long it will be before the sheep too become a subject of the past. A shepherding neighbour of mine in Badenoch is fond of reminding me that the area now has only two shepherds when in former years it supported 27 families.

Boreraig and its westerly neighbour Suisnish were 'cleared' in the mid-19th century. The villagers were sent to Campbeltown from where they set sail for the new world on the Government ship *Hercules*. Many of them died from smallpox. Those who refused to go were burned from their homes.

The landowner of the time, Lord MacDonald, argued that the people had wasted good land and it would be better for them, and it, if they were removed. Typically altruistic of his type. Once the people had gone, the lands were rented to flock masters from the south. Fertile ground which had supported generations of crofters was used as grazing for sheep.

In 1852 a report on the Highland clearances in the *London Times* concluded with the remark: "It is thus clear that the Highlands will all become sheepwalks and shooting grounds before long." Prophetic words, but what now as we face a new millennium? Lamb prices have reached an all-time low and few sporting estates, if any, are economically viable. Subsidies to hill farmers are being cut and one wonders what the next turn of the wheel will offer to lost villages like Boreraig and Suisnish?

Could freshly asphalted roads bring four-wheel drive vehicles and yuppie families bent on IT cottage industries to areas like this, using the heavenly satellites and terrestrial ISDN lines as cotters once used ponies, boats, creels and fishing nets? Or could the relentless quest for eco-tourism turn these ancient sites into Disneyesque heritage centres complete with interpretative facilities and simulated 'crofting experience' centres?

Don't laugh; on Cairn Gorm the new funicular train will take people to the top of the mountain where an audio-visual presentation will attempt to offer them a 'mountain experience'. Incredibly it's only the thickness of a wall that prevents them having a genuine mountain experience. It's perhaps disingenuous of me to remember that a real mountain experience doesn't make anyone any money, at least not directly, and we are heavily burdened by the common notion that land can only be considered in economic terms. Aesthetic qualities or philosophical values don't sit comfortably with a capitalist society.

From Boreraig a rough path picks it way west for a couple of miles through a no-man's-land between the rearing scarps of Beinn Bhuidhe and Carn Dearg on one side and the salt water of Loch Eishort on the other. The tears of the tides have left their mark here and it's not difficult, in the light of recent Balkan images, to visualise the ghostly lines of humanity, bowed under the weight of their possessions, picking their way east, as they did in 1859, abandoning their homes and fields behind them.

Like Boreraig, Suisnish smiles. In a spectacular setting above Rubha Suisnish where Lochs Eishort and Slapin meet, a leaning plateau of pasture contrasts with the blue of the sea, as delightful a situation as you'll find on this scenically-blessed Isle of Skye. But beyond the fields, away from the steep cliffs and its salt-laden updraughts, the husks of former homes, the stone shells of the land, cast a shadow across the sparkling seas and verdant smiles. Recent events in Kosovo emphasise all too clearly the cruel resonances in the term 'clearances'. Nowadays this is referred to as ethnic cleansing. And yet, despite the records and the newspaper reports of a 150 years ago there are still those who would argue that the Highland clearances never happened, that they were a figment of an historical imagination or at the very least an exaggeration of the truth. Incredibly, there are those who make the same argument about the holocaust. Perhaps these people need to spend time in places like Boreraig and Suisnish, or in Strath Brora, or Kildonan or Strath Halladale or Strath Naver or in hundreds of other remote locations throughout the Highlands where the sheep pick their way through the tumbled stones of former communities and the ghosts whisper of injustice and terror.

A track, built by the Board of Agriculture earlier this century in a token attempt to try to encourage the re-crofting of Suisnish, now follows the shore of Loch Slapin north to the bay of Camus Malag where, across the head of the loch, the magnificent outline of Bla Bheinn and Clach Glas rises majestically. I was glad that some things, at least, never change.

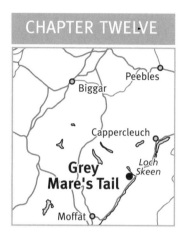

CHAPTER TWELVE

CASCADES, CATARACTS AND COOMBS

S ir Walter Scott left it on record that any poet, however poor his attainments, can write about a waterfall, and many have. Norman Nicholson refers to his 'chain of water, the pull of earth's centre', while others anthropomorphise, describing cascades and cataracts as 'the voice of the mountains'. In his typically adjectival poem *Inversnaid*, Gerard Manley Hopkins describes the course of the burn in tumultuous terms:

"His rollrock highroad roaring down
In coop and in comb the fleece of his foam
Flutes and low to the lake falls home"

A deservedly well-known poem which of course concludes with that emphatic plea for wilderness:

"Where would the world be, once bereft, of wet and wildness?
Let them be left.
O let them be left, wildness and wet;

Long live the weeds and the wilderness yet."

Although it's not the highest waterfall in Scotland, the crashing 60m drop of the Grey Mare's Tail above the A708 Moffat to St Mary's Loch road is certainly one of the most spectacular, motivating Sir Walter Scott, despite his literary theories, to pen a rather grandiose poem about those waters which hurl down the dark abyss from 'dark Lochskene/Where eagles scream from shore to shore'.

Every year, the Grey Mare's Tail draws car-loads of visitors who come to gaze at its aquatic spectacle. Consequently, the lower part of the footpath has suffered from all the tramping feet but some sterling work by the National Trust for Scotland has created some secure, if mildly unaesthetic pathwork, which carries you high above the 'roaring linn'.

The waterfall itself is created by the Tail Burn which issues from the moraine-dammed waters of Loch Skeen, a quiet and secluded stretch of water that's well set in its craggy east-facing corrie between White Coomb and Lochcraig Head. In winter the waters of the Grey Mare's Tail often freeze up, silencing the burn and turning the roaring, cascading waters into a solid gash of green ice.

Beyond the waterfall, and above Loch Skene, the south Tweedsmuir hills cut an empty, desolate quarter of the Scottish Borders. Rising between the Moffat Water and the source of the Tweed, these are well-rounded hills with boggy skirts which exude a very definite air of wet and wildness. Such geographical sogginess is well-expressed in some of the place-names, like Rotten Bottom (between White Coomb and Hart Fell) or Dead for Cauld (south-west of the Megget Reservoir), leaving little to the imagination. However, the air of desolation and the vastness of the views from the summit of White Coomb at 2,693ft/821m are fitting, for this is the highest hill in Dumfriesshire.

In an optimistic and adventurous frame of mind I once climbed this broad sprawling hill along with Hart Fell in the north. But once was quite enough, thank you. The route not only involved negotiating the aforementioned Rotten Bottom, a miserably peaty and waterlogged stretch of terrain, but ended up as a wet and soggy bog-trot in damp mist that cut visibility to a few yards. Even my map, made limp by the incessant dampness, fell apart in protest. A shorter and scenically superior route is to climb White Coomb from the top of the Grey Mare's Tail before descending into the hill's north-eastern corrie which forms a fine craggy backdrop to Loch Skeen.

Desolate it might be but the views from the summit of White Coomb are wide ranging, from Criffel in the west to the Eildons in the east and from the Solway Firth to the distant outline of the Lake District fells. In spring and summer colourful displays of wild flowers decorate the ferociously steep banks of the Grey Mare's Tail and feral goats roam the hills – you can usually smell them before you see them. Be particularly careful on the path beside the waterfall and don't be tempted too close to the edge; although it is well made the path does traverse above very steep drops and several accidents have occurred here.

The route of ascent is fairly straightforward, if steep in its upper stretches. Leave the NTS car park beside the A708 and take the obvious footpath which follows the bank of the Tail Burn, with spectacular views of the Grey Mare's Tail ahead of you. Follow this path above the falls to where it begins to level off. Cross the burn well-above the falls and head west over rough ground to Upper Tarnberry. An old wall, with a footpath beside it, leads up Rough Craigs, avoiding the steepest slopes. Follow the wall but note that it doesn't lead directly to the summit cairn; instead it passes about 100m to the north.

From the summit descend north for half a kilometre and drop down the steep slopes beside the Midlaw Burn to Loch Skeen, described by an 1891 Scottish Mountaineering Club hill-walking party as: "a lovely little loch, lying in a veritable cradle of bare stony slopes topped by precipitous crags." Well-popular with anglers, Loch Skeen is one of the jewels of the Borders but nowadays is more infested with raucous black-headed gulls than Sir Walter Scott's romantic vision of screaming eagles. Having said that I once camped above a small bay of Loch Skeen and was alerted by a familiar screech. It wasn't a golden eagle but a peregrine falcon, slicing through the air in its swift gliding flight that sent fear and alarm through the raft of gulls on the water's surface. On its narrow, clean-cut wings the peregrine glides at deceptive speeds and when it swoops on its prey in the air the force of its death-dealing blow can be so terrific as to sever the victim's head from its body. It's no wonder the gulls went quiet.

From the southern shore of the loch you'll pick up the Grey Mare's Tail path again which plunges down the hill on a parallel course to the waterfall itself:

"White as the snowy charger's tail,
Drives down the pass to Moffatdale."

CHAPTER THIRTEEN

AN EXPLORATORY TREK IN THE KUMAON HIMALAYA

As the trails of Nepal and Pakistan become more and more overcrowded and as more and more trekkers' lodges and tea-houses open up it seems as though many of the cultural attractions of the Himalayan countries have become diminished by an increasing westernisation. There is a danger that trekking into previously little-known areas could expose that part of the Himalaya to the excesses of the trekking industry but occasionally the terrain of such areas is just too wild to attract the masses. The Panch Chuli area of the Kumaon Himalaya in India is one such area...

It was while watching a television programme about a motor cyclist who claimed that riding his big Harley Davidson brought him closer to the land that I thought of Colin Fletcher's law of 'inverse appreciation'.

The writings of Colin Fletcher have probably inspired me more than any living author. A Welshman now domiciled in the warmer, gentler climes of northern California, Fletcher was the first man to walk the arid length of the Grand Canyon and his book of that journey, *The Man Who Walked Through Time,* is a classic of foot travel adventure. In the past 30 years Fletcher has become the guru of North American backpacking. Wise and articulate, yet at the same time intensely private and not a little curmudgeonly, Fletcher's wilderness philosophy shines through his writings like the sun bursting through the canopy of the forest. His 'law of inverse appreciation' is pertinent to backpackers and hikers the world over.

Fletcher suggests you can only come close to the land, that is you can only learn of its rhythms and read its small print, by walking on it. The less there is separating you from that environment, the more you are able to appreciate it. Most walkers are well-aware that the bigger and more efficient your means of travel, the further you become divorced from the reality through which you are travelling. For example, if you drive along a motorway in a luxury coach at 70mph, you are completely and utterly sequestered from the landscape, other than the visual appreciation of what you see through the smoked glass window. Likewise, driving along a dual carriageway in a car you don't get much contact with the land. Riding a Harley Davidson doesn't bring you a whole lot closer. Take a bicycle down a country lane and you can begin to connect with the landscape around you but not as much as you would if you were to dump the bike and start walking.

An obvious parallel is that a solo yachtsman learns more about the sea than a passenger on the QE2.

But Fletcher's law has an interesting corollary. He claims your appreciation varies not only according to what you travel 'in' but also according to what you travel 'over'.

By walking along a footpath you begin to appreciate the fine detail that turns a pretty countryside into a living, vibrant landscape. Other senses are brought into play too: you can smell the resinous effect that warm sun has on a pine tree, you can hear and appreciate the intricacies in the song of a skylark and you can feel, on your very skin, the breath of wind that shimmers through the grass.

But finest of all is to leave the footpath. Even a minor path can be an impediment to your appreciation, especially if it is eroded by the trudge of countless boots. Paths and trails take you by the hand and lead you where they want you to go, following the route of others. Once away from the trail you can gain the cognitive freedom that allows you to literally follow your own nose, to break new ground and really break free.

This is what exploratory trekking is all about.

Eliminate any hint of a footpath, ease your way across viciously steep slopes hundreds of feet above the river, slash and cut a route for days on end through virgin forests of rhododendron and bamboo and cross tumultuous glacial rivers on newly-cut tree trunks, and you begin to understand something of the pioneering nature of this unique form of travel.

The sheer thrill and excitement of negotiating a way through wild, unexplored territory is something few can enjoy in this shrinking world and the simple yet profound satisfaction of standing on top of an unclimbed Himalayan mountain, albeit a comparatively minuscule one, is something never to be forgotten.

Very few western mountaineering expeditions, and certainly no trekking groups, had penetrated the extensive forests which skirt the lower slopes of the Panch Chuli range in the Kumaon Himalaya of India. A Scottish expedition of Bill Murray, Tom Weir, Douglas Scott and Tom McKinnon flirted with the area in the 1950s and in the early '90s an Indo/British expedition, including Chris Bonington, Stephen Venables and Victor Saunders, took advantage of the lifting of a ban to foreign visitors and climbed Panch Chuli 2, the highest peak in a glorious cirque of high mountains. Victor, keen to return to the area, believed the area offered the potential for a good trek. At the time I was looking at possible destinations for a TGO readers' trek and the double delight of trekking with such a delightful character as Victor Saunders in a largely unknown area of the Himalaya was too good an opportunity to miss.

I had known Victor for some time and was aware of his reputation as a strong and resourceful mountaineer. Swarthy and dark haired, his eyes intelligent behind his rounded John Lennon specs, Slippery Vic was one of the most energetic individuals I had ever met, a hyperactive character whose penetrative mind seemed incapable of relaxing. The only time he quietened down was when he was asleep or playing chess; at other times he was a bundle of nervous energy.

I asked him how he had earned the nickname Slippery Vic.

"I've no idea," he replied with a look that suggested he didn't wish to continue the conversation. But our sirdar, Jaideep, told me later.

"It was on an earlier British/Indian expedition," he explained. "The climbers were in the mess tent discussing logistics and it seemed that every time a particular idea was put forward Victor would find a reason to disagree with it. After several hours of arguments one of the Indian climbers, with charitable patience, proclaimed: 'Mr Victor, I think you are a very slippery customer.' The adjective stuck."

The area Victor had suggested for our trek was in the extreme northeast corner of India, very close to both Nepal and Tibet. Sandwiched between the massifs of Nanda Devi and Api lies the beautiful mountainous region of Kumaon. Until quite recently much of this area was within the so-called 'Inner Circle' and was completely off-limits to all foreign visitors. However, in the early '90s, a new Governmental ruling effectively opened up the area around the striking Panch Chuli group in the very heart of Kumaon.

Victor Saunders was one of the few westerners to have previously visited this area as a member of the 1992 Indo-British expedition to Panch Chuli, the first group to have been given permission to visit this area for more than 30 years. Our trip was the first trekking group to visit the area and was given the opportunity of making an extensive exploration of this almost completely untrodden area around the high basin of the Panch Chuli Cirque.

The basic outline of the trek was simple. We would travel by bus from New Delhi, up through the Himalayan foothills of Kumaon to a remote and dusty mountain village called Mathkot. From there we would trek up terraced hills, over a forested ridge to reach the Pyanshani Valley, a deep cut trench in the hills which was still virgin jungle in its lower reaches. We hoped to find a route through the jungle which would take us up-valley, following the Pyanshani river, to our eventual destination, the Panch Chuli glacier. Here we hoped to make a high camp and explore some of the lower hills and passes.

It sounded straightforward but the differences between following a well-trodden route, aided by experienced porters and an able sirdar, with a multitude of tea-houses along the way, and this form of pioneering trek soon became obvious. When Victor was here three years before it was early in the season, pre-monsoon. In post-monsoon October the pleasant shepherds' paths which he remembered with such fondness were covered with vicious nettles. Our porters suggested another route, which due to the difficulties of the terrain and the fact that they were very inexperienced (if you want to trek in an area with no history of trekking you ain't gonna find experienced porters!), took us almost six days instead of the planned two. But, as we constantly reminded ourselves, this was exploratory trekking!

It has become a cliché to suggest that India blasts your emotions apart. Preconceptions of Delhi were exploded within hours of our arrival. Having flown into the city late the night before, 17-year old Gregor and I slipped out of the hotel before breakfast. It was his first visit to a third world country so as a responsible father I thought we could begin our explorations early in the morning before the daily hubbub of the city got going. But even at seven in the morning we were soon surrounded by a bedlam assortment of beggars and magicians, snake charmers and carpet dealers all keen to unload us of the weight of a few rupees. For Gregor it was a baptism of fire but he coped with it well.

Squalor and deprivation live here cheek-by-jowl with grandeur and wealth, and guilt, surprise, shock and delight are feelings that become confused and intermingled in this whirligig of cultural diversity. In contrast, the mountain villages bring a welcome return to sanity, a slower existence where even *manyana* is too hurried and urgent. Here, where the terraced fields are still tilled by oxen, where seeds are scattered by hand, exists a medieval world largely untouched by the 20th century, where the natural inquisitiveness of the local folk is warm and innocent.

This is an area with an indigenous population that is as yet untouched by the consumerism of the west. No trekking groups and very few mountaineering groups come this way, looking, looking. There are no gaudy tea-houses here, no trekkers lodges with adverts proclaiming the delights of yakburgers or Coca-Cola. Few children run from the houses to greet you, hands held out in expectancy as is now customary in Nepal and Pakistan. Instead the children are inquisitive but shy, hiding behind their mother's sari, their eyes wide in wonder…

At one point, as we passed through a small town, I asked one of our head porters if he could find me a Coca-Cola. He went off and returned about an hour later shaking his head in what I thought was disappointment but which was in fact delight. "I'm sorry Mr Cameron," he said, head shaking from side-to-side. "I'm afraid I have some bad news, but also some good news."

I asked him for the bad news first.

"There isn't a bottle of Coca-Cola in the entire village," he informed me. "But the good news is I found a shop that sells beer."

After a couple of days of wandering along the cobbled paths through the tiny villages, it was a shock to reach the jungle. The well-maintained path suddenly degenerated into a faint and narrow track, dropping into steep gorges and thickets of bamboo, and climbing loose, muddy banks. Occasionally we would burst clear of the stifling shrubbery into the intense heat of the sun, where the track would vanish into shoulder-high deer grass and nettles.

We climbed up and across the steep shoulders of the mountain, fighting against the grain of the land, constantly aware of the steep, grassy slopes below us that dropped vertiginously into swirling, glacial rivers. The entrance to the Pyanshani Valley, our route to the Panch Chuli glacier, lay enticingly close and it was frustrating to find ourselves looking down on to it. As day turned to dusk, we made a determined effort to ease our way down the steep, craggy slopes. Aware that a simple slip could have serious consequences, we moved slowly and carefully by the light of our head torches, groping for holds, digging the edges of our boots into the grassy hillside for security. One of the porters, a shepherd, convinced us of the value of local knowledge as he managed to thread a route down through the craggy outcrops. It was a relieved band of trekkers that pitched their tents beside the roaring river that night.

With more jungle-bashing ahead we were glad to get the vertiginous slopes behind us but yet another problem faced us in the morning. We had to cross the torrent of the Balati River which careered down from its glacier high above. Cutting down a couple of trees, we formed a makeshift bridge, a fragile and rickety structure, and rigged up handrails from which we looped sling harnesses. It was a tedious business, our lack of balance made to look pathetic by the ease with which our barefoot porters crossed the greasy poles. But despite their natural dexterity, we almost lost one of them a couple of days later. Showing excess bravado, he slipped and fell into the torrent, the weight of his load pulling him under. He was swept downstream and, luckily for him, into an eddy where he was dragged to safety by his frantic companions, his load becoming wedged between boulders in midstream.

Interestingly, this aroused mixed emotions within the group. Concern for the near-drowned porter was virtually outweighed by the realisation that his load, now in great danger of sinking, could contain someone's kitbag. Making use of an old log to form a rickety bridge, Victor volunteered to creep along it to retrieve the sodden holdall. Roped up and firmly belayed he managed to grab it but his return was made even more precarious by the weight of the water-filled bag pulling him back towards the boiling waters of the river. As he dragged the bag ashore everyone watched with bated breath as he opened the zipper to check the contents. It contained two store tents. The relief was almost tangible... and the porter recovered quickly.

There was a fair amount of relief, too, when we reached the site of our base camp, a beautiful spot just below the grey snout of the Panch Chuli glacier. Here we had flat sandy pitches, clean fresh water and a magnificent view of the Panch Chuli peaks, mountains famed in Hindu mythology as the five cooking pots – some say the five fires – the highest some 22,650ft (6,905m).

We also enjoyed a change of routine. Instead of packing up camp every morning and walking through until dusk we enjoyed the luxury of a static camp. No-one appreciated this more than our cooks, Farookh Ahmed and Abdul Salaam. It's no exaggeration when I say the food night after night was of the highest quality. Large quantities of fresh vegetables were carried throughout the trek and there was a delightful absence of western-style dehydrated grub. Now that we had a base for a few days these guys really went to town and we enjoyed a nightly exploration of the delights of Indian gastronomy. On one memorable occasion we returned from a long glacier walk to a platter of mouth-watering cheese pakora. On another, just as our palates began to tire of spicy food, Farookh produced the unexpected delicacy of egg and chips. Just the thing for a jaded palate!

From the very beginning, ever since we heard Victor speak of the wealth of unclimbed peaks, we had harboured a strong desire to climb something. It's not every day that a bunch of walkers gets the chance to first-foot a Himalayan mountain. We set our sights on a small peak which we christened Little Bainti Peak. The upper slopes rose from Little Bainti Col, which we thought might offer access into the adjoining valley but in fact such a route would have been barred by the complex and crevassed Bainti glacier.

This was a day to remember. Under a cloudless sky we climbed high above the glacier on a long flower-covered ridge. Around us, dwarfing our little hill, the giant peaks of Panch Chuli rose to eyeball-searing peaks, their snow-covered summits contrasting vividly with the intensity of the blue sky. On one hand this was no more than severe hill-walking – the gradient wasn't excessively steep, we were well acclimatised and there were few objective dangers to worry about. It was all rather carefree. But we weren't oblivious to the fact that we didn't know what was around the next corner. We could have come up against a crevasse-filled glacier, we could have been faced with a ring of high-level cliffs which barred further progress. All we could do was take each section at a time, enjoy it to the full and keep an eye on the clock. With darkness falling at just after six, we reckoned we would have to start our descent by 2pm.

The long access ridge topped out into a huge boulder-filled cwm, about half a mile in diameter, on the far side of which another ridge gave access to what looked like another high cirque. Fortunately, we could drop down into this cwm without having to use a rope and after negotiating the remains of a retreating glacier and tentatively climbing up a steep ice field, we reached the final scree slopes of our little peak.

On reaching the summit ridge the views exploded on our consciousness like a bursting dam. From the upper cwm we were exposed to one of the finest mountain panoramas any of us had witnessed. Away across the lower Panch Chuli slopes the peaks of the Nanda Devi massif rose into the sky and beyond them the great mountains of the Garhwal Himalaya were arrayed across the horizon. East, towards the Nepalese border, the complex and crevasse-ridden Bainti glacier flowed down its inexorable course from a ring of unclimbed 20,000-footers.

We could have sat there for hours, backslapping and taking photographs of each other with one of the most incredible backdrops any of us will ever experience. But we were aware of the big descent before us. Though reluctant to leave our high eyrie, we were content at having achieved such an ascent after the frustrations of our walk-ins, and thrilled in the knowledge that our little 15,340ft (4,677m) peak had been climbed for possibly the first time. It was a reward all of us will cherish.

CHAPTER FOURTEEN

Lochinver

Elfin

Coigach

Ullapool

COIGACH AND THE
FIDDLER

It was the ancient Norse who gave Ullapool its name. Ulli's Steading was then, as it is now, a gentle oasis amid a harsh, mountainous landscape. But drive north from the town, over the spine of the Rhue peninsula and you enter another world.

Ardmair is a magnificent spot, well-loved by caravanners and campers. From the campsite a spit of white shingle curves gracefully out into the bay pointing towards the sanctuary of Isle Martin. Beyond, protecting the bay from the Minch gales, the Summer Isles float alluringly on their sea of green. Flocks of dunlin and ringed plover feed on the salt flats, gulls wheel overhead and brightly-coloured fishing boats bob and dip on the water. But for all these attractions of sea and shore it is a mountain which dominates the scene.

An extensive wall of weathered Torridonian sandstone commands the northern shore of the bay, an ancient relic of one of the oldest land masses in the world. Below the sandstone lies a platform of crumpled Lewisian gneiss, said by some to be well-over 1,000 million years old, toughened by heat and pressure deep within the Earth's core. The long sandstone wall runs slightly south of west to north-east, from Garbh Choireachan to Speicin Coinnich, and is collectively known as Ben Mor Coigach. The hill's protective cap of Cambrian quartzite has, like those of many of its neighbours, long since gone but the bare bones of this venerable relic still rise straight from the sea to almost 2,500ft (760m), a mile-long wall of seamed buttresses, gullies and cliffs, a living archive of this spinning rock we call the Earth.

While that seaward wall is impressive it's really only a front, a simple facade that hides an intricate, complex system of peaks, ridges, corries and lochans. This area of Coigach is a gem of a wilderness area. Unspoiled and challenging, it begins to express itself more fully as you drive further north on the A835. Ben Mor Coigach, at 2,438ft/743m, is the highest summit, but the other main peak of the area, Sgurr an Fhidhleir (2,306ft/703m) rises to a sharp and dramatic point about a mile along a broad north-west ridge from Ben Mor. It's a high eyrie of a summit, the culmination point of a huge blade of rock that rises from the bare moorland close to the reflective waters of Lochan Tuath.

The 10-mile traverse of these two hills brings together all the finer characteristics of a walk that blends sea and mountain in that distinctive combination that you only find on Scotland's western seaboard. You'll experience such a blend on Skye and Rum of course, and the best mainland example is probably Ladhar Bheinn on the Knoydart peninsula but there's a peculiar quality to the blend here in Coigach, as though the spaciousness of the vast seascape emphasises the height of the hill, and you catch a notion you're mounting a staircase to the heavens. Indeed, it's perhaps not too fanciful to imagine the traverse of Ben Mor Coigach's long south-west ridge beyond Ardmair Bay as a high-level promenade to Tir nan Og, beyond the shimmering ocean of the Celtic twilight.

At Drumrunie junction on the A835 a minor road runs west towards Achiltibuie. As everyone else rushes off to climb Stac Pollaidh, or fester on the pale yellow sands of Achnahaird Bay just a few miles along the road, park your vehicle and cross the river just east of Loch Lurgainn. A faint path, rising steadily on the right bank of the Allt Claonaidh will take you as far as Lochan Tuath, which mirrors the mighty north-west prow of Sgurr an Fhidhleir, the peak of the fiddler, probably the most impressive peak in the area. Walkers don't follow the prow: that's the domain of rock climbers who'll find a long and exposed climb of Very Severe standard, a relatively moderate grade in this day and age which belies the objective dangers of loose rock and vegetated ledges.

South of the prow, a prominent heather-filled gully climbs steeply up to the bealach between The Fiddler and Ben Mor Coigach in the south and from there easy slopes lead to the summit of Sgurr an Fhidhleir itself, a stunning place with magnificent views over the peaks of the Inverpolly National Nature Reserve – Cul Mor, Cul Beag and the improbable outline of Stac Pollaidh itself. This hill has been described as a 'mountain straight out of a fairy tale', with a ragged and spiky crest looking for all the world like some primeval stegosaurus.

Once you've drunk your fill of the views, retrace your steps back to the broad bealach and climb the easy, grassy slopes to Ben Mor Coigach itself. The mile-long south-west ridge towards Garbh Choireachan is the highlight of this glorious walk. Enjoy the succession of rocky towers and good sandy paths which make this ridge such a delight and take time to take in the views out over the Summer Isles and, on a good day, across the Minch to Harris and Lewis. Given reasonably clear weather you'll see the Cuillin of Skye, the Torridons, An Teallach, the Beinn Dearg hills and the magnificent spread of northern hills from Inverpollaidh to Assynt. Immediately below your feet lies Isle Martin, an unpopulated square mile which was recently gifted to the local Isle Martin Trust by the RSPB in the spirit of 'land reform and devolution'. This little nature reserve is the first land the RSPB has transferred to community ownership and, indeed, the first land it has given away in Scotland.

It's well-worth scrambling out to the end of the ridge before making your way back to the summit of Ben Mor Coigach. Descend now to the small bealach below Speicin Coinnich, then down steepening slopes to the long ridge of Beinn Tarsuinn. Make your way along the ridge, continue over the summit and down steep, heathery slopes back to the Allt Claonaidh and the boggy path back to the road.

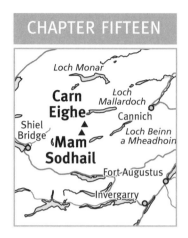

CHAPTER FIFTEEN

Loch Monar

Carn
Eighe

Loch
Mallardoch

Cannich

Shiel
Bridge

Mam
Sodhail

Loch Beinn
a Mheadhoin

Fort-Augustus

Invergarry

CONTRASTS OF AFFRIC

The constant drum roll that had filled my dreams all night had ceased and I was being shaken awake. "Look outside," I was told, "It's as clear as a bell." Sure enough, the tent had stopped shaking and there was no longer a dull throb of heavy rain on the flysheet. I glimpsed out of the tent door and was greeted with a view of crystal-clear sharpness and hills that etched their shape against a clear sky.

If anyone deserved a bit of good luck my mate John and I did. Just 24 hours earlier we had arrived in Gleann na Fiadh in a thick pea-souper of a mist. The waters of Loch Beinn a'Mheadhoin and Loch Affric had been as still as glass, reflecting all the dank and grey depression of the morning. After pitching our tent we had climbed an old stalkers' path to the Bealach Toll Easa, the high pass which connects two Munros: Tom a'Choinich and Toll Creagach. We climbed both but saw little, other than the wavering point of a compass needle. That night I prayed for better weather.

It was with the shame of the unfaithful that against all my

expectations I realised the miracle had happened. Inside half an hour we had breakfasted, dressed ourselves in clothes still damp and cold from the day before and were off, the cold air nipping and chivvying us along the track.

Gleann na Fiadh is a northerly offshoot of Glen Affric and a great horseshoe of hills protect its upper reaches. Two real giants form the head of the glen – Mam Sodhail, the rounded hill of the barn, and Carn Eighe, the cairn of the notch, the highest mountain in Scotland north of the Great Glen. Good ridges form the connecting horseshoe and our initial task was to gain the ridge from the waterlogged glen. An ancient stalkers' path carried us part-way up into Coire Mhic Fhearchair and a stiff climb over rocky terrain led us on to the Garbh Bealach at the foot of our ridge.

Sadly, a build-up of clouds spoiled our view to the hills of the north but their dark forms couldn't obscure the wildness of the landscape, across the silhouetted form of the Lapaichs to the Strathfarrar hills and beyond.

Too cold to linger we began to climb again, the stalkers' path now reduced to anonymity among the loose scree and boulders of the ridge. At one point our way was apparently barred by a series of steep and jagged 'gendarmes', fine rock pinnacles that tempted our scrambling instincts. Instead we negotiated a route through and around them, treading delicately, like the Old Testament character Agag.

All too soon we were on Carn Eighe and we took shelter from a mischievous wind behind the wall that encircles the triangulation pillar. It was too cold for anything other than a quick bite and a swig of hot coffee but the break gave us enough time to consider whether we should continue north, to take in Beinn Fhionnlaidh as well. This hill is one of the awkwardly-placed Munros that lies out on a limb, mocking the Munro-bagger in its isolation. You either take it in on a round like this, adding another three miles and a 1,000ft of climbing to your journey or you leave it for another day. Curiously, another Munro not far to the west of here, Mullach na Dheiragain, involves an even longer diversion to reach its summit cairn from its nearest neighbour, Sgurr nan Ceathreamhain. Hills like these test the commitment of Munro-baggers and test their will-power to the full. It's all too easy to leave such hills for another day and then, as you approach eventual 'compleation', you discover you've a handful of such hills still to climb, scattered around various parts of the country. Such are the joys of the Munro-bagging game.

Since I had climbed Beinn Fhionnlaidh twice before I had little inclination to hike out to its summit on a winter day when light was short. Reminding ourselves it would be dark just after four and with the fine weather of the morning now deteriorating sharply, we left Beinn Fhionnlaidh for a better day. John, who hadn't climbed it, muttered various excuses in self-justification... I smiled and promised to come back with him.

From Carn Eighe the main ridge drops to the south-west, then south, across a high bealach to reach the steep summit slopes of Mam Sodhail. This top was once an important survey station in the primary triangulation of Scotland in the 1840s and, as a result, boasts an astonishingly large cairn. With the mists now flirting around its stony walls it looked for all the world like an ancient broch, and we felt disinclined to stop. Three great ridges radiate from Mam Sodhail and we took the most northerly, down over the Mullach Cadha Rainich towards Sgurr na Lapaich. I'd never descended from Mam Sodhail this way before and what a surprise it was – a delicately tight and curving ridge flanked on both sides by slopes that fell away steeply into the glens below.

With sunlight piercing the clouds like great spotlights we stopped to enjoy the spectacle. Each beam appeared to light up a distant hill, highlighting it from its neighbours and exaggerating its splendour. This was Scotland at her glorious best and we were sorry to leave. The previous day we had walked through a still, damp shroud of grey cloud. Today, we were rewarded for our patience and enjoyed a superb 14-mile mountain traverse. We tramped down the glen in silence, collected the tent and headed for home, reaching the car as darkness fell. In the pale gloaming the ancient pines of Affric stood like dark sentinels, the waters of Loch Beinn a'Mheadhoin still, smooth and black. It was a sore temptation to stay on for another night, enjoying yet another contrast to the conditions we had experienced over two short days, the special atmospheres that make hill-bashing in Scotland such a glorious love affair.

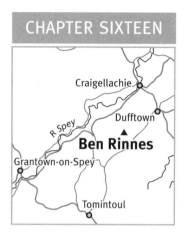

CHAPTER SIXTEEN

Craigellachie

R Spey

Dufftown

Ben Rinnes

Grantown-on-Spey

Tomintoul

DEMON VOICES AND
DEMON DRNK

G reylag geese grazed in the fields which rolled down to the River
Spey and snowdrops and crocuses brightened the road verges.
The pale green tint on the birches emphasised the promise of
spring but, less than a thousand feet above, the snow was still deep and the
wind had a razor edge to it.

The breezes that blow off Ben Rinnes, the north-eastern terminal point
of the Grampians, are legendary. Nearby Ballindalloch Castle dates from
the mid-16th century but a local tale suggests the stone masons and
builders had a hard time during its construction. No sooner had the walls
reached a certain height than they were knocked down by some unknown
agency. This occurred so many times that the laird set up a special night-
watch to discover who was responsible for the vandalism. Early in the
morning, the story goes, a great wind swirled down from Ben Rinnes and
not only blew the newly-built walls down but pitched the laird and his
cronies into a holly bush. Three times a demoniac voice was heard above
the rushing of the wind, saying: "Build on the cow haugh." The laird, well-
aware of what might happen if he ignored the warning, built his new castle

on the lower, less-attractive site instead.

It could have been the same demoniac voice that was trying to convince me to stay in the warmth of the car rather than expose myself to the raw coarseness of the northern wind. The mischievous breeze was already drifting powder snow across the narrow Glack Harness road between Ben Rinnes and Meikle Conval but tantalising glimpses of blue skies between the snow flurries were enough to cast out the demon voice and turn my thoughts to the demon drink instead.

Lying just a few miles south-west of Dufftown, Ben Rinnes lies in the heart of whisky country. Someone once wrote that while Rome might have been built on seven hills, Dufftown was built on seven stills, and from the 2,755ft/840m summit of Rinnes you can look down on more than a dozen distillery towns and villages: Aberlour, Keith, Cromdale, Dufftown, Rothes, Knockando, Ballindalloch, Craigellachie, Carron, Glenlivet, Tomnavoulin and Advie, all associated with the names that stir the blood of any whisky enthusiast: Balvenie, Glenfarclas, Glenlivet, the Mortlach, Cragganmore, Tamdhu, Glenrothes, Glenfiddich, Carndow, Tamnavullin – the epithets of the waters of life and the lifeblood of these entire regions of Moray, Nairn and Banff.

Indeed, this major whisky producing area extends about 50 miles to the west and about 25 miles south of the Moray Firth and the waters of both the Monadhliath and Grampian mountain ranges contribute to the northern reaches of Strathspey. Not content with this, Speyside whiskies are distinct from other malts, tending to be lighter in 'weight' while still carrying their own character on the palate. Not as peaty and heavy as, say, Islay malts, the whiskies of Speyside are still full-flavoured but in a more subtle, delicate way – water of life indeed.

As I tramped up through the snow drifts it didn't seem too fanciful to imagine the basic elements of this *uisge bheatha* as the provision of the mountain – the melting spring snows, the roaring burns, crystal clear and cold, the rolling slopes of peat that were once used to fire the distilleries and the patchwork fields of barley below me in Glen Rinnes.

Rising boldly above the Laich of Moray, Ben Rinnes offers a magnificent viewpoint across the Moray Firth to the mountains of Ross, Sutherland and Caithness. On a clear day you can see Ben Nevis in the west and

Buchan Ness in the east and, beyond Corryhabbie Hill on the opposite side of Glen Rinnes, Lochnagar and the arc of the Cairngorms form the distant horizon.

From Glack Harness a track, then a narrower footpath, runs all the way to the quaintly-named summit, the Scurran of Lochterlandoch, offering a glorious afternoon's walk the comparative ease of which is out of all proportion to the mountain's height. The name of the hill comes from the Gaelic Beinn Rinneis, which possibly means 'headland hill' but the word 'rinn' in Gaelic means a sharp point and while this north-eastern hill couldn't really be described as pointed it does boast distinctive granite tors on its summit which give it a spiky appearance. It's a well-formed hill nevertheless, its slopes easing themselves gradually down to the waters of the River Spey on its north side and considerably more steeply on its southern Glen Rinnes side.

Despite my earlier reluctance to face the wintry conditions it was curiously exhilarating to battle through the snow drifts and clouds and arrive by the summit tor just as the clouds broke. I could empathise with the Rev James Hall of Edinburgh who, in 1803, climbed Ben Rinnes on a cold and cloudy day. His written account tells of becoming lost and frightened but, when the mists cleared, he proclaims the experience as "a secret enjoyment, a calm satisfaction and a religious fervour which no language can express". Such quasi-spiritual encounters are not unusual in the mountains and I've often found it curious that even non-religious people often revert to such pious language when describing such encounters.

If you can arrange transport, a complete traverse of Ben Rinnes is well-worthwhile, continuing west from the summit down the length of the Lynderiach Burn to Bridge of Avon. Alternatively, descend, as I did, in a south-west direction to the Hill of Knockashalg before dropping south-east to Wester Clashmarloch in Glen Rinnes and a quiet road walk back to Glack Harness. I think it's also highly appropriate, after climbing such a worthy hill as Beinn Rinneis, to toast yourself from a hip flask with a little dram of *uisge bheatha*, the water of life that flows from the very flanks of this north-eastern hill. As Robert Burns once wrote:

"Freedom and whisky gang thegither,

Tak aff your dram."

CHAPTER SEVENTEEN

CAIRN GORM – AN ARENA
OF CONFLICT

I've lived in the shadow of the Cairngorms for almost 30 years
and my relationship with these high, wind-scoured
mountains is a passionate one. They are my hills of home and
my love affair with them shows no sign of waning – indeed as I
become older I find myself discovering more of their subtle
attractions. But in recent years the Cairngorms have come to
symbolise a growing conflict between conservationists and
developers, an open hostility that goes way beyond any simple
argument over ski development. In this essay, rather than
reiterate all the arguments, I've tried to offer some solutions for
the future.

Before I try to make any sort of prophesy about what's likely to
happen to the high tops of the Cairngorms in the next 25 years perhaps
I can take a look back at what was written about Cairn Gorm some years
ago, on the basis that we can all learn from our mistakes and try not to
make them again in the future. Indeed, perhaps we can be encouraged

by some of the good things that have happened since we realised those mistakes were, in fact, mistakes...

Almost 25 years ago, the Aberdeenshire poet Nan Shepherd wrote these words:

"Aviemore erupts and goes on erupting.

Bulldozers birze their way into the hills.

Roads are made, and re-made, where there were never roads before.

Chair-lifts swing up and swing down (and a small boy falls from one and is killed)

A restaurant hums on the heights and between it and the summit Cairn Gorm grows scruffy, the very heather tatty from the scrape of boots (too many boots, too much commotion, but then how much uplift for how many hearts?)

Reindeer are no longer experimental but settlers.

The Nature Conservancy provides safe covert for bird and beast and plant (but discourage vagabonds, of whom I have been shamelessly one – a peerer into corners). Ecologists investigate growth patterns and problems of erosion, and re-seed denuded slopes.

All these are matters that involve man. But behind them is the mountain itself, its substance, its strength, its structure, its weathers. It is fundamental to all that man does to it or on it."

Things don't change much in 25 years, but not all is bleak. Some good things have been happening in the Cairngorms in the past few years.

The National Trust for Scotland bought the Mar Lodge Estate on the southern side of the Cairngorms and is rebirzing, if I can borrow Nan's term, the bulldozed track up Beinn a'Bhuird, a track that was originally gouged out of the landscape to serve some ill-advised and ill-fated ski development. The NTS has also embarked on a severe cull of red deer to help regeneration of the native woodlands and has promised to remove the deer fencing that the old Nature Conservancy Council built around various plantations.

The Forestry Commission has been cutting down its exotic conifer species in Glenmore and leaving the native Scots pine. About ten years ago a sort of glasnost came over the commission and it granted access to forests all over the place, encouraging visitor access. Thanks to the sudden change that came out of that glasnost, it is today seen as the friend of the outdoors enthusiast.

The story of what's happened at Creag Meagaidh is one that every rural politician and every Highland landowner should be made aware of. By reducing numbers of sheep, the woolly locusts, and red deer, the antlered locusts of the countryside, regeneration of trees and associated undergrowth and subsequently associated bird life has been nothing short of phenomenal.

What we're realising, both in the UK and abroad, is the dire need to divorce ourselves from the buzzword of the '90s that was 'sustainable development', whatever that means. I'll mention Larry Hamilton of the World Conservation Union later but he recently told me that buzzwords for the foreseeable future, based on new attitudes from around the world, are 'repair and rehabilitation'. It's restoration – a healing of the damage that we've done in the past in the name of progress or, dammit, in the name of what we've called 'sustainable development'.

Do you know there are plans to restore Glen Canyon on the Colorado River? Are you aware of plans that are afoot to demolish the dam at Hetch Hetchy in Yosemite National Park, the dam and reservoir scheme that many believe brought the life of John Muir to a premature end when he and the Sierra Club failed to stop developers? I believe Muir might do a wee birl in his grave when that comes about – indeed he might even do a wee birl in his grave when Scottish National Parks come about too…

You might be familiar with the achievements of John Muir, who emigrated from Scotland to America just over 150 years ago, and I think the most fascinating aspect of this man's life was that he had a prophetic understanding of the natural world that went way beyond the normal scientific activities of his contemporaries. Muir had the ability to gaze deeply into the beauty and mystery of Nature.

Where other scientists of the 19th century recognised a myriad diversity of individual creatures, rocks, rivers and mountains, John Muir saw everything in the natural world as one great flow of interconnected life-forms, a single, unitary web of creation in which everything – energy, stars, planet, continents, mountain ranges, oceans, rocks, rivers, plants, animals and bacteria – was linked together.

John Muir gave truth to those lovely lines of Francis Thompson: "Thou canst stir a flower, without troubling of a star." That we are all part of an immense, complicated web of created life and whatever we do to one part of the web will ultimately have repercussions on other parts.

The truth of this was brought home to me when I visited Cairn Gorm with Professor Larry Hamilton, who I have just mentioned. Larry is vice chairman of the mountains committee on the World Conservation Union, which is part of the United Nations – UNESCO. He travels the world looking at environmental problems.

Larry wanted to look at the proposed funicular scheme in Coire Cas and when we arrived at the top of Cairn Gorm he was overwhelmed by the view across the high arctic plateau towards Ben Macdui, Beinn Mheadhoin, Cairn Toul and the other high tops. He then told me he'd visited the ski developments in Coire Cas a couple of times and couldn't fully understand what all the problems were. It was only when he stood on the summit and gazed around him that he realised that you could not treat Cairn Gorm, or Coire Cas or Coire na Ciste for that matter, in isolation, for these corries, indeed this mountain, are part of a much greater whole and whatever we do to Coire Cas, whatever we do to Cairn Gorm, will have repercussions throughout the rest of this mountain range, soon to be our second National Park. It's a case of cause and effect.

Coire na Ciste and Coire Cas have been developed for years, so what's the effect been on the rest of the Cairngorms?

Well, increased access by road to high-level car parks has meant considerable damage to plants and flora in areas where, because of the altitude, regeneration is incredibly slow. The past ten years have seen an amazing enlargement of the footpath network, emanating from the summit of Cairn Gorm, where people have had access by the ski chairlift and from the Coire Cas car park, across the Northern Corries on to Lurchers Meadow and beyond.

Because of this easy access there are many people going on to the Cairngorms who are perhaps unfamiliar with the skills of navigation, people who build and add to lines of waymarking cairns across the plateaux. As they remove boulders to add to the cairns, the holes that are left fill up with water, freeze and expand and in turn become water courses in which mosses and sedges and grasses are washed away, which of course affects the insects and the birds and so on and so forth.

Much of the extremely fragile arctic heath that normally flourishes in the high and cold environment of the Cairngorms has simply been trampled to death and wide ranging dogs run amok among the seasonal clutches of ptarmigan and dotterel.

Cause and effect. Do something to one part of the web and you affect another. Pick a wild flower and you disturb a star.

In a sense it grieves me to say it – it's the paradox of the outdoor writer and broadcaster – but there are too many people tramping the high tops and plateaux of the Cairngorms; or, to be more correct, there are too many people gaining easy access by high-level entry, either by the chairlift or by the Coire Cas car park, people who wouldn't normally want to climb all the way there.

Now, some of you might say, the funicular train proposals will cure all that. Hasn't an agreement been made between the Cairngorm Chairlift Company and Scottish Natural Heritage that users of the train will be enclosed within the top station and that there won't be any access to the open mountain?

And is it not true that climbers, cross-country skiers and hill-walkers will be discouraged from using the Coire Cas car park by, possibly, draconian parking fees and isn't there an agreement that the road between Glenmore and Coire Cas will have double yellow lines painted up either side of it to stop folk parking on it?

Well that's great. A local councillor told me a while back that walkers and climbers could then treat the Coire Cas road as 'a long walk-in', betraying his complete ignorance of the whole concept of the 'long walk-in'.

I want to draw your attention to a recently-published report called *Trends and Motives affecting Participation in Active Outdoor Pursuits*. It was written by psychologist and mountaineer Robin Campbell for Scottish Natural Heritage and its purpose was to look at the motivations of hill-goers, to look at their personal psychological factors and values and to speculate on possible future trends within mountaineering and the implications of those trends for SNH and its policies.

Under a section called *Green Policies and Climber Ambivalence* it says: "The climbing communities have always been identified with 'green' policies, no doubt because enjoyment of the mountain environment is such a strong motive. As the best known example, in America the Sierra Club has for many years mounted effective campaigns against land uses that damage mountain land and wildlife. In Scotland the preservation of mountains and mountain wildlife owes much to mountaineers such as Arthur Russell, Percy Unna, Bill Murray and Adam Watson. However, the struggle for preservation has to deal with enemies within as well as without.

"Most climbers, if pressed, will sign up for the principle of the 'long walk-in' for example, but the very same individuals when pursuing some private goal will resort to their mountain bicycles. Likewise, although climbers and their representative organisations express spirited opposition to the plans for a funicular railway to the summit of Cairn Gorm, I have a nagging feeling of certainty that they would form a queue to use such a facility as soon as it was in place. Better, quicker access to a resource is desperately hard to resist, and recent climbing history provides many examples, such as the huge numbers of winter climbing routes in the Northern Corries since the opening of the Cairngorms road, and the similar present enthusiasm for the western corries of Aonach Mor in Lochaber (based on easy access via the Nevis Range chairlift system)."

Campbell concludes by saying he is sure: "that ambivalence will always be with us. The common good will always be set aside in favour of individual gain and it will always be useless to expect restraint in the use of a facility once established, even from those who deeply deplored the facility and fought hard to prevent it."

I wonder how long the Cairngorm Chairlift Company can maintain a closed-loop funicular train with no access to the upper part of the mountain?

It sounds great in theory but let's look at the facts. For a start, at a cost of some £14m to get the thing up and running, there will a hellish strong imperative in future years to make this thing work.

With declining snow cover due to global warming, declining tourist numbers due to the initial novelty value of the train ride wearing off, or when other, newer visitor attractions take away the share of a diminishing number of tourists, cause financial problems as many people, infinitely more expert than me, have suggested then the imperative will be to throw more money at the project and seek new customers. Climbers, hill-walkers, botanists, geologists, Uncle Tom Cobley and all, if Robin Campbell is correct in his assertions, will be queuing to be taken to the summit, just like the old chairlift.

The access management problem which was to be solved by the building of a closed-loop funicular train will in turn, I prophesy, become the problem all over again, legal agreements or not. Even at the time of writing, the management of the chairlift company is considering how tolerant it can be of 'leakage' from the closed-loop system and chairlift staff will not be instructed to deter people from leaving the top station. The chairlift management is also aware that it needs the walkers and climbers and others to make its summer funicular train viable and, while keen to protect the integrity of the wildlife sites on flanks of Cairn Gorm, it will, I strongly suspect, make legal moves to open that top station for access to the mountain's summit.

Okay, so what's the answer? I believe there are two things to be done:
1) Damage limitation, and
2) Restoration and healing of the Cairngorms.

The heart has been torn out of Coire Cas. Tens of thousands of tons of concrete has been poured on to the slopes and we now have a funicular train structure that is irreversible. So how can we limit the damage that will do to the rest of our proposed National Park?

What we have to do, every one of us, is to police that closed-loop circuit and resist any temptation to use that train to reach the plateau. We have to hold the chairlift company and SNH to their agreement. We have to make sure the damage does not spread to the rest of the massif.

Secondly, we have to restore and heal the damage that has already been done to the high tops by the high-level access of the past 30-odd years. Let's take what is happening in Coire Cas as an opportunity, rather than a problem.

I would like to see the Coire Cas road closed to every vehicle, other than those carrying passengers for the funicular. People should buy their funicular tickets in Glenmore, not Coire Cas. Likewise, skiers during the snow season. The road-end should be in Glenmore, not Coire na Ciste or Coire Cas, with shuttle buses taking people up to the funicular. The present car parks in Coire na Ciste and Coire Cas should be closed and landscaped as naturally as possible. The focus for entry to the Cairngorms should be taken away from Coire Cas and the funicular. There is even a strong argument in favour of closing the road at Coylumbridge, with shuttle buses running up to Glenmore. If they can do it in Yosemite Valley, with four million visitors a year, why not here?

I would like to see an integrated wildlife and adventure playground based in Glenmore, with forest trails, cross-country ski loops and mountain bike loops in the forest. I would like to see more of an integration between the forest and the mountain, so that those going to the mountain can enjoy a longer, holistic experience of the area: a long walk-in through the forests, climbing steadily beneath increasingly-smaller Scots pines and montane scrub, up past a tree-line that must be encouraged to be much higher than it is today, and on to mountains that are as remote and isolated as they were 40 years ago.

Let's bring the *challenge* back to the Cairngorms, the challenge of walking and climbing on remote, distant mountains. Fewer numbers will take up that challenge but many will be content to walk in the revitalised forests, forests of natural species rather than densely-packed fast-growing conifers.

And most important of all, we have to fight for the Cairngorms National Park to be made an area of *preservation*, not of opportunistic development, sustainable or otherwise. A National Park is exactly that, an area of national or, in the Cairngorms' case, international importance.

On the final slopes to Little Bainti Peak with the crevassed Bainti Glacier behind.

On the long ridge of Ben Mor Coigach in Wester Ross.

Members of the Cairngorm Mountain Rescue Team training above a snow-covered Loch Avon.

Devastation and demolition in Coire Cas. The unjustifiable cost of a funicular train.

Stob na Doire and Stob Dearg on the Buachaille Etive Mor ridge.

Crossing Upper Oliver Dod on the Kingledoors horseshoe.

Testing our crampons on the icy walls and leaning seracs of Mount Rainier.

Approaching the summit of Mount Rainier in the Pacific North-West of the United States.

Descending to the Bealach na Sgairne from A'Ghlas-bheinn, Kintail.

Scotland's grandest corrie? Coire Mhic Fhearchair of Beinn Eighe.

The amazing landscape of Evolution Valley, Sierra Nevada.

While community involvement in a future National Park Board is vital, the future of that National Park should not be left solely in the hands of local interest groups.

There must also be an understanding and an ongoing education of what these mountains mean and can offer society today and I don't believe we can better the prophetic vision of John Muir.

Perhaps his clarion call, coming down through the decades, will teach us that the main value of experiencing wild places like the high tops of the Cairngorms is not simply the conquering or collecting value of mountains or rock and snow and ice routes, or long distance walking trails, or the benefits of fresh air and exercise or even the economic advantages that walking or climbing brings to rural communities.

These things are all fine and good but the vital lesson that John Muir, the wilderness prophet, brings to us as we stand at the beginning of a new millennium, is that the real value that comes from experiencing these wild places is a transcendence of ego boundaries, a sense of growth and of being part of some greater entity. Not seeing man as the anthropocentric owner or master of the biotic community, but as an equal partner in it.

We have to learn to see these forests and mountains as places that are vital for a society that is increasingly becoming sequestered from those things that were once held to be sacred; indeed we need to recognise that forests and mountains are part of our society, an integral part of our civilisation.

The existence of wilderness should be seen as a compliment to civilisation, something that complements society. Edward Abbey once wrote that any society that feels itself too poor to afford the preservation of wilderness, or lacks the desire to preserve wilderness, is simply not worthy of the name of civilisation.

Professor Hamilton fervently believes that as we go forward into the new millennium it's not enough to be thinking only in terms of sustainable development, we should be considering repairing much of the damage that's been done in the past as well.

"We really do need to treat these Cairngorm mountains, and especially the alpine-arctic zones, with much greater care than we have in the past. We have to learn not to throw more technology at mountains because snow isn't coming down as it used to, so I believe a rethink would be in order to get rid of some of the more unsightly aspects of this particular development and push for future development to be further down the mountain where it can be handled in a better fashion.

"In this new millennium the watchword for the world is 'repair, restoration, rehabilitation and healing'. The term 'sustainable development' is old hat – that was the watchword for the past decade or so. We need to embrace this new watchword and we see it happening in other countries – we're looking at some of the mistakes we've made, some of the things we thought were good but time has shown them not to be so good, so we're now tearing them out and if necessary relocating smaller scale developments to places where they won't do so much damage."

There are many who would like to follow through on Larry Hamilton's advice and remove all skiing development from the Cairngorms, then close Cairn Gorm for a hundred years to allow the mountain's vegetation to regenerate, in his words 'to permit healing'.

But it's a call that inevitably will fall on deaf ears, not a particularly pragmatic solution to the problems that face the Cairngorms. But perhaps by making such an extremist call we will make a point.

No-one can ever claim that the writer Jim Crumley will get splinters in his bum by sitting on the fence. But that's exactly the ailment he believes the conservation bodies are suffering from and the only way those splinters can be removed is by a sharp, painful operation.

But before the cure, what is the conservation measure he's so critical of? It's compromise. This is what he says:

"The Government has created the Cairngorms Partnership, a laborious talking shop of all the mountain's vested interests – a forum which guarantees that radical voices will be smothered, radical solutions shouted down, in the perpetual quest for that holiest of bureaucratic grails, compromise.

"But compromise has given the Cairngorms what it has now, which is insidious dereliction. The devastating power of the compromise culture is seen in the response of conservation organisations to the preposterous proposal for a funicular railway on the Cairn Gorm ski slopes, not a funicular railway – a gondola! You can almost hear the fearful voice at work… 'Mustn't be seen to be negative… must make a positive contribution. Propose a less-damaging alternative, eh? Damage limitation… that's the answer!'"

As an illustration to back up his point he quotes from Aldo Leopold's *Sand Country Almanac* in which Leopold suggests that modern conservation is, to a large extent, local alleviations of biotic pain, which are necessary but which should not be confused with cures. And Crumley's cure for the Cairngorms is simply to remove the skiing.

Is such a solution possible? Would anybody ever admit that the initial approval of planning permission away back in the '50s for the first ski development on Cairn Gorm was a mistake? If there is even a hint of regret, or the tiniest suggestion it was a mistake, then surely Crumley's cure isn't all that far-fetched; or, as he suggests, is conservation in the Cairngorms to be limited by its own lack of ambition?

Sadly it will be and I don't believe the fault falls entirely in the lap of the conservationists. There are too many vested interests in our mountain landscapes, interests that fear the very word 'conservation'. They associate such a word with job losses, lack of investment, lack of profitability and a fall in the value of their deer- and sheep-infested land.

And while we maintain a countryside watchdog quango that sees Cairn Gorm as a 'sacrificial' mountain, institutes talking shop after talking shop, and continues to dole out money to landowners to build miles of deer fencing, then there is little hope for the sort of conservation that Jim Crumley feels passionate about.

It's surely the responsibility of the conservation bodies to educate, to argue with reason and prove that conservation can mean jobs, can encourage visitors, can heal the landscape for the betterment of everyone. Henry David Thoreau once said that in wildness is the preservation of the world. We'd better believe it, and teach others to believe it too.

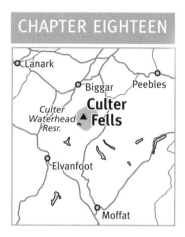

CHAPTER EIGHTEEN

DODS OF HILLS ON THE KINGLEDOORS HORSESHOE

It was ostensibly a Backpackers' Club outing to the Borders but plans for a two-day walk with a couple of wild camps were put on hold when the weather forecast suggested storm-force winds and torrential rain. A Friday night camp in the field opposite the cosy Crook Inn near Tweedsmuir seemed a better option and gave us an opportunity to wait and see if the weatherman's timing was accurate.

It wasn't and Saturday brought a brief window of cold and bright weather that gave us an opportunity to put some miles in, climb some hills and camp high in a wild and lonely corrie. Fortunately we were settled in our tents when the weather eventually unleashed it's vile and lasting storm. As a result Sunday morning saw us pack up sodden wet gear and struggle back to the Crook Inn in torrential rain. Curiously, no-one complained.

Despite the fact that we hadn't slept well, were soaked through and were cold and hungry, we all agreed the trip had been a resounding success. I was reminded of something the American writer Edward Abbey had once said. He had been out on a long hike and had been caught out by darkness and bad weather. Lacking a tent or bivouac bag, he took shelter in a shallow cave:

"The rain came down for hours in alternate waves of storm and drizzle and I very soon had burnt up all the fuel within reach. No matter. I stretched out in the den, pillowed my head on my arm and suffered through the long night, wet, cold, aching, hungry, wretched, dreaming claustrophobic nightmares. It was one of the happiest nights of my life."

Such happiness usually comes in retrospect and it's perhaps as well we're adaptable creatures with selective memories. Our Borders weekend was a success because we cut our losses to suit the conditions and what we lost in terms of our original plan was compensated by the sheer delights of an area that was new to all of us.

The Culter Fells reach out over a huge area of border country, hills that form part of the historic Druim Alba, the watershed, or the spine of Scotland. Bounded on the west by the nascent Clyde and on the east by the Tweed, the Culter Fells are relatively low hills, rounded and smooth-topped and they range out in extended ridges, slender and undulating, above long, deep valleys. Culter Fell itself is placed central to the whole group and rises to a respectable 2,454ft (748m). There are no Munros or Corbetts here but there are five Donalds, the Scottish lowland hills which are above 2,000ft (610m), and four of these can be climbed in an 11-mile horseshoe ridge walk which rises above the Culter Waterhead Reservoir.

You can gain access to the Culter hills from a variety of points. Coulter village itself lies south-west of Biggar on the A702 and a minor road linking Coulter and Broughton runs south of Goseland Hill giving access from Kilbucho. Two long, sinuous valleys, formed by the silvery watercourses of Holms Water and Kingledores Burn, run south-west from Tweedale and separate the ridges of Upper Oliver Dod, Coomb Hill and Culter Fell itself. The first two ridges run parallel to each other on either side of the Kingledoors valley, connected above the lonely valley head by the tops of Coomb Dod and Hillshaw Head.

This Kingledoors horseshoe walk, starting and finishing at the Crook Inn, was more or less the route we decided on once the weather altered our original, more ambitious, plans. The sun might not have shone on us but good fortune did, for the 12-mile route we cobbled together turned out to be an excellent walk, an ideal outing for this fag-end time of the year.

The Crook Inn, near Tweedsmuir, is no stranger to walkers. The nascent Scottish Mountaineering Club held its first official meet here in February 1891 and ever since it's been a popular rendezvous point for walkers. Indeed, as we left the car park to start climbing on to Crook Head behind the inn a bus load of ramblers appeared. As we headed for the cold heights they rambled into the warm lounge for morning coffee.

From Crook Head a broad close-cropped ridge runs in south-west, rising and falling over Nether Oliver Dod and Upper Oliver Dod. I've no idea as to the history of the said 'Oliver' but a 'dod', as a descriptive term for a bare, rounded hill, is not uncommon in the Borders and the Lake District. It actually describes these hills very well.

Beyond Upper Oliver Dod there is a long drop through deep clagging heather before a trio of tops lifts you to the edge of a large forestry plantation, the upper edge of which forms the route to the western summit of Glenwhappen Dod. It's here that you have to turn north, over Coomb Dod and Hillshaw Head, with its lovely views down to Culter Reservoir into which Culter Fell dips its toes.

From the next top, the evocatively-named Gathersnow Hill, you could, if you felt fit enough, digress north to Culter Fell but it would involve a big descent and another long climb. Probably better, with the short days at this time of the year anyway, to stick with the undulating Glenwhappen Rig to Broomy Law (there is another Broomy Law in the Minch Moor hills above Yarrow and I've often wondered if it has any connection with Glasgow's Broomielaw) where you can descend into the valley and pick up the track that leads to Kingledores Farm. In decent weather and with the longer daylight hours of summer you could continue on the ridge as far as the col before Benshaw Hill where a footpath drops down directly to Kingledores. From the farm the line of an old railway parallels the A701 back to the Crook Inn and its cosy inglenook fireplace.

CHAPTER NINETEEN

GUARDIAN OF GLEN ETIVE

sk any hillgoer for their ten favourite hills in Scotland and you can bet your last dollar that the Buachaille Etive Mor will be mentioned. Ask them for their top three hills and I'm pretty certain the Buachaille will still be in there, challenging for top spot, for this squat pyramid, filling the acute angle formed by Glen Etive and Glen Coe, dominates its surroundings like no other mountain in the country.

There's a certain bend on the A82 Tyndrum to Glen Coe road over the Moor of Rannoch where the Buachaille suddenly comes into view. The mountain is still some distance away but the sudden glimpse of its rhyolite flanks never fails to take the breath away. Rising from the flat, bare mattress of the Rannoch Moor, this big shepherd of Glen Etive stands guard over both Glen Etive and the gaping jowls of upper Glen Coe, its shape and pointed peak the very epitome of a dream mountain – or a nightmare, depending on your attitude to steep rock, snow-clad slopes and ice-choked gullies.

A visitor to the nearby Kingshouse Inn, in 1792, was singularly unimpressed by the view of the Buachaille, describing it as "a carcass of a mountain, peeled sore and hideously disgustful". Charles Dickens didn't like it either, but he was a city man: "an awful place," he wrote, "scores of glens high up, which form such haunts as you might imagine yourself wandering in, in the very height and madness of a fever." Dorothy Wordsworth, a keen hill tramper herself, was more impressed, if a little overawed: "A great peak, black and huge, as if with voluntary power instinct, upreared its head."

It's easy to be overawed by the Buachaille for its main peak, Stob Dearg, looks higher than its 3,351ft/1,021m. Great rock walls rise from the flat moorland bedrock, splintered and riven by deep gullies which partition well-known features: Crowberry Tower, the Rannoch Wall, Slime Wall, Curved Ridge, the North-East Buttress, names which bring a quickening of the spirit to anyone with a passion for this magnificent lump of rock. My own passion for the hill evolves from years of climbing in both summer and winter; bumming around its flanks, taking from its solid presence something of its spirit, evoking from it some sense of belonging, a relationship that helped shape my own nascent mountaineering lusts into something much more lasting and worthwhile.

It takes little effort to recall memorable days here; climbing some of the great classic routes like Agag's Groove or January Jigsaw, long, exposed and steep climbs made easy by a profusion of big holds. Or climbing John Cunningham's classic Crow's Nest Crack on a freezing day when the cold rock numbed the fingers. Happy times too filming the BBC series *The Edge: 100 Years of Scottish Mountaineering* when I had the privilege of interviewing some of the gruff stalwarts of the Creag Dhu mountaineering club at Jacksonville, their wee howff at the foot of the hill, before watching Jimmy Marshall and big John MacLean climb Bludger's Revelation for the cameras. Both climbers were in their 60s when we shot the film, but both made the climbing look ridiculously easy.

But the Buachaille isn't just a climber's mountain and the traverse of its four-mile long ridge now puts two Munros in the bag: Stob Dearg and Stob na Broige (3,130ft/955m), one conveniently at either end of the ridge. While some walkers will be happy to tackle the airy and sinuous Curved Ridge, which as the name suggests curves a route up the Rannoch face of the mountain, others will happily head round the corner to

Lagangarbh, where the more open aspect of Coire na Tulaich, directly behind the Scottish Mountaineering Club hut, offers a less horrific prospect for those who like to keep their feet on the ground.

A footpath crosses the River Coupall and climbs steadily up the corrie where it steepens out considerably towards the top. At this point the going is rough, over scree and loose boulders, and it's far easier to take to the rocky ribs on the right where some easy scrambling offers a little solidity under the feet and makes upward progress less traumatic.

Once you've topped out on the bealach above, a scree-covered ridge leads to the Stob Dearg summit to your left. As you approach the top the ridge begins to narrow in a rather satisfying way and, after one or two false summits you'll reach the large cairn which appears to sit on the very edge of nothing, with the great boggy mattress of the Rannoch Moor spread out before you like a map.

From Stob Dearg a superb high-level promenade runs roughly south-west, linking three other tops, each of which is worthy of Munro status. Just over a mile away, Stob na Doire's conical north-east face looks particularly impressive and beyond it the ridge twists its way over stony ground on the gradual rise to Stob Coire Altruim. The Buachaille's newer Munro, Stob na Broige, is easily reached over a series of undulations and offers extensive views down the length of Glen Etive towards Ben Starav. To return to your starting point you're best to head back over Stob Coire Altruim to the bealach between it and Stob na Doire, from where rough slopes, many of them becoming badly eroded, lead down into the Lairig Gartain. There a wet and boggy footpath squelches you back to Altnafeadh and the A82.

The wear and tear on this descent from Stob na Broige is the inevitable legacy of the creation of new Munros. Spidean Coire nan Clach of Beinn Eighe in Torridon, another new Munro, has suffered a similar fate and land managers have admitted they can't keep up with the pace of erosion. When a mountain top is given Munro status the ensuing hill traffic is considerable. Perhaps the Scottish Mountaineering Club should consider a moratorium on new Munros, if only on ecological grounds.

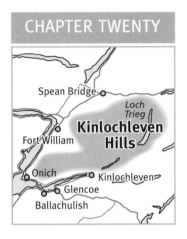

CHAPTER TWENTY

HILLS OF THE
DEAD END

"**A**bove and over all, the mystery of the night and the desert places hovered inscrutable and implacable. All round the ancient mountains sat like brooding witches, dreaming on their own story of which they knew neither the beginning nor the end. Naked to the four winds of heaven and all the rains of the world, they had stood there for countless ages in all their sinister strength, undefied and unconquered, until man, with puny hands and little tools of labour, came to break the spirit of their ancient mightiness."

The words of Patrick MacGill, the erstwhile 'navvy's laureate', describing the hills that frown down on the Argyll village of Kinlochleven.

In 1906 the British Aluminium Company opened a plant in Kinlochleven, turning what was a tiny settlement of two or three farmhouses and a shooting lodge into a 'model village' to house the hundreds of itinerant workers employed on the smelter project and later, once the operation was up and running, into a factory town serving what became a major centre of industry. To provide the power for the aluminium smelter the Blackwater Reservoir, four miles to the east of the town, was created by damming the high glen and slowly filling it from the burns and streams that endlessly pour off the black flanks of the surrounding hills. Today, the reservoir's dam holds back 4,000 million cubic feet of water and is constantly fed by the record-breaking sluices of Lochaber rain.

Children of the Dead End, MacGill's semi-autobiographical account of life as an itinerant worker in the early years of this century, graphically describes the terrible isolation and horrendous conditions the navvies had to endure as they toiled against the broken earth in those hills above Kinlochleven: "We were men despised when we were most useful, rejected when we were not needed, and forgotten when our troubles weighed upon us heavily."

MacGill's book vividly portrays the horror of the times and contemporaneous accounts verify his descriptions. The nearby Moor of Rannoch is also a silent witness to those who succumbed to its chilling wintry horror as they left the warmth of the Glasgow train at Corrour to make their way on foot to the worksite at Blackwater. Those victims of cruel hypothermia were still being discovered many years later – they had no-one to report them missing.

There's also a cruel sense of irony in the timelessness of those mountains described by MacGill, for their "spirit of ancient mightiness" remains unbroken. Instead it's the smelter that's been run down while the hills remain, steadfastly undefiled and unconquered. Once again the workforce "has been rejected when not needed" but paradoxically there is a bright ray of optimism shining on the area. Tucked away at the head of the fjord-like Loch Leven, Kinlochleven nestles at the foot of the Mamore Forest and is completely dominated by high peaks and soaring ridges, the same mountains which ironically offer hope for a resurgent 'green' economy.

The highly popular West Highland Way, the 96-mile long distance trail that runs from Milngavie to Fort William, passes through Kinlochleven bringing welcome revenue, and jobs and plans are afoot to set up a walking centre here, complete with bunkhouses, an outdoor centre and camping facilities. Few villages are so naturally blessed with such a beautiful situation and such close proximity to wild areas. Indeed, mountaineer Hamish MacInnes once wrote of it as a, "deplorable town in a delectable setting". The hill slopes around the village boast a remarkable network of stalkers' paths some of which are followed on an excellent half-day outing which visits the lonely Loch Eilde Mor.

The route offers a good mid-level circular walk that produces extensive views down the length of Loch Leven and across to the high tops of the Mamores and the northern corries of Glen Coe's serrated Aonach Eagach ridge. Using old footpaths and stalkers' tracks it climbs the western slopes of Meall na Duibhe, behind the village, before following an old pipeline track above the deep gorge of the Allt na h-Eilde. This pipeline runs from Loch Eilde Mor to help feed the Blackwater Reservoir, which lies south-east of Meall na Duibhe.

Just above the pipeline a good path runs north all the way to the outflow of Loch Eilde Mor, where the river is crossed by another footbridge. Cross it and continue on the muddy path which skirts the headwaters of the loch to meet a major track which runs west to Mamore Lodge, once used as a shooting lodge by King Edward VII.

Continue west, descending steadily as the track follows the curves of the southern slopes of Na Gruagaichean into Coire na Ba, where it crosses the Allt Coire na Ba by a footbridge and turns back on itself, descending south then west, to Mamore Lodge hotel. You can descend from the hotel by a tarmac road but it's much better to continue past the buildings and out of the trees with a wonderful view down the length of the fjord-like Loch Leven, the Pap of Glencoe on the left and Beinn na Caillich on the right like twin portals. From this point look out for the amazing zig-zag footpath running up the north-east slopes of Beinn na Caillich. Such marvellous old stalkers' paths are a feature of this area.

Soon you'll see a wooden marker post on your left beside a small cairn. This post, with its white thistle emblem, indicates the West Highland Way, Scotland's first official long distance trail. The section from here, through the Lairigmore to Fort William, is one of the finest; alas, we have to turn our backs on it and drop to the left where the path soon joins the trees again for a long descent to the B863 as it enters Kinlochleven. Follow the road back to the bridge over the River Leven and the car park.

The buildings of the aluminium smelter lie empty and forlorn. Development agencies and tourist boards debate the future of Kinlochleven and the once-large workforce has dissipated. The tunnels and pipelines are now a blight on the landscape, a testament to man's transitory nature and, meanwhile, "All round the ancient mountains sat like brooding witches, dreaming on their own story of which they knew neither the beginning nor the end." Perhaps Patrick MacGill's words contained just a hint of prophecy…

CHAPTER TWENTY-ONE

FROM PARADISE TO COLUMBIA CREST

Mount Rainier lies in the Pacific North-West of the USA and is reckoned to be one of America's most dangerous volcanoes. This isn't because the mountain is liable to blow its top like near-neighbour Mount St Helens did some years ago; it's due to the fact that the mountain is unusually covered in some 35 square miles of ice and snow. When the sun hits that ice and it begins to melt, the mountain unleashes a shocking artillery fire of rock and stone. If you happen to get in the way, it can easily be curtains...

One step up, then lock-out the lower leg so it can rest momentarily before swinging it through to crunch into the icy snow above. My lungs crave oxygen and I force the breath out from between pursed lips like an accelerating steam train, searching for a rhythm – one forced breath to every two uphill strides, power breathing, forcing the lungs to work more efficiently.

Occasionally the breathing rhythm is interrupted by a frustrated curse as the rope between me and the climber behind goes taut. This umbilical cord that links us tells me when Amy is feeling tired and dragging on the rope. I curse when it seems I have to drag her up steep sections but later, in the warmth and comfort of a downtown Seattle bar, she tells me of her appreciation, the encouragement of a tight rope when she felt her lungs and legs wouldn't take her any further.

In turn I'm encouraged by another of our companions, local climber Art Rausch. He's worked for Rainier Mountaineering Inc, the guiding company that holds the concession for running mountaineering courses on the mountain, for more than ten years and his squat muscular frame oozes a sense of solid reliability. He's climbed the mountain dozens of times and is well-aware of its intricacies, its foibles and its dark side, for Mount Rainier is the largest and potentially most dangerous volcano in the United States of America.

Our route, from Camp Muir at 10,000ft (3,050m) to the mountain's summit, is essentially a long trudge across glaciers and up long intersecting ribs. There is no technical climbing involved, nowhere do you have to use your hands and the slopes by-and-large lack any sort of serious steepness. But Mount Rainier is a dormant volcano, formed aeons ago in an area we know as the Ring of Fire, a circle of volcanoes which stretches around the Pacific Ocean, a vulcanistic loop linking the Philippines and Japan, the Aleutians, the western coast of North and South America, and Hawaii. Rainier is a composite volcano built of lava and fragmented rock and while volcanologists and geologists will tell that it is unlikely to erupt again in the near future (it last erupted 150 years ago and nearby Mount St Helens erupted with devastating consequences on May 18, 1980 – that's a little close for comfort) they always add a small corollary. Rainier isn't waiting to explode so much as fall to pieces. The mountain is literally falling apart, and that's the main problem for mountaineers.

Mount Rainier's 35 square miles of ice and snow includes 26 named glaciers. When all that lava and fragmented rock is held in place by frozen snow all is well but when the sun shines the air warms up and the ice releases its hold. It's then that climbers come in for a terrifying barrage of rockfall and avalanche, and people sometimes die. I was glad of Art's company and even more glad of his knowledge of the danger spots.

Four days earlier such blackspots were far from our minds. In suffocatingly hot sunshine, we had made our way up from the trail-head in the Paradise Valley near the appropriately-named Paradise Inn, heading towards Camp Muir at 10,000ft. We were an assorted bunch of outdoor writers and mountain bums ostensibly climbing the mountain to field-test outdoor gear but few of us had all that much interest in waterproof suits and fleece base-layers. We were here, like hundreds of other climbers every year, to utilise this magnificent outdoor arena that is Mount Rainier to test ourselves against the cold and the ice, the altitude and, most vital of all, our own frailties. It would be easy to suggest it was simply us against the mountain but I've never considered mountains as combatants in that sense. Despite the potential threat of rockfall, crevasses and intolerant weather we were there to find out whether our skills and mental attitudes were capable of coping with such a potentially hostile, but wholly natural, environment. If they weren't, we could always retreat, disappointed perhaps but not necessarily defeated. For too long military and battleground metaphors have gone hand-in-hand with the simple activity of men climbing mountains.

Consider Ed Hillary's victorious outburst when he arrived back at Everest Base Camp after climbing the mountain for the first time: "We knocked the bastard off..." But in those days mountaineering expeditions were organised like a military campaign so it's not surprising that climbers were caught up in the militaristic spirit of the event. Thankfully, attitudes have changed and I certainly wasn't on Rainier to do battle or conquer anything, other than my own fears; I was there to enjoy the mountain in all its diverse glories, and that appreciation began before I even started climbing.

Before climbing the mountain in 1888, John Muir described the Paradise Valley as "the most extravagantly beautiful of all the alpine gardens I ever beheld". I guess he wasn't exaggerating too much. Avalanche lilies poke their heads through the snow and, by mid-summer, when the snow has finally capitulated to the warmth of the sun, anemone, phlox, arnica and Indian paintbrush blanket the mountain's lower slopes. Forests of Douglas fir, hemlock and Alaskan yellow cedars clothe the mountain's skirts giving shelter to pine marten, mule deer, elk and the occasional mountain lion. We allowed the warmth of the sun to penetrate our bones and breathed the pine-scented air deep into our lungs – higher up we would share the Spartan comforts of Camp Muir with an assortment of hawks, whistling marmots, grumpy ptarmigan and a scavenging fox, the creatures of the icy wastes and rocky screes.

With its glaciated dome rising high above the lush Washington forests, Rainier is to Seattle what the Matterhorn is to Zermatt or Nepal's Machapuchhare is to Pokhara, and the spirit of this 14,411ft/4,393m giant permeates the whole of the Pacific North-West. Its familiar outline has become the trademark of the region and can be seen everywhere, not only from the downtown boulevards and freeways but on adverts, posters and badges throughout the area. It's the citizen's emblem of Seattle.

Earlier in the year, Mount Rainier National Park had celebrated its centennial – 100 years as North America's fifth National Park, and 100 years as the most glaciated peak in the lower 48 states, boasting as its centrepiece the highest and most massive peak in the Cascades Range. For Seattle's residents and visitors alike when 'the mountain is out' means the rain has stopped, the clouds have evaporated and the crown jewel of the region is smiling down on the city which holds it in such proud reverence. To citizens of the Pacific North-West, Rainier is like a sacred icon and is loved by thousands who have never set foot on it, nor ever will.

Rainier is worshipped by mountaineers too. Lou Whittaker, a veteran of Everest who has lived in the shadow of Rainier all his life, told me about returning home from an extended visit to the Himalaya and seeing the mountain appear through the clouds. Despite being satiated with spectacular views of the greatest mountains on Earth he said that glimpse of Rainier had simply taken his breath away. Familiarity, in this case, doesn't breed contempt – Lou has climbed the mountain more than 250 times.

About 10,000 people attempt Rainier every year; roughly half fail to make it. Adverse weather conditions account for many of the failures and a crumpling of the will when faced with the apparently-endless snow slopes of the upper mountain causes others to slump by the wayside. But for most it is the altitude that effects them so badly and there's only one antidote – they have to turn round and descend to where the air is thicker and sweeter.

Even at 10,000ft the air is beginning to thin appreciably and so we grasped the opportunity to try to adapt to this lack of oxygen before our attempt on the final 4,500ft (1,375m) of the mountain. The handful of assorted buildings, including a basic – and I mean basic – two-seater thunderbox, at Camp Muir are well-positioned for a high-level acclimatisation camp. A stone shelter with wooden bunks offers shelter from the winds but, like most similar buildings, you only really realise its value when things are life-threateningly difficult.

I was happy to forego its acrid, freezer-like luxuries. The first night saw a squabble of climbers grab bench spaces inside RMI's wooden hut but I elected to sleep outside, bivvying below a star-studded sky. Occasionally during the night I awoke gasping for breath. My body, relaxed in sleep, had fallen back into a sea level mode of breathing, deep and regular, until the thinness of the air had me gulping for breath. But each time I awoke it was the beauty of the night sky that made it more difficult to fall asleep again.

When John Muir stopped here in August 1888 little did he think the place would someday be named after him. By all accounts it was a cold and windy night and Muir and his companions built wind-breaks from rocks. They shivered the night away and it was next day that E S Ingraham, who was to have the nearby glacier named after him, dubbed their bivouac spot Camp Muir. One wonders if there was a hint of ironic sarcasm in the name, a friendly dig at Muir's reputation for being at one with nature, in all her moods? We'll never know.

Touring the Pacific North-West coastal regions Muir hadn't intended taking part in a climbing expedition but the spirit of Rainier took a firm hold of him. "I didn't mean to climb it," he later explained to his wife, "but got excited and soon was on top."

Reading his account of the ascent of Rainier you can't help but reach the conclusion that while Muir was regarded by many to be one of the finest mountaineers of his day he was more comfortable in the role of a wanderer, a roving spirit, a stravaiger. Climbing a mountain tends to be a focused, singular activity – in many ways you are constrained by the geography of the mountain and the linear route up and down it. Such a restriction can easily curb the sensation of freedom that wilderness wandering offers.

Reflecting on his successful ascent of Rainier, Muir appears uncharacteristically subdued: "The view we enjoyed could hardly be surpassed in sublimity and grandeur, but one feels far from home so high in the sky, so much so that one is inclined to guess that, apart from the acquisition of knowledge and the exhilaration of climbing, more pleasure is to be found at the foot of the mountains than on their frozen tops." Perhaps, at 50 years of age, he was missing the warmth and comfort of the Californian sun?

We enjoyed better weather than Muir's party and made the most of the cloudless skies that were made even more dramatic by the white fluffy temperature inversion that lay below us, submerging the lower valleys like a great ocean. Only distant Mount St Helens pierced the cloud, like a volcanic island on a sea of white. For four days we relaxed and played at being mountaineers, testing our crampons on icy walls and practising crevasse rescues, desperately hoping we'd never have to do it for real. At night we huddled together in the hut and planned future trips, sharing mountain experiences and brewing endless mugs of tea and all the time our bodies were adjusting, acclimatising to the thinner oxygen content of the high mountain air. Soon we'd be ready to tackle the upper slopes.

On the evening of our fourth day we decided that early the next morning we would have a crack at the summit. The weather forecast was promising and after dinner we would try to get some sleep before breaking camp at about 2am. Sleep, needless to say, was as rare as the oxygen and few of the climbers even noticed a fox as he scavenged round the tents looking for scraps of food. Packing and grappling with frozen gear in the icy cold of the pre-dawn hours tends to focus the mind and wildlife watching comes way down the list of priorities

Alpine starts are curiously nervous affairs, as the increasing queue to the Muir Camp toilet testified. The frigid air numbs the fingers, making it difficult to thread crampon straps through buckles, and a dimmed brain refuses to function properly. Haunting doubts and concerns are magnified out of all proportion by the Cimmerian blackness of the night and the mind, dimmed by lack of sleep, is open to all forms of suggestion. Perhaps that's why, in a subconscious search for a good omen, I remembered the legend of The Changer.

The North American Nisqually tribe believed that Mount Rainier was originally a female monster called Tahoma who sucked people to her billowing breast. Tahoma was eventually challenged by a supernatural being called The Changer who, in the form of a red fox, eventually overwhelmed Tahoma and changed the streams of blood that ran down her sides into roaring creeks and rivers of water. Higher up, the frigid temperatures caused those streams to take the form of tumbling rivers of ice. In a few short hours the morning sun would in turn begin to change those rivers of ice into something far more liquid, potentially releasing tons of unstable rock that had been trapped in the frozen fingers of the night. Luck, or the lack of it, plays a big part in such mountain ascents so I was glad to have seen that old dog fox. I took his presence as a good omen.

With the head torches of the rope teams ahead of us strung across the darkness of the Cowlitz Glacier like garlands of fairy lights, our turn came to step out on to the ice, gingerly trying to gauge the pace of the person in front and behind, watching the rope for fear clumsy, cramponed feet would trip over it, sensitive to each pull or tug of this umbilical cord that tied us together.

Some of the local guides had referred to our route as the 'dog run', a reference to the fact that it is the mountain's trade route, and earlier we had been encouraged to discover that the route was the most direct it had been for years because of record snowfalls. Despite this, there were parts of the route where the snow had gone, leaving gaping sections of scree and loose talus – not an ideal walking surface for crampon-clad boots. As we climbed the rocky spur that separates the Cowlitz Glacier from the neighbouring Ingraham Glacier soft curses broke the night air;

we were pirouetting on crampon points that slipped and glanced off rocks, sending sparks into the darkness.

Above the spur lay the first of our resting points – the Ingraham Flats. Below us the Ingraham Glacier flowed its way down towards the distant forest, and away to the west the sky was just beginning to display the pink and orange threads of dawn. It was still cold and we were thankful for this as the next section of route was potentially the most dangerous.

On the other side of the Ingraham Glacier, a narrow dirt track eased its way across the top of a huge chasm to reach another rocky rib known as Disappointment Cleaver, so named because early climbers thought they must be close to the summit, when in reality there was still a good 2,000ft of climbing to go. As we tip-toed across the 12-inch-wide ledge to the rib we were all too aware of the drop below us. But the chasm wasn't the real problem, it was the icefall above the trail that caused us concern. In 1981 ten climbers and an RMI guide perished here when a serac collapsed on the icefall, sending thousands of tons of ice and snow down on to the climbers. All 11 are still entombed within the ice shroud of the glacier. We weren't too disappointed to reach the foot of the Cleaver, we were just glad to reach its relatively solid ground.

From the top of the Cleaver we zigzagged up seemingly endless slopes of dazzling white snow and ice, crossed snow bridges over yawning crevasses and periodically glanced up to see more snow slopes stretch up towards the sky. We became automatons, one step in front of the other, power-breathing and rest-stepping as we had been taught by the RMI guides at Camp Muir. And then that delicious moment came when the snow slope became sky, when the incline levelled off and we stumbled on to the rim of the summit crater, a huge snow-filled arena big enough to take 20 football pitches. The bad news was that the summit, Columbia Crest, lay on the other side of the crater, a good 15-minute walk away; the good news was that the walk to the summit was mostly flat, with only a short climb to the actual top.

We reached the top in the company of another group of climbers and there were the inevitable hugs and kisses, mostly with complete strangers, bound together by the fleeting experience of reaching the summit of a major mountain at the same time. We took time to gaze around at distant Mount Hood, Mount St Helens, the other peaks of the magnificent Cascades and the distant outline of the Olympics before the long, knee-creaking descent back to Camp Muir. From Paradise to Columbia Crest, Mount Rainier had been uncharacteristically benevolent and, before I stumbled into the hut at Camp Muir to celebrate our success with a few cans of beer, I couldn't resist throwing a few squares of chocolate on to the ground as a little gesture of thanks to that old fox. Perhaps I was being unnecessarily superstitious but it seemed to me that The Changer, the spirit of Rainier, had looked kindly on us.

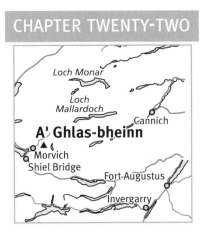

CHAPTER TWENTY-TWO

IN THE ACCLIVITIES OF
THE MOUNTAINS

A' Ghlas-bheinn, which dominates Strath Croe at the head of Loch Duich in Kintail, was described in an early Scottish Mountaineering Club guide as "not a particularly interesting mountain, but its ascent forms an agreeable variation on the walk from Loch Duich to the Falls of Glomach."

The very latest word on the subject from the Scottish Mountaineering Club, in its new and updated guide to *The Munros*, is equally disparaging. "A rather small and insignificant hill," it says, and goes on to gloss over the route in half-a-dozen lines.

A' Ghlas-bheinn undoubtedly suffers from its close proximity to the high and shapely peaks of Kintail, in particular corrie-sculpted Beinn Fhada to which it appears to have been stuck on as some sort of mountaineering addendum. All the guidebooks (including my own guides to the Munros) suggest you climb both hills in one outing, with an ascent of A' Ghlas-bheinn obligatory only because it reaches Munro height, and therein lies the nub of the problem.

The lure of doubling their Munro-tally for the day is too great for most baggers and one of the great delights of post 'Munro-compleation' is the freedom to spend more time on individual hills, as the Cairngorm poet Nan Shepherd wrote: "Often the mountain gives itself most completely when I have no destination, when I reach nowhere in particular, but have gone out merely to be with the mountain as one visits a friend with no intention but to be with him."

A' Ghlas-bheinn's certainly an old acquaintance of mine, this grey-green hill of Kintail which jauntily cocks a snook at its bigger and more popular neighbours, and in both its complexity of form and sequestration from the other hills of Kintail it offers a multi-optional day out, especially during winter months when daylight hours are in short supply.

Because it's normally climbed as an addendum to Beinn Fhada most hill-walkers climb A' Ghlas-bheinn from the Bealach na Sgairne, the high pass which links the two hills together, trudging up the mountain's long south-east ridge and over its interminable false tops knowing full-well they have to return to the bealach the same way before tackling Beinn Fhada. Others climb Fhada first, and tackle A' Ghlas-bheinn when the legs and lungs begin to display the first symptoms of fatigue, when the thoughts are beginning to turn to the first pint of beer in the Kintail Lodge Hotel. No wonder so many walkers belittle A' Ghlas-bheinn. It deserves better treatment than that.

From Loch Duich-side A' Ghlas-bheinn appears as a retiring, knobbly hill, with long, gnarly fingers reaching down towards Strath Croe at its foot. The broadest of these fingers represents the hill's west ridge, the most popular, albeit relatively uninteresting, route of ascent or descent, but it's worthwhile combining the ascent of A' Ghlas-bheinn with a visit to the Falls of Glomach on the north side of the mountain, leaving the multi-topped south-east ridge to the Bealach an Sgairne for the descent, a complete 13-mile traverse of the hill giving the possibility of superb views in all directions.

The Falls of Glomach route is well-signposted from Innis a'Chrotha in Strath Croe. A footpath links with the old Forestry Commission car park at Dorusduain before heading north through the Dorusduain Wood to the confluence of the Allt Mam an Tuirc and the Allt an Leoid

Ghaineamhaich. A bridge crosses the latter stream and a good footpath begins to wind its way up the hillside before climbing gradually to the 1,700ft (518m) Bealach na Sroine. Those uninterested in the aquatic display of the waterfalls can leave the path here and climb over the Meal Dubh shoulder of A' Ghlas-bheinn and on towards the summit but the Falls of Glomach, said to be the second highest falls in the country, are worth at least a peek, especially after wet weather when the feeder streams are swollen and the falls are consequently a greater spectacle.

The top of the falls lie about a mile beyond and 600ft (183m) below the Bealach na Sroine. From here the Allt a' Ghlomaich plunges some 500ft (152m) into a deep and rocky cleft. Needless to say great care should be taken on the normally wet path which skirts the top of the falls.

As you grind your way back up to the Bealach na Sroine consider the experience here of Frank Smythe, a fine Himalayan mountaineer and well-known writer who, at the time of his visit to the Falls of Glomach in 1942, was a squadron leader in the Royal Air Force, teaching commandos mountain warfare in the Cairngorms. Smythe wrote of seeing a "a pitiful procession" coming towards him.

He described a band of people climbing up a narrow defile before him, when, "concealed men leapt to their feet and brandishing spears, axes and clubs, rushed down with wild yells on the unfortunates beneath. There was a short, fierce struggle, then a horrible massacre. Not a man, woman or child was left alive: the defile was choked with corpses."

Smythe was convinced he had been given a backward glimpse into some ancient page of Highland history, the kind of psychic experience which, curiously, is comparatively widespread among hill-going folk. On his home hills of Ettrick the border shepherd James Hogg once witnessed the apparition of a drove of Highland cattle accompanied by three drovers.

"It is quite evident," he later recorded, "that we must attribute these appearances to particular states of the atmosphere, and suppose them to be shadows of realities; the airy resemblance of scenes passing in distant parts of the country, and by some singular operation of natural causes this expressively imaged in the acclivities of the mountains."

Once you've climbed A' Ghlas-bheinn from the Bealach na Sroine and descended the long and bumpy south-east ridge to the Bealach na Sgairne, it's worth knowing that the name of this pass can be translated as the pass where the stones make noise. That loose interpretation of the Gaelic refers to the wind 'sighing' or 'murmuring' through the rocks, as well as the sound of falling rocks. Bear that in mind if you hear any strange sounds, for apparitions have been experienced here too. On the trail that winds its way downhill back to Strath Croe some walkers once passed a tall, thin man with a white beard, hand-in-hand with a small girl wrapped up in a cloak and a hood. After making some local enquiries they were convinced they had met the ghosts of Osgood Mackenzie, the great botanist and creator of the Inverewe Gardens, and his daughter Mhairi. Mackenzie who had died some 30 years previously.

CHAPTER TWENTY-THREE

IN THE THRONE ROOM
OF THE MOUNTAIN KING

I had intended climbing the two Munro summits of Torridon's
Beinn Eighe but I was waylaid by a corrie, stopped in my tracks by
a change of focus.

I had climbed the summits before, several times over and had passed
through the corrie and over its scree-clad flanks often enough but today
there was something in the stark contrast between shadow and light on
the cliffs, the slight wind-ruffle on the loch and the two-tone shades of
the triple-tiered cliffs that made me slow down, drag my feet and change
my plans for the day. Aware of the antiquity of the mountain's ancient
rocks, I wanted to linger in its timelessness.

Many mountain commentators are of the opinion that Coire Mhic
Fhearchair of Beinn Eighe is the finest corrie in Scotland, a claim that is
difficult to contest (close contenders would be Toll an Lochain of An
Teallach or perhaps the An Garbh Choire of Braeriach). Dominated by
a great triple buttress of light grey quartzite which soars from an equally
impressive plinth of red sandstone, the precipices loom over a rock-
cradled lochan which spills over the corrie lip in a series of fine
waterfalls and cascades.

Unlike Beinn Eighe's other corries, Coire Mhic Fhearchair (the corrie of the son of Farquhar; try *corrie vic feracher*, with the 'ch' harsh, as in *loch*) doesn't feel as though it's shut into the mountain and despite its north-facing aspect its open nature attracts a fair share of sunlight, more often than not highlighting the chocolate brown of the Torridonian sandstone and the glistening white speckles of quartzite on the upper tiers of the cliffs.

Earlier in the day I had left the National Trust for Scotland car park on the Glen Torridon road and climbed the path beside the Allt a' Choire Dhuibh Mhoir which rises gently into the narrow confines of Coire Dubh Mor, a wonderful situation with the great flank of Beinn Eighe on your right and the castellated buttresses of Liathach on your left – two of the finest mountains in the country.

Shortly beyond, another track carried me around the northern flanks of Sail Mhor, with views across a lochan-splattered glen towards Beinn Dearg and Baosbheinn, before rising steeply and suddenly into the cathedral-like grandeur of Coire Mhic Fhearchair. Bounded on the left by the scree girt slopes of Beinn Eighe's highest summit, Ruadh-stac Mor, and on the right by the steep, broken cliffs of Sail Mhor, the softly lapping waters of the lochan reflected a scene of savage beauty, a ruffled image of a scene that has changed little in millions of years, the throne room of the Torridonian mountain king.

The mountains of Torridon are said to be the oldest in the world. Raised as a vast plateau 30 million years ago and carved into their present shape, it has been suggested that really they are no older than the Alps, at least in their present form. What is really ancient is the rock of the original chain, now exposed as the grey quartzite caps, reckoned to be 600 million years old. The sandstone below them is even older and the platforms of gneiss on which they stand are believed to be in the region of 2,600 million years old. It's no small wonder they exude an air of primeval dominance. No small wonder that I, in turn, felt the insignificance of mere humanity.

Instead of climbing the scree gully to the summit of Ruadh-stac Mor, my original plan, I sniffed around the corrie's inner recesses like a dog in a new kennel, searching out the resonances of the corrie's more recent history – the remnants of the aircraft that crashed here in 1952, the slivers of metal cold to the touch. I eased up the lower moves of a rock climb first completed more than 100 years ago by Dr Norman Collie, one of the founding fathers of Scottish mountaineering who, with a lovely sense of exaggeration, had described the last section of the route as, "not quite but very nearly AP". The route most certainly steepens out but isn't quite 'absolutely perpendicular' as he suggests. I gazed along the line taken by Chris Bonington and the late Tom Patey in 1960 when they completed their Upper Girdle Traverse, a long horizontal route that followed the natural fault line between two layers of quartzite, and recalled with some fondness a climb, The Gash (severe, 200ft/61m), I had enjoyed many years ago with a friend now long-gone, the victim of an avalanche in the Alps.

I lingered in the corrie for much of the afternoon, time slipping by without much notice. From somewhere close by I heard the raucous cry of a peregrine but failed to actually see it. A flock of black-headed gulls floated on the loch, scavengers attracted by the crumbs left behind by hill-walkers, and a pair of ptarmigan drew me away from their chattering brood by dragging their wings along the ground in mock injury. But for most of the time I simply sat, back against a flat rock that could be several thousand million years old, in silent wonder, trying as I've so often tried before to grasp some meaning behind such a time-scale. And, as has always happened before, I failed completely, aware only of my own mortality...

For those who prefer to visit Coire Mhic Fhearchair as part of a 12-mile circular route taking in the two Munros of Beinn Eighe, the route to the first summit of Ruadh-stac is now fairly straightforward. A sketchy footpath follows the north-eastern shore of the lochan and climbs through a jumble of rocks to reach a prominent gully in the south-east recess of the corrie. Badly eroded and filled with scree it offers an energetic scramble on to the eastern enclosing arm of Coire Mhic Fhearchair which runs out north to Ruadh-stac Mor, 3,314ft/1,010m, climbing gently over white quartzite screes to the summit.

Return along the ridge you've just climbed to the top of the access gully from the corrie below. Climb now in a south-west direction towards the eastern end of the dome of Coinneach Mhor from where the main Beinn Eighe ridge runs south-east over another rough col before climbing a steeper, narrower rocky ridge to the second Munro, Spidean Coire nan Clach (3,258ft/993m). The best route of descent is to return west to a trig point and a prominent south-south-east spur from which you can drop steeply into Coire an Laoigh where a stalkers' path can be easily followed to the A896 in Glen Torridon. A short walk back on the road returns you to the car park from where you started.

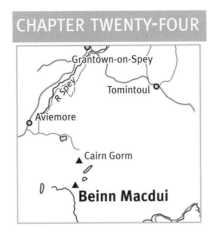

CHAPTER TWENTY-FOUR

Grantown-on-Spey

R.Spey

Tomintoul

Aviemore

▲ Cairn Gorm

𝑂 ▲ **Beinn Macdui**

INSIDE AND OUT ON THE
ROOF OF SCOTLAND

I t was the novelist and poet Nan Shepherd who suggested that a mountain has an inside. She wasn't referring to its deep volcanic core but to its corries and chasms, its deep clefts and precipices that are often even more enticing than its summit. And nowhere can you experience this sensation more than on the roof of Scotland, the elevated levels of the Cairn Gorm to Ben Macdui plateau.

Up here you tend to look down on the sensational rather than gaze up at it from below; boulder-strewn slopes drop away below your feet, silent shining lochs float below you and broad chasms split the mountainsides to reveal dizzying depths and it's all thanks to the slow, grinding processes of glaciation and the endless scouring of a cruel arctic climate. The rivers have played their part too for these Cairngorm mountains are hills of circumdenudation, carved out of their original plateau blocks by erosion and subsequently re-shaped and re-moulded by the fast-flowing waters that continue to deepen the valley floors.

It's been a prolonged process and through the aeons of geologic time, as the scouring and the grinding and the reshaping has gone on, the mountain's interior has gradually been revealed for all to see and an 11-mile wander over Ben Macdui, Britain's second-highest hill, exposes you to the best of it.

A rough path leaves Cairn Gorm's Coire Cas and follows the Allt Coire an t-Sneachda up into the clench of its eponymous corrie, at first over slopes of rock and heather, then over heaths which glow golden in the evening light before tumbling into a jumble of granite rocks and boulders, some the size of a minibus. Already you will have experienced something of the Cairngorms' character. Even at this early stage in the walk you might have been entertained by the wonderful aerobatic displays of meadow pipits or the guttural outbursts of the red grouse might have told you to 'go-back, go-back' in no uncertain terms. Higher in the corrie you might even have heard the joyous song of the cock snow bunting or the throaty call of the ptarmigan, the arctic grouse which inhabits these high, but not so lonely, places.

The inner recesses of Coire an t-Sneachda, the snowy corrie, cast a shadow across the blue-green waters of its lochans and a wall of gully-riven cliffs and buttresses forces you to consider where you go from here. An unlikely path, known locally as the Goat Track, traces a weakness through the cliffs to the right lifting you through a series of tight zig-zags on to the high plateau, just east of Cairn Lochan. From here a well-worn track grooves its way across the grassy uplands and boggy flushes towards Britain's highest named tarn, Lochan Buidhe, the small yellow loch. The walking is easy and comparatively flat and your eyes are drawn to the shapely outline of Cairn Toul and Sgor an Lochain Uaine in the west. On a glorious summer day it's hard to believe you're treading slopes that are above 3,000ft (914m) high. In the depths of winter you'd need little convincing.

The Macdui route now runs south from Lochan Buidhe, over scree and boulder slopes, a trail hideously lined with way-marking cairns which appear to grow bigger every year. Even the regiments of committed cairn-kickers, of which I am proudly one, have given up on these giants. Only a bulldozer could flatten them effectively. I can understand people's desire for way-marking cairns but why can't they be small affairs, like the 'ducks' of North America or the traditional inukshuk of the Arctic Inuit people? Sadly, we're afflicted by the tradition of adding a stone to every cairn we come across; like a dog pissing up against a tree we have to somehow leave a mark of our passing.

After a spell of boulder-hopping a short and sharp pull takes you on to the western slopes of Macdui's north top. Traverse the slopes of granite scree and enjoy the clumps of purple moss campion which stand out starkly against the gunmetal grey of the ground. This remarkable plant flowers successfully, year after year, amid the desolation of its upland desert where little else grows, a miracle of survival.

As you traverse these otherwise bare slopes, the other big hills of the western Cairngorm massif come into view: Cairn Toul, Sgor an Lochain Uaine and Braeriach, forming the rugged walls of the An Garbh Choire, the big rough corrie, one of the finest examples of a glaciated corrie in Scotland.

Soon the gravelly path meanders past a series of stone wind-breaks to the broad summit of Ben Macdui, crowned by a giant cairn and a view indicator. On a good day you can see the Lammermuirs in the south and Morven in Caithness in the north but such good days are few and far between. East of the summit the mountain begins to expose itself in dramatic form, its slopes opened up and revealed in a series of great corries and chasms. The rocky depths of Coire Sputan Dearg give way to the great bowl of Coire Etchachan and its loch, whose shores caress the 3,000-foot contour, before that corrie gives way to something even greater, the long slit trench that holds Loch Avon, the sparkling jewel in the Cairngorms' crown.

A footpath plunges steeply into the trench, dropping you into a confusion of huge boulders and tiny emerald-green lochans. Ahead of you, below the gaunt square-topped monolith of the Sticil, lies the Shelter Stone, a particularly huge boulder which has come to rest on lesser stones leaving a gap, or a recess, below it. There is enough space for a dozen or so people and it's probably the best-known howff in the country. A mini-interior if you like, which has offered shelter and protection to generations of visitors.

Cross the river now and follow the north shore of Loch Avon to Coire

Raibeirt. Another path climbs steeply up the corrie and returns to the Cairngorm plateau south-west of Cairn Gorm itself. Finally, cross the plateau and return to the car park by descending the long ridge of Fiacaill a' Choire Chais.

CHAPTER TWENTY-FIVE

THE WAY OF THE PROPHET

The Sierra Nevada mountains of California have touched the spiritual consciousness of backpackers and mountaineers for generations. No-one could expound on these transcendental aspects of the Sierra Nevada better than the wilderness prophet himself, John Muir. His writings and philosophies are as powerful today as they were when he wrote them, a rich and puissant voice echoing down through the decades, a voice for our times as well as his own...

Stretched between the southern boundary of Sequoia National Park and the northern boundary of Yosemite National Park, California's Sierra Nevada is the highest mountain range in the contiguous US.

Similar in size, shape and dimension to the European Alps, the mountains, crags and granite domes of the Sierras lack the moist tendencies of the European weather and instead are blessed with the finest climate of any mountain range in the world. Wall-to-wall sunshine guarantees wonderful conditions for extended mountain journeys through alpine meadows, past turquoise lakes and across steep talus slopes, above natural forests of pine, starting perhaps in the hot desert-like conditions of the eastern Sierra and finishing among the lush redwood groves on the western slopes. The whole area is a veritable paradise and it's little wonder the Sierras have captivated the spirit of outdoors people for well over a century-and-a-half.

To celebrate our silver wedding anniversary, my wife Gina, myself and our two sons enjoyed two weeks' memorable backpacking around the Yosemite high country. So captivated were we by the landscape that Gina and I promised ourselves a return visit to walk the 220-mile John Muir Trail, all the way from Yosemite to Mount Whitney in the south of the range. While the name of John Muir is synonymous with the Sierra Nevada and, in particular, Yosemite Valley, most folk don't realise he wasn't the principle architect of the trail that bears his name.

On a clear spring morning in 1884 a 13-year-old boy gazed across the fields of alfalfa on his uncle's farm near Fresno, California. Stretched across the far horizon lay the mountains of the Sierra Nevada, named centuries earlier by pioneering Spaniards, and as far as the young Theodore Seixas Solomons was concerned it was "the most beautiful and mysterious sight" he had ever seen.

So thrilled was he that he imagined himself "in the immensity of that uplifted world, an atom moving along just below the white, crawling from one end to the other of that horizon of high enchantment". Solomons later claimed that it was on this very day that he first envisioned the "idea of a crest-parallel trail through the High Sierra".

Between the years 1892 and 1897 Solomons visited the High Sierra every summer, gradually pushing a route south from Yosemite and bestowing hundreds of place names, about 60 of which remain today. In the years that followed other adventurers continued Solomons' work, particularly Joseph Nisbet LeConte, son of the renowned geologist Joseph LeConte, and Bolton Coit Brown. Both were members of the highly influential Sierra Club, which had been founded in 1892.

In 1901 the Sierra Club, led by its president and founder, John Muir, held its first annual meet in Yosemite Valley. Ninety-six members attended and included in the group were Muir's daughters Wanda and

Helen, the landscape artist William Keith and the chief of the US Biological Survey, C Hart Merriam. All five individuals were later to be commemorated with Sierra place names.

During the early years of the 20th century more and more outdoorsmen were visiting the high country of the Sierra Nevada – indeed the Sierra Club repeatedly held meets in Yosemite, King's Canyon and the Mount Whitney region. Realising that not many people would attempt the arduous journey along the length of the mountain range until a proper trail was established, and perhaps thinking of the vast new territory that would become accessible for their annual outings, the directors of the Sierra Club suggested to the California State Legislature that it would be in the public interest to construct and maintain a trail running the length of the Sierra.

In 1915 work began on the trail, named in honour of John Muir. Several years later gangs of workmen had constructed a well-engineered path which stretched from Yosemite Valley and the southern ramparts of the Sierra Nevada mountain range near Mount Whitney. By the mid 20s the 220-mile John Muir Trail was completed. The Sierra Club's Francis Farquhar spoke for many outdoor enthusiasts when he wrote that the new path was: "a magnificent memorial, a highway for devout pilgrims blessing the memory of the prophet who was the first to sing the praises of this glorious sequence of mountain, meadow, pass and lake."

Farquhar's words describe the spiritual emotions that were aroused in these early pioneers of the Sierras, emotions that still boil up and bubble over in those who extol the mountains today. But no-one could expound on the transcendental aspects of the Sierra Nevada better than the wilderness prophet himself, John Muir. His writing and philosophies are as powerful today as they were when he wrote them, a rich and puissant voice echoing down through the decades, a voice for our times as well as his own:

"Then it seemed to me the Sierra should be called not the Nevada or Snowy Range, but the Range of Light. And after ten years spent in the heart of it, rejoicing and wondering, bathing in the glorious floods of light, seeing the sunbursts of morning among the icy peaks, the noonday radiance on the trees and rocks and snow, the flush of the alpenglow and a thousand dashing waterfalls with their marvellous abundance of irised spray, it still seems to me above all others the Range of Light, the most divinely beautiful of all the mountain chains I have ever seen."

Our first night on the John Muir Trail was particularly memorable – for the wrong reasons. We'd had a long, hard day and, still jet-lagged from our flight, we hadn't really organised our camp. All our food was in bear barrels, plastic tubs that bears can't open but my son Gregor had mistakenly left his wash kit hanging on a bush in front of my tent. At about two in the morning I was awakened by a noise and looked out the open door of my tent to see an enormous black silhouette reaching up to take the wash kit. I roared as loud as I could, grabbed my cooking pot and lid and clashed them together to make as much noise as possible. The bear fled.

I should have felt triumphant but I didn't. My heart beat like a drum for what seemed like hours and I started at every little sound. I was a nervous wreck, even though I knew that the bear, all 300lb of it, was as terrified of me as I was of it.

Next night we cleared up the camp site, organised our bear barrels and left nothing lying about for the temptation of roaming bears, little realising how richly rewarded I would be for our efforts. As I lay in my tent watching the last trickles of daylight fade beyond the spires of Cathedral Peak a huge brown bear padded slowly into our camp. In that peculiar ursine way he appeared clumsy yet strong, his thick fur chocolate brown with lighter markings on his massive rump. He stopped and twisted his short stubby neck, his head small and round and his muzzle pointed.

As he gazed at us I felt none of the alarm that I had experienced the night before. The bear's nose was black and twitched slightly but it was his eyes, his remarkably tiny eyes, that I recall. So dark, so impenetrable, showing no sign of fear or alarm. It seemed like minutes, but I'm sure it was no more than three or four seconds, before he turned and slowly waddled off into the woods again but in those few instants, as the bear and I looked directly at each other, I was aware of the almost overwhelming wonder of the moment, the immensity of gazing directly into the beautiful world of nature.

It had been a vitally important encounter. The night before we had been careless and as a direct consequence I had been scared witless by a bear and the bear had been scared witless by me. Not the kind of experience that leads to wilderness contentment. The second night we didn't tempt the bear's presence but, nevertheless, our evening visitor was welcome and, in a curious kind of a way, welcoming. Indeed the experience reminded me of John Muir's belief that such encounters had a mystical ability to inspire and refresh. "Nature's peace will flow into you as the sunshine into the trees," he wrote. "The winds will blow their freshness into you, and the storms their energy, while cares will drop off like autumn leaves."

As far as backpacking trails go the John Muir Trail is possibly the finest in the world, carrying you 220 miles from Yosemite Valley through Yosemite, Sequoia and King's Canyon National Parks, Inyo National Forest and the John Muir and Ansel Adams Wilderness areas. It finishes on the summit of Mount Whitney, at 14,491ft (4,418m) the highest point in the contiguous states of America. Recollections of wandering through scented pine forests, camping by turquoise lakes set in mountain cirques and climbing over a succession of high mountain passes, most of them higher than 12,000ft (3,660m), will linger with me for the rest of my life. It was, without doubt, the finest backpacking trip I have undertaken anywhere but it was more than that. It was as though I'd had my eyes opened and in the context of a 220-mile journey through Muir's Range of Light I recognised something in wilderness that I hadn't quite understood before. The English language has a paucity of words to describe it, but 'spirituality' will probably do for now.

It would probably be an exaggeration to suggest my bear encounter held any resonances of a spiritual benediction, a baptism into wilderness, but Muir, and indeed many others, would certainly claim such an experience. A friend of mine, Graham White, editor of *Sacred Summits – John Muir's Greatest Climbs*, writes of being "haunted by the experience" of walking the John Muir Trail and others talk of life-changing encounters. This intensity of spiritual discovery to be found in the Sierra Nevada is not entirely unusual, and is well recorded in Adrian Cooper's fascinating book *Sacred Mountains*. A number of contributors were drawn to the Sierra and although they found the Californian mountains an easy travel destination they all described their surprise and frustration at feeling 'ill-equipped' and 'unprepared' to encounter the often profound experiences they found there. One of the book's contributors, Danny, a motor mechanic from Los Angeles wrote:

"It was as if I was a beached whale out there. I had no education in looking at the sacredness you immediately feel there. And no way of dealing with any of what I found at first... about all the sacredness I felt there."

His companion Jed experienced similar sensations and it wasn't until they read the writings of John Muir that they began to form a more satisfying and compelling relationship with the Sierras. Both men, in particular, quoted these words of Muir's: "Brooding over some vast mountain landscape, or among the spiritual countenances of mountain flowers, our bodies disappear, our mortal coils come off without any shuffling, and we blend into the rest of Nature, utterly blind to the boundaries that measure human qualities into separate individuals."

Both Danny and Jed had been used to looking at mountains in a logical way, studying physical landscapes in scientific terms and while they were both familiar with the work of John Muir it wasn't until they had "both been through this 'wall' of major and complete bafflement" that they began to understand something of Muir's philosophy and its importance in the understanding of mountains as a 'spiritual and holy thing'.

John Muir had been raised in a strict Calvinist household so it's perhaps not surprising that he habitually used Christian imagery to give depth when describing his experiences, never more so than when outlining the transformation into what became his religion of the wilderness.

Muir experienced a fairly gradual initiation into this 'religion'. He had travelled widely, to Canada, Cuba and Florida and indeed had set out on a 1,000-mile journey to the Gulf of Mexico in 1867. It was a journey of discovery. On his first excursion through the southern states to Florida, he gradually realised that man had become fearful of nature, caused largely by his anthropocentric views which saw wilderness as an ungodly chaos.

As he walked through Florida, Muir tried to reconcile a particular fear he had of alligators because he was desperate to try to love all creatures, a fundamental in his belief that man had ignored the natural laws in favour of his own unfounded beliefs and as a result had failed to live in harmony with the wilderness. But it was the following year, on his first visit to the Sierra Nevada, that Muir encountered for the first time a land that showed no evident sign of civilisation, a land that was wilder and more spectacular than anything he had witnessed to date.

On his first sighting of Yosemite Valley Muir was spellbound and his subsequent writings were enriched with a sense of awesome wonder.

"From end to end of the temple, from the shrubs and half-buried ferns of the floor to the topmost ranks of jewelled pine spires, it is all one finished unit of divine beauty, weighed in the celestial balances and found perfect," he exclaimed.

With Christianity playing such an important part in his upbringing (as a child he could quote the whole of the New Testament and much of the Old), it's evident how much Muir relied on spiritual idiom when describing the transforming experience of his own wilderness baptism. This phenomenon occurred one night as he explored the underside of a large waterfall.

"I was gazing up and out through the thin half-translucent edge of the fall, when suddenly all was dark, and down came a dash of outside gauze tissue made of spent comets, thin and harmless to look at a mile off, but desperately solid and stony when they strike one's shoulders."

Feeling dazed and overwhelmed by his experience, Muir returned home and went to bed. Next day:

"I awoke sane and comfortable, some of the earthiness washed out of me and Yosemite virtue washed in… Wonderful that Nature can do such wild passionate work without seeming extravagant, or that she will allow poor mortals so near her while doing it."

It was as though Muir had been initiated into a secret sect, fully converted by a new, indwelling spirit and, like the baptism of the Holy Spirit so often described by charismatic or Pentecostal Christians, Muir had found release and salvation in what Nature offered him. But, while his experience might have been novel, it wasn't entirely new – American transcendentalists and English romantics had been writing about the redemptive qualities of Nature for a long time. Thoreau and Emerson in

America and Wordsworth and Coleridge in England had already hinted at such spiritual release but had all stopped short at suggesting Nature played an important role in their personal salvation. These 19th century writers, while recognising Nature's ability to illuminate the divine within an individual, believed their own intellects provided the ultimate answers in the search for religious truth.

One vibrant and obvious characteristic of Muir's beliefs is his oneness with the natural world, perhaps not surprising in one who claims to have been personally baptised into wilderness. Here was a man who was completely at home in the outdoors, often travelling over the mountains with little other than a crust of bread and a twist of tea, a mountaineer in the truest sense of the world, a climber who was apparently fearless. Indeed, it's rare for Muir to be given the full credit he deserves as one of the great mountaineering explorers of his era.

In *Sacred Summits – John Muir's Greatest Climbs*, Graham White celebrates Muir the climber as well as Muir the naturalist. According to White, Muir's epic climbs and summit experiences stand comparison with those of any other mountaineer of his time.

Muir made solo-ascents of a number of unclimbed 13,000ft (4,000m) peaks, particularly in the Sierra Nevada mountains, 20 years before mountaineering was constituted as a sport in Scotland. But such was Muir's contribution to the discovery and exploration of the high Sierra that it's sometimes forgotten that he was pretty widely travelled. As well as making the first ascents of Cathedral Peak, Mount Ritter and Mount Whitney in the Sierras, he also made early ascents of Mount Shasta and Mount Rainier in Washington State. He also travelled extensively in Alaska and, later in his life, made a visit to his native Scotland.

While many of Muir's mountain ascents came about as part of his explorations, mapping the distribution of the giant redwoods, exploring the canyons and carrying out the first botanical and geological studies of mountain wilderness areas, there is little doubt that he took great delight in the physical expression of climbing, almost giving it a spiritual dimension. He once suggested that "Christianity and Mountainanity are streams which flow from the same source". As such, he appears to have cultivated his own list of climbing ethics, characteristics which include the importance of climbing as a solitary activity, a preference for the extended adventure and long walk-in, an ascetic disregard for the comforts of food, shelter and clothing and a profound respect for all forms of life. He was, in fact, on a continual search for spiritual transcendence in the mountains.

Where Muir differs from many of his contemporary mountaineers, and certainly from the majority of modern climbers, was in his motives for climbing. There was no peak-bagging mentality in Muir's make-up. In the introduction to his book Graham White writes: "Muir's approach to mountaineering was nature-centred rather than human-centred and the 'quality' of the experience was more important than the 'quantity'. Muir was interested in the whole experience: the canyon's depths, or the alpine meadows, were just as inviting as the mountain peak. Every rock, every plant and animal encountered on each step of the whole journey was to be studied and experienced to the full: with mind and body, intellect and emotion, spirit and soul. For Muir, the highest peak attained was only the mid-point and climax of a circular pilgrimage, rather than the terminus of a summit assault."

Many of us are aware that wild country has a mystical ability to inspire and refresh. "Climb the mountains and get their good tidings," Muir said. For all those "bound by clocks, almanacs… and dust and din" and limited to places where "Nature is covered and her voice smothered", Muir claimed wilderness was essential, so much so that, in an obvious plagiarism of the words of Henry David Thoreau, he concluded, "in God's wildness lies the hope of the world – the great, fresh, unblighted, unredeemed wilderness".

And what of the Sierras?

"Mountains holy as Sinai," said Muir. "No mountains I know of are so alluring. None so hospitable, kindly, tenderly inspiring. It seems strange that everybody does not come at their call. They are given, like the Gospel, without money and without price. 'Tis heaven alone that is given away."

I'll say 'amen' to that…

CHAPTER TWENTY-SIX

MEALL A'BHUACHAILLE
AND THE KINCARDINES

I suspect it was nothing more than a whim that took me for the first time on to the Kincardine Hills. I'd only intended stealing two or three hours from a busy schedule, just enough time for a leisurely stroll over the Thieves' Road, the Rathad nam Mearlach, from Glenmore through Ryvoan Pass and a climb over the wee Meall a'Bhuachaille, but the intoxication of late summer went to my head.

The walk begins and ends at Glenmore Lodge, the National Mountaineering Centre near Aviemore, and continues through the lovely Pass of Ryvoan past the Lochan Uaine, the Green Lochan, so-named because local legend has it that the faery folk once washed their clothes in its waters. It certainly is an enchanted spot with the translucent green waters reflecting the grey screes of the intriguingly-named Creag nan Gall, the hill of the Stranger, but one wonders what the Glenmore faery folk think of the ugly fence and railway sleeper staircase that's been built. Such utilitarian vandalism, no-doubt created with the best of intent in the name of erosion control.

This Ryvoan Pass is the route of the ancient Rathad nam Mearlach, which ran from here to the glens of Lochaber. The western clans followed its quiet byways on cattle raiding forays to and from the fertile lands of Morayshire, avoiding all the large centres of population in Badenoch.

The woods below Ryvoan Pass were loud with exuberant birdsong, blue tits, great tits, chaffinch and willow warbler, but the mewing call of a buzzard seemed to greet the warm sun with all the resignation of the summer's fag-end. Soon the first frosts of autumn would begin nipping the leaves and the greylag geese would be winging their way south through the great defiles of the Lairig an Laoigh and the Lairig Ghru. The heather's fading and the bracken had already given up its hold on life.

From Ryvoan Bothy, a good footpath runs up through the heather to the higher, steeper slopes of Meall a'Bhuachaille. It's a fairly hefty pull up to the summit on an increasingly eroded path, with one or two steep, rocky sections that might just require the use of hands, but the views make a good excuse to stop for a breather. Gaze down on the broad, ochre-coloured moors of Abernethy Forest and the gentle sweep up to the sharply-defined top of Bynack More. Let your eye be led up the length of Strath Nethy to the high saddle which overlooks Loch Avon, that most secretive of Scottish lochs, hidden by the enormous bulk of Cairn Gorm brooding over its the row of scalloped hollows that are the Northern Corries.

So many times I've arrived on this summit to be blown behind the huge cairn in search of some shelter from the winds that scourge the place, but today the usually exposed cairn seemed warm and welcoming. It was good to loiter instead of cower, for this really is a grand vantage point with its unobstructed views of the Cairngorms across the green foreground of Glen More. Anywhere else Meall a' Bhuachaille's comparatively lowly elevation of 2,657ft/810m would be fairly significant but, although dwarfed by the bulk of the Cairngorms, this 'rounded hill of the shepherd' is magnificently positioned to allow you to gaze down the full length of Glenmore into the heart of Badenoch, to the Laggan hills and beyond.

Slithering down the western slopes of Meall a'Bhuachaille in ankle-deep peat I looked towards the path that traces its way up Creagan Gorm on the other side of the bealach and, as I've done so many times in the past, considered extending my high-level walk over it and its north-western neighbour Craiggowrie. Normally I would wander up Meall a'Bhuachaille on a summer evening, then hurry down through the Glen More woods to reach the Lochain Bar in Glenmore Lodge before closing time but today the warm weather and distant views encouraged me to sacrifice some time. The schedules and deadlines could wait...

I was glad I continued. The high-level traverse over these Kincardine Hills, over Creagan Gorm and Craiggowrie, is a fine one, a roller-coaster ridge of easy walking. On one side lie the great V-shaped jaws of the Lairig Ghru, the rounded, scalloped summit of Braeriach and the steep-sided ridge of the Sgurans while on the other the flatter lands and forests of Strathspey roll on towards the Morayshire coast. I couldn't understand why, in 20-odd years of living here, I had never climbed these two hills before.

From Craiggowrie it's an easy enough descent to the Slugan track which runs back through the Glenmore Forest Park towards Loch Morlich but I wanted to continue just a little further to a small, rounded hill that I did know quite well, a hill I had visited many times – Creag Chaisteal, the castle crag. This little bare-topped hill has been described as the 'last of the Cairngorms', a foothill of some significance in times past. A dun, a Pictish fort, crowns the summit and at its foot, according to the writer Alasdair Alpin Macgregor "you can see the outlines of a prehistoric lake dwelling deep below the waters of the loch".

I've never seen this crannog myself, even in times of low water, but I like the link between the loch dwelling and the Pictish fort, the spirit of place it implies. On the other side of the loch is the site of a late 14th century battle where some Cummings were treacherously slain by the Shaws but, happily, this Creag Chaisteal is nowadays a peaceful corner, dressed beautifully in birch and pine, its rocky hollows holding pools of rain water. Another peaceful corner, a round drystane dyke on a hill at the end of the loch, recalls a recent sorrow. The dyke encircles a tiny graveyard, overgrown with heather. Here lies the remains of the wife of

Sir Herbert Ogilvy, 19th Baronet of Inverquharity who died on September 20, 1940. Eleven days after her death, their son, Henry Iain Ogilvy of Pityoulish and his girlfriend, Lucy Scott Robson, were killed while climbing Sgoran Dubh Mor, the same Sgoran Dubh Mor which can be clearly seen from the graveside, rising its head into the clouds away beyond the loch and the forest of Rothiemurchus. Their epitaph reads: "They all loved Pityoulish and Pityoulish loved them."

CHAPTER TWENTY-SEVEN

NO SUMMIT HERE
JUST SPACE

It's a vast expanse of stony ridge and green hollows of turf and moss, drained by a profusion of sparkling clear streams. A high tableland like a vast raised moor, it's a favourite feeding place of red deer and a haunt of Arctic-type birds like ptarmigan, snow bunting and dotterel. Although it's not much lower in elevation than the great plateaux of Braeriach and Cairn Gorm, this is no rocky, boulder-scree moonscape. Greener and softer than its neighbouring plateaux, the Moine Mhor lacks the harshness and stony desolation of these other Grampian mountainscapes. This is another world, a place of infinite contrasts spoiled only by the jarring outline of the bulldozed track that has ripped across the plateau's undulating surface.

For all that this Great Moss offers a lonely solitude, green rather than grey, tending to the gentler end of harsh, a soft pearl in a crown of hard diamonds. Its billowing acres flow south from the Sgurans and the impressive head of Loch Einich and over Mullach Clach a' Bhlair to upper Glen Feshie. Bounded on the east by the huge swelling bosoms of Monadh Mor and Cnapan Mor its peat-hag ridden heartland is gnawed deep by the River Eidart, a tumultuous watercourse fed by some of the highest streamlets in the country.

A few years ago a good friend and I climbed on to the Moss from Coire Garbhlach, a long, sinuous corrie which bites its way greedily into the Moine Mhor plateau from Glen Feshie in the west. I would describe writer and broadcaster Jim Crumley as a similar spirit, a soul mate, whose views on landscape protection and whose criticisms of conservation bureaucracies have caused some to describe him as an extremist. I suspect he rather likes that description. As a landscape and wildlife writer his work is inevitably compelling, his prose elegant and creative and through the years I've known him I've often fed on his enthusiasm and thoughtful imagery. He's also an ideal hill companion with a deep and passionate love of the Cairngorms, as his book, *A High and Lonely Place*, well-illustrates. I took him on his first visit to Coire Garbhlach and, after climbing up the length of the corrie and floundering in steep, soft snow slopes up to the corrie's rim, we eventually managed to ease ourselves over the edge. I could almost feel Jim's gasps of astonishment.

"You emerge from Coire Garbhlach to find yourself nowhere," he later wrote. "Oh, there are points of reference, but between any of these and your stance on the rim of the corrie there is just the rolling, dipping, flattening, climbing, sprawling dimensions of Am Moine Mhor, the Great Moss. You have not climbed to a summit at all, but to a space."

Such a sensation is particularly apparent under the winter's soft mantle of snow. In past seasons I've seen the Moine Mhor when not a rock, blade of grass or clump of heather protruded from the snow – an endless blanket of white offering no relief to sun-strained eyes. Under such conditions even the vast Cairngorm landscape is made to look puny by the deep infinity of the blue sky above. At this time of the year, well-described by Scotland's travelling people as 'the terror time', the deer have fled to the lower glens in search of food, the ptarmigan, now white coated and camouflaged, are also down low, the golden plover have gone to the milder coasts and the swifts which haunt these lonely Grampian slopes and which habitually dance in the warm summer breezes are wheeling in the sunshine of Africa. The Moine Mhor is now a high and lonely place indeed, but no less spectacular for that, and offers a variety of high-level explorations among its glacial hollows and rocky knolls, the *roches moutonnées* of the geologic world, preferably by touring ski.

One of the Moine Mhor's jewels is Loch nan Stuirteag, nestling snugly in the grassy depression that forms the watershed between Monadh Mor and the long slopes which fall from Cairn Toul, Sgor an Lochain Uaine and its neighbouring Einich Cairn massif. This high pond, this loch of the gulls, is well-worth a visit for it's a place of desolate beauty, the reed-edged waters lapping gently on tiny sandy beaches. A hundred and fifty years ago cattle were grazed here; now it's regarded as wilderness.

Behind the loch, Monadh Mor lifts its rounded head, its long flat-topped ridge stretching south, a sore temptation for Munro folk. Its highest point is mid-way along the ridge. To bag Monadh Mor and then cross the steep bealach and grab Beinn Bhrotain fills a summer evening well from a high camp, but at this time of the year an expedition to these two hills is a major undertaking from the Glen Feshie side. A shorter route is possible from White Bridge in Glen Dee, particularly when you can ride a mountain bike from Linn of Dee to the slopes of Carn Fiaclach Beag. From there follow a route over Carn Cloich-mhuilinn to Beinn Bhrotain and Monadh Mor. Either descend the way you came or follow a route by Loch nan Stuirteag down into lonely Glen Geusachan. It's still a long way for the short days of winter but, if time is available, sit for a while between these two big hills, just above the screes of Coire Cath nam Fionn, the Corrie of the Battle of the Fingalians.

As the breeze sighs coldly up from Glen Geusachan, let your imagination wander back through the mists of time to an era as old as these hills themselves. Who fought in this Battle of the Fingalians? Who won? Only the remaining rocks can tell of the deeds of that once proud race. The distant voice of Ossian, Fingal's bardic son, casts little light on the matter:

"Though the plains of our battles are dark and silent, our fame is in the four grey stones. The voice of Ossian has been heard. The harp has been strung in Selma. Come Ossian, come away, come fly with thy father on clouds. I come, I come, thou king of men."

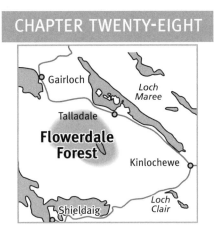

CHAPTER TWENTY-EIGHT

Gairloch

Loch Maree

Talladale

Flowerdale Forest

Kinlochewe

Loch Clair

Shieldaig

NO TIMELESS WONDER
IN FLOWERDALE

The Flowerdale Forest is a curiously halcyon name for what is essentially the northern boundary of Torridon in Wester Ross, an area more often associated with rough, tough mountains rising from a rocky landscape patterned by streams, bogs and lochans. An unforgiving landscape, a wild landscape, a challenging landscape, and heaven help any soul who is taken in by the gentle suggestion of pastoral woodlands.

Flowerdale is a traditional deer forest and trees are conspicuous by their absence. Instead, a number of mountain peaks rise sheer from the watery mosaic which forms their plinth. Two of them in particular, Baosbheinn (2,871ft/875m) and Beinn an Eoin (2,805ft/855m) face each other across the slit trench of Loch na h-Oidhche, presenting a superb, if tough, 15-mile walking route among some of the oldest rocks in the world.

These mountains were raised as a vast plateau some 30 million years ago. The rock of the original chain, now exposed as the mountain's quartzite caps, are reckoned to be 600 million years old but the sandstone below them is even older and the platforms of gneiss on which the mountains stand are thought to be in the region of 2,600 million years old, abstract periods of time that I find difficult to comprehend. Not only does this gneiss underlie all Highland rock, it covers a huge geographic area far outwith these shores, from the distant Ural mountains of Russia through the vast Greenland archipelago and across Canada to the Rockies.

Not only does such geology bind distant continents together but it's been said that geology is also the womb of history. Now, with my car parked near the old barn beside the A832 Loch Maree to Gairloch road, I had some space to try to get to grips with this whole amazing concept of geologic time and space. A stalkers' path begins on the opposite side of the road, just beyond the outflow of the Am Feur-Loch, and runs for almost four miles from the road to the crossing of the Abhainn Loch na h-Oidhche. From there on the security of the footpath is abandoned for a high route of rock and heather.

The landscape became increasingly wild as I walked south, the path climbing gradually to meet the Abhainn a' Garbh Choire below the western rocky slopes of Meall na Meine. Ahead I caught the first glimpse of Baosbheinn's row of tops but my first peak, Beinn an Eoin, still hid itself shyly behind Meall na Meine, the mossy peak.

It wasn't long before Beinn an Eoin did come into view but first I had to cross the Abhainn Loch na h-Oidhche. Fortunately the river was low and I managed to cross virtually dryshod and, after two hours of relaxed walking, it was time to leave the footpath and start climbing. Around me the big hills burst through the Earth's emaciated skin like sandstone skeletons, a living museum of geologic history. My understanding of geology is sketchy in the extreme but the archives of these ancient rocks offer a hint of explanation, particularly when we look at the small print which explains something of this spinning rock we call Earth.

The steep scramble up Beinn an Eoin came as a shock after the relaxed walk-in, a thousand feet of rock and grass to reach the final fringe of weathered sandstone outcrops. These have long lost their quartzite caps to the relentless frosts and winds and protrude from their gneiss bedrock like rows of toothless gums. I pushed on to the broad scoured-sandstone ridge and saw it stretch before me into the haze. Beinn an Eoin's ridge is generally fairly broad, a high promenade of mossy grass and sandstone slabs, but after a mile or so the slope suddenly steepens and begins to narrow appreciably. Almost subconsciously I slowed down and scanned the slope ahead for the easiest line. I needn't have worried. As so often happens in hazy conditions, the shapes look bigger or steeper than they are and I happily followed pleasantly angled sandstone slabs all the way to the summit, the cairn perched dramatically on a small plateau at the end of a four-foot-wide section of ridge. This then, was Beinn an Eoin, the peak of the bird.

A jog down rock shattered slopes on the west side of the hill dropped me very rapidly to the old cottage of Poca Buidhe. The stone bothy (locked) nestles naturally among some huge boulders but it's easily betrayed by its rusting iron roof. From here, the route to Baosbheinn lies across a broad swathe of weather-scoured sandstone slabs and boulders, with a liberal scattering of pools and lochans. I didn't linger; clouds of biting clegs made sure of that. Early afternoon saw me climbing through the sandstone crags on Ceann Beag, the southern summit of my second hill, Baosbheinn.

Resting on a rocky platform, looking over and beyond Loch na h-Oidhche, I realised for the first time that Beinn an Eoin and neighbouring Beinn Dearg are made up of stratum-upon-stratum of rock, horizontal layers mounted one on top of the other, exact replicas of the strata that I was now climbing on Baosbheinn. But I could now see clearly, as I moved my eye downhill, that the rocks were becoming older, from the relatively young sandstone peaks which once upon a time were probably graced by quartzite caps but which were now toothless, down through the aeons of time to the darker, older lower slopes and the bedrock of ancient gneiss. Millions of years had created them, millions of years were wearing them down. We tend to consider mountains as timeless creations but here was evidence that even these ancient leviathons fall prey to the steady progression of quantum-time. I might still have lacked the explicit insight into the meaning of 300 million years but at least I now felt more at ease with the concept.

I climbed on over Ceann Beag and over two subsidiary summits to the final pull on to Baosbheinn's main summit, Sgorr Dubh (2,871ft/875m). The ridge continues north to its terminus on Creag an Fhithich from where I could drop down the north-east slopes back to the rock-splattered moorland just north of Loch na h-Oidhche. Baosbheinn, the wizard's hill, had cast its spell on me, and I regained the path back to the road well-aware of my own fleeting timespan amid the hoary giants which dominate our landscape.

CHAPTER TWENTY-NINE

THE HEART OF SCOTLAND
– A LAND REDEEMED

For some time I'd dreamed of a long distance trail in Scotland that would take at least a couple of weeks to walk and traverse some of the finest countryside in the Highlands. The West Highland Way, running from the outskirts of Glasgow to Fort William, was justifiably popular and I'd walked between Fort William and Aviemore several times, a superb week's walk through some of the wildest landscape in the Central Highlands. But could there be a route that linked Glasgow and Aviemore to form a unique heart-shaped trail through the heart of Scotland? There was.

The ragged line of the Farragons dominated the horizon across the broad expanse of Strath Tay, a little-visited hill area which lies in the shadow of Perthshire's finest peak, Schiehallion. Broad, knobbly ridges run from Meall Tairneachan in the west to Farragon Hill itself, two Corbetts which form the highest points of a huge forested area between Loch Tummel and Strath Tay. Beyond those hills lay the key to the rest of my route...

When planning any long distance walk there are always one or two points that are crucial to the whole journey. So far, from my starting point at Milngavie just north of Glasgow (my route shared its first few miles with the West Highland Way), the route had been straighforward, but north of the Farragons the natural barrier of Loch Tummel and its east-flowing river threatened to halt further progress north. I had little inclination to swim over the loch, even without the 30lb pack that hung from my shoulders, but could its outflow river be crossed, enabling me to continue to Blair Atholl, up the length of glorious Glen Tilt, through the high defile of the Lairig Ghru and down to my final destination of Aviemore? I wanted to keep a north-bound momentum and not have to deviate too far east or, God forbid, too far south and I desperately wanted to avoid public roads as much as possible.

In 1902 it was recorded in the *Bathymetrical Survey of the Fresh-water Lochs of Scotland* that Loch Tummel was 2.75 miles in length with a maximum breadth of half a mile. Subsequently, a dam was built at the eastern end of the loch, raising its level by some 17ft and flooding new areas. As a result the loch is now closer to 7 miles long and has more than doubled its breadth. But the dam that caused the swelling of the loch and flooded any possible crossing points ultimately proved to be my salvation. Despite the prominent 'No Access' signs I sneaked across the dam walkway which spans the new outflow of the loch, mentally preparing some snivelling excuse should I be stopped by some zealous hydro-board official, to reach the north shore and my route to Glen Fincastle and beyond. From the top of the glen the rising road pointed directly over the hill to Blair Atholl and the Cairngorms. After the uncertainty of crossing Strath Tummel the long miles of Glen Tilt and the stony climb over the Lairig Ghru were a piece of cake.

Official long distance trails are a rarity in Scotland. The West Highland Way has been a huge success, with several thousand people taking the route between Milngavie, just north of Glasgow, to Fort William every year. The trail brings hundreds of thousands of pounds to the small communities along the way and several dozen full-time jobs have been established because of the existence of the trail. The Southern

Upland Way, with its long winding stretches through Forestry Commission plantations stifling both the views and the wayfarers' enthusiasm has been less successful. Scotland's third trail, the Speyside Way has, for some bureaucratic reason, terminated at Aviemore rather than run the full-length of that glorious river to its source in the wild heart of the Monadhliath (although following calls from walkers and community groups in Badenoch, Scottish Natural Heritage is consulting on proposals to extend the route as far as Newtonmore). The Great Glen Way, linking Fort William with Inverness, won't be officially opened for a few years yet.

As well as being a rarity, official long distance trails are curious beasts, attracting thousands of walkers who for some odd reason are reluctant to plan their own routes, averse to the idea of following their own noses instead of signposts, and disinclined to leave the beaten track established by others. Perhaps there's a comfort in knowing what the next section of trail will bring, or maybe Homo Sapiens' herding instinct is still strong in us and, like the sheep, we're happy to follow in the steps of those who have come before us. It's a pity we can't be more like goats now and again...

For some time I'd dreamt of following the West Highland Way north from Glasgow and linking its northern terminus at Fort William with the ancient Rathad nam Meirleach, the Cateran's Trail, to Aviemore, a magnificent traverse of the districts of Lochaber and Badenoch. To complete a wonderful 300-plus mile loop that would form a challenging Heart of Scotland Trail, all that remained for me to do was work out a route between Aviemore and Glasgow. I had little idea that the remaining side of the triangle would prove to be so different from the other two sections and in its own way prove to be a walk of superb variety and contrast.

At last I managed to find a few days that allowed me to put dreams into action. Sharing the first dozen or so miles with the West Highland Way the last link in my Heart of Scotland trails trio starts in Glasgow's leafy suburb of Milngavie and follows footpaths, tracks, lanes and an old railway line as far as Drymen before diving into the sprawling Garadhban Forest. After a short distance on forest tracks the West

Highland Way crosses the minor public road between Drymen and Gartmore and heads for Conic Hill and Loch Lomond. The Aviemore route parts company here, making its own way towards Gartmore for just over a couple of miles to a car park and picnic area near the Drymen Road Cottages where a trail runs through the Loch Ard Forest to Aberfoyle.

For the next 120-odd miles forest tracks, rights of way, footpaths and drovers' roads take a rough and straggling north-easterly line through forests, along lonely glens, over high passes and across the ridges that form the grain of the Central Highlands. The gables of a thousand ruins bear testament to the former communities who relentlessly worked the land while the ever-present sheep, woolly locusts of the Highlands, remind us of what replaced them. There are the remains of Roman camps and standing stones and here and there vitrified forts reflect more ancient times. The whiffs and taints of antiquity are stronger here than on the West Highland Way and there is even a greater spirit of place than on the Cateran's Trail, despite that route's historic association with the cattle rievers of old.

Ancient tribes once inhabited these districts between what we now call the Grampians and the River Forth in the south. They spoke not Gaelic, nor Pict, not even Irish but a form of 'British' that had a relationship to today's Welsh, Cornish and Breton. Known as Verturiones, these ancient people were heavily influenced by the Irish who increasingly occupied the lands, particularly during the Roman occupation. In time the northern area became known as Ath Fhodhla, or New Ireland, nowadays known as Atholl, and further south Strath Eireann, Ireland's strath, eventually became known as Strathearn. Loch Earn is derived from the same source.

Another Irish link is to be found in upper Glen Artney, just north of Callander. Where Gleann a' Chroin rolls down from the great corries of Stuc a' Chroin and Ben Vorlich, and meets Glen Artney, a house called Arivurochardich still stands, an old building fully-exposed to the winds and the rains that sweep along the length of the open glen. According to the writings of Seton Gordon, the name of the house is a corrupted form of Airigh Mhuircheartaich, or Moriarty's Shieling, another suggestion of an Irish link in the place-name chain of this vast district.

There are Roman links too. As you follow the old railway into the town of Callander you pass a field which appears to be curiously corrugated. This was the site of a Roman camp. A temporary camp, as the might of the Roman legions never quite managed to quell the Scots to the north of the Antonine Wall. There are also Roman links with Glen Almond.

From the Trossachs to Rothiemurchus it's impossible to simply shrug aside the ghosts of yesterday. They are as real as the trumpeting lapwings, the shrieking oystercatchers and the warbling curlews. Often they are as melancholy as the thin piping of the golden plover. You can't ignore the ancient shielings and the dry stone walls, or the gable walls still standing. You can't pretend there is a purity in this kind of wilderness – unless you are happy to accept that such desolate beauty has been paid for time and time again by the blood of those who came before us, a land redeemed by those who were removed from it. And while you can't deny the sorrow of yesteryear these empty lands now give undeniable joy to many; the landscape's ability to outlive and outshine our attempts, however valiant, at taming it, never fails to impress.

From the Loch Ard Forest good tracks lead to Aberfoyle. But, initially, follow the course of an aqueduct which carries water from Loch Katrine in the Trossachs to the city of Glasgow. Work on the aqueduct was started in 1855 in typical Victorian fashion – no expense spared – and the watercourse is lined with stone beehive-shaped water cisterns with black iron basketweave railings over the top. Less than 30 miles from Glasgow's city centre, the village of Aberfoyle sits slap-bang on the very edge of the Highlands. Indeed, the village sits on the geological fault line which runs across Scotland from the south end of Loch Lomond to Stonehaven on the north-east coast. All before it is lowland. To its north lie the Highlands, rich in promise.

The clans who inhabited these northern regions were, until comparatively recently, as Sir Walter Scott so succinctly put it, 'much addicted to predatory excursions upon their Lowland neighbours'. As such, Aberfoyle has had a turbulent history! Graham's *Sketches of Scenery in Perthshire*, published in 1806, explains:

"Tis well known, that in the highlands, it was in former times accounted not only lawful, but honourable, among hostile tribes, to commit depredations on one another; and these habits of the age were perhaps strengthened in this district by the circumstances which have been mentioned. It bordered on a country, the inhabitants of which, while they were richer, were less warlike than they, and widely differenced by language and manners."

You won't notice that wide a difference nowadays!

The next few miles, over the Highland Edge itself and along the Mentieth Hills to the foot of Loch Vennacher, certainly emphasise the geographical difference between those districts to the north and to the south of this geological faultline. The southern views take in some of the flattest land in all Scotland: Flanders Moss, leaning east and then opening out towards the distant blue rise of the Ochils, and across to the lowland swell of the Campsie Fells and the Kilpatricks. To the north, a jumble of high hills and mountains dominate, a raised and tumbled land, as different as chalk from cheese.

There are a handful of towns in Scotland that boast the nickname "Gateway to the Highlands" but Callander's claim is more than justified. This Stirlingshire town, beautifully situated at the confluence of the Teith and the Leny, has long been popular as a tourist resort and indeed as a centre for exploring the hills and lochs of the Southern Highlands. Indeed it's been claimed that Callander has, in proportion to its population, the largest number of hotels and guesthouses of any town in Scotland.

Despite its popularity with those who want to visit the Highlands, Callander itself is very much a lowland town. It consists of a long, broad main street from which narrower streets and lanes run south towards the River Teith which forms its southern boundary. The first bridge across the river was built in 1764 and was replaced by the present bridge in 1907.

The poet John Keats passed through Callander in 1818, describing it as "vexatiously full of visitors". The person to blame, of course, was Sir

Walter Scott whose novels and writings on the nearby Trossachs, particularly the long romantic poem *The Lady of the Lake*, caught the imagination of the 19th century public. They flocked to Callander, and to Aberfoyle, to drink-in the atmosphere of *The Children of the Mist*, *Rob Roy Macgregor* and *The Celtic Twilight*!

Behind the town the beautifully wooded Callander Craigs rise to a height of 1,100ft (335m). Views over Callander towards the distant Gargunnock and Fintry hills are nothing compared to the view which opens up as you reach the summit cairn. Gaze west along the length of silvery Loch Vennachar, its head seemingly choked by the high hills of the Trossachs. To the right you can see into the very bosom of Ben Ledi, into its great wild north-east corrie, and east your gaze carries you along the broad strath to Stirling, the Ochils and, beyond, to the dim outline of the Pentlands near Edinburgh.

Beyond the summit cairn, built in 1887 to commemorate Queen Victoria's Silver Jubilee, a footpath descends gently through young birch woods and groves of Scots pine and gives good views over the open moorland which stretches into the long dog-leg of Glen Artney. A public road runs as far as the farm at Breleny and from there a track carries you into country that becomes increasingly open and bare. Nodding its head to the peaks of Beinn Each, Stuc a' Chroin and Ben Vorlich the glen eventually bends away north-east and drops down to its beautiful, wooded lower stretch where the Water of Ruchill cascades down its deep channel towards the village of Comrie.

Small earthquakes are a common occurrence in Comrie. The village is apparently situated close to several geological faultlines. Consequently, the world's first seismometers were set up here in the 19th century and you can see models of them at a house called The Ross, to the west of the village.

The road up lovely Glen Lednock leads eventually to Invergeldie at the foot of Ben Chonzie and beyond the farm a rough track rises to a bare windswept bealach which looks down on the head of Glen Almond. Beyond its head a low pass leads down Gleann a' Chilleine to Ardtalnaig on Loch Tay, but in the opposite direction a track runs for some six miles down the length of Glen Almond, whose hillsides are largely given over to the farming of sheep and the shooting of grouse. Here and there are the tell-tale signs of former settlements, not least the memorial cairn built on the site of the Stuck Chapel, the church that once served the population of this part of the glen. Today the solitude is tangible, almost overwhelming when the mists hang low over the tops and winds sigh down the long miles of the glen.

Beyond Auchnafree the narrow-sided pass of Glen Lochan links Glen Almond with Glen Quaich, where a hill track climbs above the waters of Loch Freuchie and makes its way over a high, partially-forested plateau and down to the wonderful Birks of Aberfeldy and the wooded glen of the Moness Burn, celebrated in verse by no less a worthy than Robert Burns, who visited the area in August 1787. The town itself is claimed by some to be the exact geographical centre of Scotland.

Rough paths follow the northern banks of the River Tay and parallel the busy A827 but these run out about a mile or so short of Edradynate where a minor road climbs high above the meandering river past the farms of Blackhill and Lurgan to where another hill track begins the climb over the Farragons – past Loch Derculich, skirting the rugged eastern slopes of Farragon Hill itself before turning north-east to pass close to the summit of Beinn Eagagach at well over 2,000ft (610m). The long and winding descent to Loch Tummel at last gives views of the Atholl hills, where Glen Tilt cuts its way north in an uncompromising line towards the Cairngorms and the final splendour of the marvellous Lairig Ghru.

Once across the Tummel dam (there is a bridge further down river which leads to a series of nature trails but the dam crossing is much more direct) a quiet road runs up Glen Fincastle to where another hill path crosses over a low ridge to Blair Atholl. This is the last chance to stock up on provisions before the final 45 miles or so up the length of Glen Tilt, through the Lairig Ghru between Ben Macdui and the An Garbh Coire of Braeriach and down through the pines of Rothiemurchus to Coylumbridge and Aviemore.

Like all good routes this Central Highland Trail keeps its best till last and the long walk down Glen Tilt eventually leads to the Lairig Ghru, undoubtedly the finest mountain pass in the country.

Bill Murray once suggested that Glen Tilt is a place where the walker will never find his interest flagging; the river is continually lively, the woods are mature and varied and there is a continuous, gradual change from its lower fertility to an upper desolation where oystercatchers and lapwings provide the summer music.

There is a growing awareness, as you tramp the empty miles of Glen Tilt, of a gradual constriction as the valley narrows to a cleft, a defile, before broadening out again to a windswept and desolate beauty. The ruins of the old Bynack shieling lie here, a soft spot in the harshness of these high moors, a good place for a camp before the few miles to White Bridge and the threshold of the Lairig Ghru.

Despite the bare, Arctic-feel of the stony Lairig the resounding echoes of history still call clear. Caterans, robbers and thieves were on intimate terms with the Lairig Ghru and cattle drovers and armies have marched through its narrow defile. But, curiously, history has chosen to commemorate the vagabonds by such place names as Allt Preas nam Meirleach, the stream of the thieves' bush, or Cnapan nam Meirleach, the small knoll of the thieves. A pair of drunken tailors are remembered too; the Clach nan Taillear is the name of the rock where they tried to shelter one New Year's Eve, after trying to negotiate the Lairig after a night of merrymaking in Abernethy and Inverdruie. And who, I wonder, was the Murchus whose fort is recalled in the name Rata-Mhurchuis, or Rothiemurchus? His fate, I fear, is lost in the byways of time as are the wolves, bears and lynx who once wandered through these pinewoods of which the present forest is but a mere remnant.

Today walkers, ramblers and mountain bikers enjoy the byways of Rothiemurchus and our route, almost over, finishes at Inverdruie, just a mile or so from the dubious delights of Aviemore. Here, in the heart of the Highlands, Aviemore has become an overgrown village that has suffered at the hands of ill-conceived, over-ambitious corporate greed. The vision was for an all-year-round holiday resort that would attract visitors from around the world but the reality is a badly-designed and now semi-derelict eyesore where any planning guidelines that might have once existed have been lost in an uncontrolled explosion of urban growth.

The modern Aviemore is symbolic of a population that has been betrayed by corporate exploitation. But for all that there are pubs and restaurants here and, for those returning south, a railway station with a night sleeper to London. The lucky ones, though, will just be girding their loins for the second stage of their route, through the byways of Badenoch and Lochaber to Fort William where the really lucky will ready themselves for the final leg back to Glasgow down the length of the West Highland Way.

CHAPTER THIRTY

Newtonmore

Laggan

Etteridge

Meall Chuaich

Loch
na Cuaich ▲

Loch
an-t-Seilich

Dalwhinnie

SUPPING FROM THE HILL
OF THE QUAICH

Spring comes late to Badenoch and often arrives in such a big rush that it catches you completely unawares. One day you're weathering the full onslaught of April snow showers, wind and below-freezing temperatures, the next the birches are dressed in new minted green-gold, the skylarks are singing with a gay abandon and the curlews are piping over the moors. Even Drumochter, so often gloomy and threatening, can look vibrant on a morning like this, with new-born lambs symbolising this new year of the natural world, the advent of the annual cycle of life.

From my bedroom window I had noticed Meall Chuaich, the rounded hill of the quaich, lift its snow-streaked head above a sea of early morning mist. Lying at the northern end of the great upland plateau that rises east of the A9 at Drumochter, the hill is held in the clench formed between Strathspey and Glen Truim and is separated from the rest of the Drumochter hills by the deep bite of Coire Chuaich. This big corrie is both Meall Chuaich's curse and its saving grace. While it effectively sequesters the hill from the other Drumochter Munros, Carn na Caim and A' Bhuidheanach Bheag, making it awkward to climb all three together, the great scooped out hollow does give Meall Chuaich an identity as a totally separate hill.

Because of this isolated position, Meall Chuaich, at 3,120ft/951m offers wide ranging views over Badenoch and Strathspey towards the high Cairngorms, across the Spey to the lumpy tableland of the Monadhliath and along the length of Loch Ericht towards the distant Ben Alder group. It's well worth the easy climb up from the A9.

Meall Chuaich also neighbours the haunted hills of Gaick, claimed by the late Seton Gordon to be "the most supernatural place in Scotland". Here dwells the Leannan Sith, the faery sweetheart who ensnares lonely hunters with her beauty, and the Sprite o'Gaick, a tiny green-suited figure who has allegedly appeared to stalkers and gamekeepers. Fanciful tales perhaps but a distinct part of the fabric of these hills, interwoven with the winds and whispers of former times.

Eager to catch as much of the spring sunshine as I could, I lay for a while on the shore of Loch Cuaich, scanning the crags of Stac Meall Chuaich for a hint of peregrine and feeling the pulse of life quicken around me. The birch twigs were a deeper wine, the buds were turgid with suppressd growth and lapwings and oystercatchers competed in vocal chaos. Higher up, on the hill itself, dark spots and patches appeared on the rumps of mountain hares and ptarmigan. A stray bumblebee even floated over the old lacklustre snow in search of flowers, languid in the unexpected warmth.

Meall Chuaich is a big, rounded hill, its distinguishing feature the broken crags that fall steeply down to Loch Cuaich on its north-west fringe. It's a straightforward ascent to the summit and makes a great jaunt at this time of the year. A private road leads from the A9 to Loch Cuaich and just to the south of the loch a footpath runs past a locked bothy and crosses the Allt Coire Chuaich which runs down from the big rounded hills of Gaick. On the north side of the stream a path has been worn through the heather straight up the hill's south-west ridge to a flatter, stony area by Stac Meall Chuaich. From there it's a straightforward walk up the stony ridge to the big summit cairn.

It was good to linger by the summit cairn, a small island of rock in the high acres of snow. To my complete surprise I was joined by a flock of snow buntings, eager for any crumbs that I would leave. They rose on white wings from the white snow surface and, flying low across the face of the large cairn, resembled a sudden snow flurry. I ate my sandwiches, enjoying the rich benevolence of the warm sun, and rather than return to Loch Cuaich by the same route, wandered off east down the long slopes of Coire Chuaich, a high and lonely place infested with red deer herds. Lower down, the snow patches were dotted with deer, no doubt cooling themselves off, and they were loath to run off as I appeared among them. Lower down I picked up a rough footpath which took me back to Loch Cuaich.

Meall Chuaich is the hill of the quaich, and you can toast yourself on your return with a drink from the waters of Loch Cuaich, waters that are led down an aqueduct which runs from the loch itself to Dalwhinnie, part of an intricate hydro-electric system of dams, power stations and tunnels. A plaque at the end of Loch Cuaich pronounces: "Chuaich-Seilich Tunnel, 22,310 feet, completed 1940." Loch an t-Seilich lies in nearby Gaick where the waters from those high, rounded hills flow through this underground tunnel to Cuaich, down the aqueduct to Dalwhinnie and Loch Ericht, which curiously has a dam at both ends, and from Ericht's south-western shores drains to Rannoch Moor, which in turn feeds the Tummel-Pitlochry system.

A friend of mine once told me a tale about his father who had worked on the Chuaich-Seilich tunnel. As he was setting out to work one morning he was stopped by an old man who asked him for a bite to eat. Anxious not to be late my friend's father thought briefly of ignoring the old fellow but there was something in the old man's manner that made him stop, take a couple of sandwiches from his 'piece' and give them to the stranger. He was thanked and then, almost as an afterthought, warned that under no circumstances should he go to work that day. Taken aback, my friend's father walked on, then turned round to say something but the old man had vanished. Deeply disturbed, he went home. It was later in the day that word was brought to him that several of his close friends had been killed in a tunnel collapse.

A chilling tale to end what had been a day full of the promise of spring.

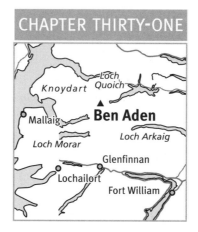

CHAPTER THIRTY-ONE

THE BARREN ROCKS
OF ADEN

Knoydart is almost surrounded by water. Jutting out into the Sound of Sleat with all the independent character of an island, it's bounded in the north by the narrow fjord-like Loch Hourn, a long and dark neck of water, hemmed in by high hills, and in the south by the more open waters of another sea loch, Loch Nevis. Island-like it might be in character and in atmosphere but the peninsula of Knoydart is nevertheless firmly attached to the mainland, held forever in the grip of a rugged tract of mountains known as the Rough Bounds of Knoydart.

The Rough Bound's only hamlet, Kinloch Hourn, is better served by boat than it is by its switch-backed, single track road which stretches across the empty moors from Glen Garry. The head of Loch Nevis is even more remote and has no need of a road at all. Only the mountain bothy at Sourlies and a ruined farmhouse greet you as you drop down to the loch shore from the heights of the Mam na Cloich Airde and the four-hour trek from the head of Loch Arkaig. In between Kinloch Nevis and Kinloch Hourn steep sided mountains form a wall of invincibility, most notably the knobbly summit of Sgurr na Ciche, the popular jewel of Knoydart, and a squat, muscle-bound mountain called Ben Aden. If Sgurr na Ciche is the most public symbol of the Rough Bounds of Knoydart, then Ben Aden is its most sacred private icon.

Ben Aden, 2,910ft/887m, is one of the most retiring of all the Corbetts. At a push you could climb it in a day by trekking round the western extremity of Loch Quoich from the Kinloch Hourn road on a nasty bulldozed track, climb the hill and get back out the same way, but that would be tantamount to rape. Surely our finest hills are worthy of more imagination, more aesthetic consideration? Any other route requires a night or two in a tent or bothy, no hardship surely in an area where lingering is well rewarded. My own choice was a long, circuitous route of some 27 miles around Ben Aden, exploiting the old deer-stalkers' paths that lace this area, camping out in the company of drumming snipe and warbling curlews.

I would contend that backpacking, with simple needs carried on your back, is the only practical way to explore the Rough Bounds. But while such a means of travel offers rich rewards, solo backpacking can sometimes be a mixed blessing. While vulnerability sharpens every sense, intensifying both the awareness of risk and the moments of bliss, these pleasures are often overshadowed by the realisation that the moment can't be shared. Having said that, it's only by walking alone that you can fully understand the indiscriminate natural power of the landscape and recognise the insignificance of the human voice raised against it. The Rough Bounds evoke this power like nowhere else in Scotland.

My route took me from Strathan, at the head of Loch Arkaig, over the boggy Bealach Feith a' Chicheanais and down into upper Glen Kingie. From there a wonderful stalkers' path runs up towards the head of the glen, gradually gaining height, and just as you think it's taking you off in the wrong direction it suddenly turns back on itself to zig-zag over a high pass between An Eag and Sgurr Beag. In a little Corbett-bashing spree I left my pack on this pass and nipped, unladen, over the Munro of Sgurr Mor to Sgurr an Fhuarain and back again before dropping down another zig-zagging stalkers' path into Coire Reidh and down its length to the rocky shores of Loch Quoich.

Camping at the head of the loch I was in a perfect position to climb Ben Aden next morning by way of Coire na Cruaiche and its rocky east-north-east ridge. This approach from the north is a dramatic one, much more preferable to the long slog up the south-west face of the hill which seems to be the popular route. Close to the head of Loch Quoich a slit-like trench holds the dark waters of Lochan nam Breac; above it, Ben Aden hurls down knolls and corries, dark crags and tumbling ridges, a mirror-image of those exaggerated Victorian paintings that epitomised the era of the Celtic Twilight.

And it's up through those corries and tumbling crags that the route climbs, easily at first over yellowed deer grass and rocky slabs before the ridge rises in a series of bluffs and craggy steps. The route rises with it, maniacally zig-zagging from one side of the ridge to another in an attempt to avoid the steeper crags, before the ground finally drops away on all sides and the small summit cairn heralds a magnificent viewpoint. Loch Hourn and Loch Nevis naturally draw the eye out to the islands of Skye, Rum and Eigg in the west, and almost every peak in the North and West Highlands becomes visible – An Teallach and Ben Wyvis, the Kintail and Affric hills, down to the blue waters of Loch Quoich and the neighbouring hills of Sgurr Mor, Gairich and Sgurr Thuilm. Closer at hand the Knoydart Munro trio of Luinne Bheinn, Meall Buidhe and Ladhar Bheinn lift their heads above the sea of rocky knolls that contribute much of the roughness to the Rough Bounds. Sgurr na Ciche appears close enough to touch.

The rest of the day was more relaxed: a late lunch by lovely Lochan nam Breac, old shielings to be examined in the narrow pass through to Glen Carnach, fields of wood anemones, the tangy scent of the Carnoch salt flats and another camp, this time by Finiskaig at the head of Loch Nevis where I drifted off to sleep to the sounds of gulls and the sea.

Next day the weather broke and the ten miles over the Mam na Cloiche Airde back to Glen Dessarry and Strathan were spent in the overhot huddle of waterproofs. I considered myself fortunate to get at least two good days out of three – that's not bad in these Rough Bounds.

CHAPTER THIRTY-TWO

IN WILDERNESS IS THE PRESERVATION OF THE MIND

Modern life has given us all kinds of benefits, from computers to chilled champagne, but the highly-charged lifestyles that often go hand-in-hand with such benefits often cause us physical and mental breakdown. The main problem is that our psychological processes are still largely stone-age and we have yet to mentally adapt to the fast and furious lifestyle modern living demands. Many individuals are discovering that one way to avoid the breakdowns caused by 21st century life is to return to an earlier, less complicated form of existence, even if only for a few days at a time...

The American writer and ecologist Henry David Thoreau once wrote: "In wildness is the preservation of the world." It was a credo deemed so important that another great writer and ecologist, John Muir, thought it worthy of plagiarism.

Muir, the wilderness prophet, later wrote: "In God's wildness lies the hope of the world – the great, fresh, unblighted, unredeemed wilderness."

But as modern man becomes increasingly urbanised, the resulting shift away from such wildness has largely sequestered us from the values of nature. Those of us who live in large towns and cities have become less exposed to the natural world and unless we make a determined effort to return to such wild places for recreation then it's unlikely we will be able to recognise, let alone take advantage of, its healing qualities.

A number of years ago a hill-running accident (I tripped and fell down a crag) left me with a broken wrist, a broken ankle and 40 stitches in my head. During my period of convalescence I was aware that I was becoming stressed. I wasn't sleeping well, I had become short tempered and comparatively slight setbacks cast me into depression. I wasn't very pleasant to live with. While I was thankful to be alive it wasn't until I was well enough to hirple out into the forest that I began to feel better mentally. Fortunately I recognised, almost immediately, the healing nature of exposure to such wild places and those excursions, though short, quickly became a crucial element in my recuperation.

Today increasing numbers of people are recognising the value of such a return to nature and many are embracing a more fundamental credo and another plagiarism of Thoreau's words – in wildness is the preservation of the mind.

Fairly recently I bought a CD by a favourite singer of mine, an American monk and musician called John Michael Talbot. Inside the cover he had written: "We live in a frantic and fast-paced modern world. God wants us to slow down and return to a life of real spiritual quality. He has called us like a father, He has wooed us like a lover, He has warned us through His prophets. He has even warned us through the erratic nature of a rapidly deteriorating ecology. Yet, we continue to ignore him, moving faster and faster, like a driver grown drunk with technological power speeding carelessly towards our own destruction."

I found those words powerful and compelling and, reflecting on them, I realised it's hardly surprising that more and more people, stressed out by the pressures of modern living, are trying to slow down and return to a life which, if not wholly (or holy) spiritual, is less frantic.

Thankfully, walking through a pristine and unspoiled landscape allows us to do just that. We can find renewal in the stillness of a forest, or on a wind-scoured mountain top – the drift of cloud against the sky, the movement of sun and shadow, the warbling, liquid call of a curlew. And I'm convinced such encounters with nature can reduce the stress in our lives simply because they speak to us of eternal values, things that have always been, as ancient as the duration of days. And all of them, the flight of a bird, the sound of the wind surf in the trees, the beauty of a sunset, are completely and utterly unplanned – none of it has been previously arranged or rehearsed by man. And that I believe, is the important issue.

Large portions of our lives are governed by schedules imposed upon us by other people. In our capitalist society we are urged to work harder and work longer hours, not for our own personal satisfaction (although there is often a deep satisfaction in reaching targets and goals) but to satisfy the unquenchable thirst for profitability of those often faceless folk we call shareholders. In years gone by individuals lived their lives in fear of invoking the wrath of the gods. Now, it seems, we live in fear of upsetting shareholders.

The problems begin when we become exhausted, debilitated, even stressed. The thirst for greater profitability is still there but we can no longer provide the means of achieving it. One of the common behavioural signs of stress is working progressively long hours in an attempt to catch up with a workload that seems overwhelming. It doesn't matter that exhausted individuals break down in the process. Modern business demands corporate success. The health and welfare of individuals, it would appear, is of secondary importance.

Thatcherism inflicted on our culture that most frightening and culpable of working practices, the short-term contract, a system of employment that pitched ordinary hard working people into a cauldron of fear and uncertainty. Consider the pressures such an employment system creates: employees work their butts off for three months in the hope that their contract will be renewed. Employers use the contract, and the uncertainty of its renewal, to dangle like a carrot under the noses of the work force to encourage it to work harder and for longer hours. It's no wonder that stress levels have reached record heights, it's not surprising that depression and suicide statistics are higher than they have ever been. We live in a highly pressurised society in which many of the stress-inducing elements are beyond our own control. Can it be of any surprise that our young people turn to drugs to help take their minds off the problems that face them?

Running parallel to this pressurised life-style is another comparatively modern phenomenon. Over the last century our steady urbanisation has also ensured a steady divorce of our physical lives from the natural world, so that we no longer consider ourselves a part of it. Indeed it was Carl Gustav Jung's belief that the crisis of our world today has two root causes: one is this divorce of our physical lives from the natural world, so that we no longer feel ourselves a part of it; the other is the over-development of our rational, analytical consciousness at the expense of the instinctive, intuitive side of ourselves that is expressed in dreams, myth, fantasy and art. According to Jung we have become cut-off from both inner and outer nature. We've lost trust in the traditional faiths, the spiritual side of our nature has been subdued and the resultant loss of meaning in the lives of many people is reflected in statistics for depression, suicide and mental illness.

Not long ago, in a seminar with businessmen in which I was trying to teach the value of seeking solitude, one of the participants stated categorically that his mind worked entirely rationally. He never, according to him, thought intuitively or instinctively. His thoughts were always logical, sane and rational.

I asked him if he was married? He said he was, so I asked him if he loved his wife? He said he did. I then asked him if he liked music? Yes, he did. Did he appreciate art? Of course he did. He was becoming a little impatient with me so I told him that love, and an appreciation of music and art, were not entirely logical or rational, or analytical, but thought processes that had their foundation in the intuitive side of our brain. He wasn't as wholly logical as he believed he was. None of us are!

So what is this condition we call 'stress'? In our western culture it's probably one of the most misused words in our vocabulary and part of the problem is that it's not amenable to a simple definition. Curiously, the condition in itself is not an illness, although it can lead to a wide range of illnesses, some potentially fatal. Neither does it have a specific cause but, more usually, a number of different causes. It doesn't even lead to a specific set of physical, emotional or mental responses, because every individual is different.

It's perhaps helpful to consider the word 'stress' as one that has been imported into the language of the doctor's surgery from the science of physics. In physics, stress is used to describe a metal's response to a force applied to it. The metal either bends and returns to its original shape when the force is released or it snaps under the force. In people, stress can affect us in different forms; acute stress tends to be periodic and almost momentary, while chronic stress is either recurrent or lasts for a longer period of time. Acute stress is usually triggered in the majority of individuals in the face of potentially life-threatening situations but it can also be caused by more mundane events, even something as simple as not knowing the answer to an examination question.

Stress can also be anticipatory, that is the stress arises from the person's anticipation of certain moments or periods of threat, or danger.

Common stress indicators generally fall into one of five categories. Signs can be physical, with headaches, a stiff neck, sore muscles, pounding heart, indigestion, loss of appetite, insomnia, feelings of general fatigue and increased use of alcohol and tobacco. Or they may be emotional with depression, nightmares, irritability, irrational fear, anxiety, crying for no reason, violent mood swings and disturbing thoughts manifesting themselves for no real apparent reason.

Inevitably there are mental signs: an inability to concentrate, boredom, indecision, establishing inflexible guidelines which lead to deeper problems both spiritual and relational with a loss of purpose, loss of meaning, loss of self-confidence or loss of values leading to a loss of intimacy, a sense of isolation, intolerance and often loneliness.

My experience is that walking through wilderness can genuinely alleviate the symptoms of stress. There is a great freedom in being able to walk where we want to: through the woods, up a mountain, along the coast. We can go fast, we can amble, we can walk with others or we can walk alone. We can walk for an hour, a day, a week or a month. We can think great thoughts, or simply empty our minds. We can meditate, we can pray, we can dream up verses of poetry or we can simply look around us and wonder at the magic in every view. All these choices are ours; no-one makes them for us. Furthermore, we can change our choices according to the minute-by-minute requirements and fancies of our minds and bodies, our own personal rhythms.

"Personal rhythms are as much a part of our structure as our flesh and bones," says Bertram Brown, one-time director of the US National Institute of Mental Health. Walking lets us adjust our lives to these rhythms. When our rhythms are at a low ebb we can cosset ourselves by walking slowly or simply lying down in the middle of a flower filled meadow. When we feel strong and purposeful we can test ourselves by climbing a mountain, by finding trails that require us to wade streams or scramble up crags, by walking hard until we gasp for air. Whatever our rhythmic needs, walking and wilderness offer the answer.

Statistics clearly show that more and more of us are becoming aware of the recreational benefits of mountains and forests. We are stimulated by the endorphins that are released in our bodies by exercise, we are thrilled by the far-flung view, enchanted by the beauty of our surroundings, encouraged by taking time-out with friends. But can it be that these places also help us reduce the levels of stress in our lives?

There is little doubt that it can be difficult to harbour pent-up anger or anxiety when standing at the edge of a mountain watching the sky turn gold and red at sunset. Yet there's much more to this wilderness-as-stress-relief concept. For instance, when you start walking, your brain and body operate as one unit, and muscle use, followed by muscle relaxation, produces brain relaxation. It just might be that for your brain to function at its best, your body has to exercise. Many psychologists agree.

Dr Hans Salye has been studying stress for decades. Each of us, he believes, possesses at birth a given amount of what he calls 'adaptional energy'. When that energy is used up, we experience a mental or physical breakdown. One way to avoid such a breakdown is by deliberately directing stress at various body systems. "Often," Dr Selye writes in his book *Stress Without Distress*, "a voluntary change of activity is as good as or even better than rest... for example, when either fatigued or enforced interruption prevents us from finishing a mathematical problem, it is better to go for a swim (or a walk) than simply to sit around. Substituting demands on our muscles for those previously made on the intellect not only gives our brain a rest but helps us avoid worrying about the other."

Dr Horst Mueller is a clinical psychologist in Alberta, Canada, and he's an advocate of the simple camp-fire: "Its flickering light brings you into an alpha-wave state," Dr Mueller says. "Alpha wavelengths are those created by meditation and deep relaxation; they lower stress and give you an overall sense of enhanced well-being and creativity."

Dr William F Thorneloe is a hiker and psychiatrist from Atlanta, Georgia. He says walking down a trail creates a meditative, Zen-like state. When walkers experience this state: "they have little awareness of hills or obstacles, such as streams and scrambles," Dr Thorneloe says. "They become transfixed in thought, emotion, or a sense of simply 'being there'."

Other research suggests that the mental demands of making muscles function actually stimulates your brain, blood vessels and denser nerve connections with the effect that the simple act of walking actually keeps your brain in shape – and a healthy, well-tuned brain helps you deal with the complexities of life, the complexities which often result in unacceptable high levels of stress. Dr Clinton Weiman, medical director of one of the world's largest banks, found that employees had less disease – high blood pressure, obesity and so forth – if they worked under an optimum amount of stress. Either too much or too little was associated with more disease.

It's been suggested that as you walk in the wild places you fall into a simpler life, reminiscent of our aboriginal ancestors. You become the hunter-gatherer and life becomes incredibly simple. The potential for stress still exists but the causes change. The phone might not be ringing but what's that hot-spot on your heel? Could it be the start of a blister? Or what are the chances of finding a good flat camp site with fresh water nearby? Does that black cloud on the horizon suggest the beginnings of a storm? It's safe to assume that such simple anxieties can be traced to our prehistoric forefathers but it's how we deal with, and indeed use those anxieties that's important.

Like us, our ancestors had a little bump of tissue at the base of the brain called the hypothalamus. This organ secretes hormones which speed up our heart rate and breathing, raise our blood pressure, flood our body with epinephrine (adrenaline), and generally get us active. Consider a Fred Flintstone scenario: a caveman is sitting at the mouth of his cave when, suddenly, out of the woods steps the menacing shape of a sabre-toothed tiger. Fred's body reacts instantly and his entire nervous system comes into play. There is a decision to be made, quickly if not instantaneously. Does he stay and fight or does he run for his life? The fight-or-flight response, still very much a day-to-day reaction in the animal kingdom, is still integral to our modern-day mental make-up. The problem is most of us don't recognise it.

This 'fight or flight' term was first coined by an American psychologist, Walter Cannon, an early pioneer in stress research. Cannon made the point that man's most basic instinct was survival. Like other animals, humans have automatic adaptation and survival responses such as shivering when cold or automatically avoiding physical pain with a reflex action. These responses are governed by the nervous system with apparently no conscious effort on the part of the individual. The physiological response to acute stress is one of the body's most sophisticated survival mechanisms – it prepares us in seconds to face potentially life-threatening events and deal with them effectively.

Today we rarely face the need for the kind of fight-or-flight response of Fred Flintstone, yet we still have the same automatic stress responses that our ancestors had. We don't face life or death situations on a daily basis but aggressive and over-demanding bosses, budgets, deadlines and examinations often feel just as bad, and our nervous reactions are often identical to those of our frightened ancestors. A number of things can happen simultaneously: our digestion slows down so that blood might be directed to the muscles; our breathing becomes faster to supply more oxygen to the muscles; our heart-rate speeds up forcing blood to the parts of the body that need it; perspiration increases to cool the body and allow it to burn more energy; muscles tense in preparation for action; chemicals are released which make the blood clot more rapidly; and sugars and fat pour into the blood to provide fuel for quick energy.

Put crudely, the body goes into high alert and a number of hormones are elevated during the stress response.

In their book *Stress Management*, Edward Charlesworth and Ronald Nathan highlight three of these hormones: norepinephrine and epinephrine – more commonly known as adrenaline – which are generally increased in exercise-induced stress, and cortisol which increases in response to psychological stressors.

Generally speaking, norepinephrine increases heart rate and blood pressure, and epinephrine releases stored sugar, both of which tend to help in our preparation for vigorous physical activity. Cortisol aids the body in the same way but, unfortunately, one of its other functions is to break down lean tissue for conversion to sugar as an additional source of energy. Cortisol also blocks the removal of certain acids in the bloodstream and when it is elevated in the blood for prolonged periods of time it can cause ulcerations in the lining of the stomach because of increased acid formation. Ever heard of stomach ulcers?

Charlesworth and Nathan go on to suggest that emotional stress responses with excess of cortisol have been the main reason why man, once the prey, is now the predator, paradoxically preying on himself. It's been a long time since any of us have had to run from a sabre-toothed tiger. We're told that our brains have evolved and our thinking processes have become increasingly complex but along with that evolution we've become confused by the simple conflict of hormonal activity versus perception. We have largely become creatures of habit who are upset by change and become easily agitated by anything that affects our daily routine or our habits; in short, our harmony. Some of us have adapted better than others and see these changes as an opportunity rather than a problem – an excuse to fight, rather than take flight. Indeed, a certain level of stress is necessary in the competitive world we live in and without it there is little doubt that life's sabre-toothed tigers, and bosses, would always win.

Sadly, most people fail to turn stress into a positive force in their lives. Instead, stress creates all sorts of physical and psychological problems like depression, anxiety, sleeplessness, mood swings and even cancer. The essence of it is this: our ancient psychology is failing to adapt to a modern way of life and the simplest way to overcome the problem is to return to the wilderness, as often as possible.

Safety aside, it's probably best to walk alone. Take the opportunity to embrace the wilderness on your own, allow it to soothe those jangled nerves and enjoy the freedom to make your own decisions about where to go and when. Walking companions can be great but, when trying to relieve stress in the wild places, small talk is an intrusion. Let common sense tell you when walking alone could be potentially dangerous. Experienced hikers will be happy to walk alone, inexperienced walkers less so. In that case, don't go into potentially difficult terrain. Restrict your outings to natural forests, or along a coastline. You don't necessarily have to climb a mountain to allow Nature's blessings to touch you.

For the same reasons, leave your mobile phone at home. A ringing telephone is in itself one of the prime causes of stress and the very sound of a mobile phone going off can be enough to set the whole nervous system jangling. Leave word of where you are going and when you'll return. Mobile phones have no place in the wilderness. Ever!

Go out for as long as you can. While it can often only take a few hours in the wilds to allow you to calm down and relieve tensions it's much better to get out there for a few days. I'm aware that some folk won't be able to cope with their own company for very long but it's really only after a few hours that the mind begins to ease out the superfluous thoughts and channels in on the big questions which need answers. You need time to let the mind flow, you need time to meditate, you need time for the mind to sort out the jumble of different thought processes which all fight for attention. In short, you need time to clear your head!

Don't be tempted into making up a schedule. The worst thing you could do is plan to knock off several Munros today and another two or three tomorrow. Try and depend entirely on your body flow; if you feel like it climb your Munros, if you don't, sit down somewhere with a beautiful view and just enjoy it. If necessary don't do anything more ambitious than contemplate your navel. Timetables and schedules should be left at home.

Listen to the birds. Birdsong is one of the most wonderful gifts of creation: the trill of a skylark, the crooning of eider ducks on the bay, the golden sound of the curlew. These are age-old gifts which are uplifting and beautiful. Take time to enjoy them.

Likewise, watch the wildlife. Take time to sit still and watch, quietly and unobtrusively. You won't see a lot by bashing noisily through the woods or panting up a hillside, but you will if you simply sit quietly and look around you.

It might help to take a notebook and jot down the problems that are causing you stress. It's amazing how often they look small and insignificant when they appear on paper.

Walk in a relaxed manner: let the arms and legs swing naturally and try to think of how you use your body. Relax as much as possible; stress causes the muscles to tighten up, particularly the back and neck muscles. Gently stretch your muscles before you start walking and when you finish. When you stop for a break stretch your calves and hamstrings. Stretch your back by raising your arms as high above your head as you can, reaching gently to the sky.

Most important of all, treat your walk as a time of healing. Don't spend it thinking what your work schedule is going to be next week or how you are going to avenge your boss if you meet him in a dark alley. Like mobile phones, thoughts of bosses have no place in the wilderness.

I leave the last word to the Harvard sociobiologist E O Wilson, who wrote: "Wilderness settles peace on the soul because it needs no help. It is beyond human contrivance." The next time you find yourself getting all worked up, head for the hills. It could be just what the doctor ordered.

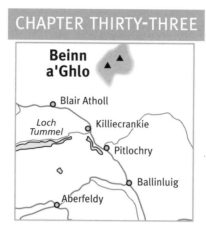

CHAPTER THIRTY-THREE

Beinn
a'Ghlo

Blair Atholl

Loch
Tummel   Killiecrankie

Pitlochry

Ballinluig

Aberfeldy

THE COMPLEX SENSUALITY
OF BEINN A' GHLO

After three days of monsoon rains the topmost slopes of Carn
Liath were still swathed in cloud. Nevertheless there was an
unexpected welcome waiting for me as I parked the car by Loch
Moraig, which nestles in green pastoral splendour among the low hills
of Glen Fender above Blair Atholl. No sooner had I switched off the
ignition than the sounds of birds filled the air, a bubbling, joyful
cacophony that couldn't fail to lift the spirits – curlew, redshank, skylark,
oystercatcher and lapwing, with a raft of black headed gulls forming a
raucous backing chorus. Their music lingered with me along the track to
the marshy skirts of Carn Liath, the first of the three Munros that make
up the massif of Beinn a' Ghlo, the chief feature of the ancient ducal
Forest of Atholl.

Lying between lonely Glen Bruar and the Cairnwell, this great deer
forest is a complex wilderness of high tops and deep-sided glens, a
billowing landscape which is split through the middle by the linear cleft
of Glen Tilt. The peat hag-ridden area to the north-west of Tilt is
dominated by Beinn Dearg, Carn a' Chlamain, An Sgarsoch and Carn an

Fhidhleir, a hill quartet known as the Ring of Tarff, while the area to the south-east of the Tilt is dominated by the triple tops of Beinn a' Ghlo: Carn Liath (3,199ft/975m), the wonderfully-named Braigh Coire Chruinn-bhalgain (3,510ft/1,070m; try *brae corrie kroo-in valagin* – just let it roll from your tongue) and Carn nan Gabhar, the highest of the three at 3,678ft/1,121m.

In clear weather the walk over Beinn a' Ghlo is straightforward, a delightful high-level stravaig of some 13 miles over some of the best ridges in the Grampians, but when the cloud is down and visibility is reduced navigation becomes complex. There are some 19 different corries on Beinn a' Ghlo (legend claims that a rifle could be fired in any of them without being heard in another) and the summits are formed by the apexes of an elaborate system of ridges and interlinking shoulders. But I didn't have to worry about fumbling around with compass bearings and maps – the optimism of Loch Moraig's bird chorus was well-placed – and as I sweated up the worn path on Carn Liath the cloud lifted above me, and the complexity of Beinn a' Ghlo's corries and ridges became evident as I rested briefly by the summit cairn. A broad ridge falls away to the north before narrowing appreciably and swinging east to end abruptly on what appears to be the blunt nose of Beinn Mhaol, an intermediary top. What you can't see from Carn Liath is the ridge twisting north again beyond Beinn Mhaol before dropping down to a high, pinched col below the south-west ridge of Braigh Coire Chruinn-bhalgain. The route climbs steeply from here, joining the hill's south ridge, before rising gently to the rounded summit.

Despite the wonderful sound of its name, and the beautifully sensuous lines of its ridges, the meaning of Braigh Coire Chruinn-bhalgain is disappointingly prosaic – the upland of the corrie of round blisters!

At first glance, the highest Beinn a' Ghlo top, Carn nan Gabhar, the hill of the goats, looks as though it is isolated from the others by a deep, steep-walled glen, but less than a kilometre from the summit of Braigh Coire Chruinn-bhalgain a high bealach, like a mighty drawbridge between the mountains, gives easy access to the col between Carn nan Gabhar and another of its outliers, Airgiod Bheinn, the silvery hill. From the col it's an easy walk over quartzite boulders to the first of three cairns. The highest top, inevitably, is the one furthest away, beyond the Ordnance Survey trig point. The return route comes courtesy of the recent popularity of Munro-bagging. Re-trace your steps back to Airgiod Bheinn and drop steeply down its south-west nose to the burn which flows from Coire Chruinn-bhalgain. From here a fairly new and rapidly evolving footpath skirts the lower slopes of Beinn Bheag and Carn Liath, roughly paralleling the Allt Coire Lagain before crossing the boggy moors to meet the track between the old farm at Shinagag and the road-end at Loch Moraig.

An alternative route climbs Carn Liath from Balaneasie Cottage in Glen Tilt, returning to the glen north of Forest Lodge via Carn nan Ghabhar's north ridge. This includes a section of Glen Tilt in the walk, a wonderfully-varied glen that's always worth a visit. Bear in mind though that you can't take a car up Glen Tilt any more – a parking place has been provided by the estate at the foot of the glen – though a mountain bike might ease the miles considerably!

Another possible route is by Gleann Fearnach on the east, which can be reached from the A924 Pitlochry road. A track runs up Gleann Fearnach as far as the remote Fealar Lodge. At Daldhu cross the watershed to the head of Loch Loch from where you can climb Carn nan Gabhar by Coire Cas-eagallach, with some easy scrambling just below the summit. If you think that route makes a big day consider the remarkable wager that was associated with Fealar Lodge and recorded in *The Times* of August 31, 1822. Lord Kennedy, a well-known sportsman (he once walked from Banchory to Inverness, a distance of about 100 miles, in 35 hours), wagered 2,000 guineas that he would, in one 24 hour period, kill 40 brace of grouse at Fealar and then ride to his seat at Dunottar, on the coast of Kincardineshire, and back to Fealar, a distance of 140 miles. He won the bet on August 12. He began shooting at 4.15am, completed the 40 brace at 8.56, then rode to Dunottar where he arrived at 2pm having ridden 70 miles in four-and-a-half hours. After resting for an hour he returned west, reaching Fealar again at 7.56pm. Not content with this, he rode back to Castleton of Braemar the same evening, reaching it at 10pm, thus adding another 14 miles to the total for the day. They obviously bred 'em tough in those days!

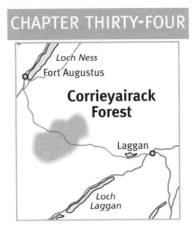

CHAPTER THIRTY-FOUR

Loch Ness
Fort Augustus

**Corrieyairack
Forest**

Laggan

Loch
Laggan

THE CORRIEYAIRACK
FOREST

General George Wade and his squad of soldiers-cum-navvies did a pretty good job on the road that runs past Corrie Yairack and over the shoulder of Corrieyairack Hill. It's only fairly recently that this, officially still a 'road', was closed to vehicular traffic, although to be fair only rugged four-wheel-drive could successfully negotiate the ruts and rough cobbles.

But it wasn't all that comfortable a ride in the early days either. In 1798, some 67 years after the road was built, the Hon Mrs Sarah Murray recorded her displeasure: "The whole road rough, dangerous and dreadful, even for a horse. The steep and black mountains, and the roaring torrents rendered every step his horse took, frightful; and when he attained the summit of the zig-zags up Corrieyaireag he thought the horse himself, man and all, would be carried away, he knew not whither; so strong was the blast, so hard the rain, and so very thick the mist. And as for the cold, it stupefied him…"

I know folk who have driven over the Corrieyairack. I've known people who have ridden a horse over it. There are those who regularly tackle it on a mountain bike and there are even those who run races over it.

For me, I'd rather walk. Working on the basis that any fool can be uncomfortable, I've never quite understood the pleasures of wrestling a Land Rover, or for that matter a horse or a bike, over a surface as uncompromisingly rutted and potholed as that found on the Corrieyairack. As a walking route it might not be the most inspiring in the Highlands – the line of goose-stepping electricity pylons that accompany the old road put paid to any claims of natural beauty – but the route does give easy access to the whole of the Corrieyairack, Aberchalder and Braeroy deer forests, and I put it to good use on a two-day wander through these hills, enjoying some relatively remote and wild areas and following in the footsteps of a bold army march which has gone down as one of the great military manoeuvres of all time.

I crossed the road from Melgarve, beyond Laggan, and dropped down into Glen Tarff on the Fort Augustus side. Rather than continue all the way to the town, I cut off to the south-west, following the Allt Lagan a'Bhainne which makes an attractive route through birch and rowan filled gorges up on to the high saucer which is dominated by two Corbetts of the same name. I'd climbed both these Carn Deargs a number of years ago from Glen Roy in the south, and that was now my destination after a superb high-level camp just below the wild bealach that joins them together.

It was a glorious early summer's morning and despite the sun and freshness around me I couldn't help but think back to some former times and events when conditions were less than pleasant. According to an old Clanranald manuscript James Graham, fifth Earl of Montrose and known in Highland Scotland in the 17th century as An Greumach Mor (the Big Graham), led his army of Highland clansmen and Irish gallowglasses over these trackless mountains in the depths of winter to surprise the Covenanter army of Archibald Campbell, Duke of Argyll, at the battle of Inverlochy in 1645. It was a master-stroke of guerrilla warfare, a form of fighting in which Montrose, and in particular his close lieutenant Alastair Macdonald of Colonsay, known as Colkitto, excelled.

Montrose led his army over a tract of land the like of which no other would have dared to march, over the wind-scoured and snow-covered hills between the Great Glen and Glen Spean, to outflank Argyll and take the Covenanter army by surprise. John Buchan, in his biography of Montrose, suggests the weather on the high hills had been deathly cold, and the march had been through a "hyperborean Hell". The upper glens were choked with drifting snow and the rocks glazed with ice, impassable save to stalwart Highland brogues.

There is some uncertainty to the exact route of Montrose's army. Some say that he followed the route of the Corrieyairack over the maze of snow-covered hills to the head of the pass at 2,500ft (762m), to the source of the River Spey, and then by way of a pass between the Spey and the River Roy, descending thus to Glen Spean and the northern foothills of the Grey Corries and Ben Nevis to Inverlochy. But others believe that the route taken was by way of the Tarff, crossing below Culachy, and then parallel to the present A82 and so to Glen Buck and Glen Turret, the valley that now lay below me. The army probably turned right into Glen Roy and then Glen Spean before marching on to victory at Inverlochy.

The narrow glen that I was now descending, Gleann Eachach, turned out to be the highlight of the whole walk, a green and lush valley with tumbling waterfalls and bird song loud trees, in direct contrast to the browns and blacks of the peat moors above. Gleann Eachach is an offshoot of Glen Turret, which in turn is an offshoot of Glen Roy – the glen of the Parallel Roads. These long parallel lines across the hillsides are believed to be the beach lines of ancient lakes which once filled Glen Roy and Glen Spean, the waters of which are long gone. I followed the lines round the head of Glen Roy and over the watershed at Meall Clach a'Cheannaiche, across the ancient Druim Alba, the mountain spine of Scotland. Once over the watershed all the rivers flow east to the North Sea, and indeed just below me the waters of the infant Spey pour gently from the river's birthplace in Loch Spey, from where it begins it's long and eventually furious route to the North Sea beyond Garmouth.

It's only a few miles from Loch Spey back to where my car was waiting at Melgarve, following the winding river and thinking how logical it would be for this to be the start or finish of the Speyside Way, rather than Aviemore.

CHAPTER THIRTY-FIVE

SUN AND SIERRAS
OF SPAIN

One of the benefits of budget airlines is that we can escape the miserable greyness of a British winter at a comparatively reasonable cost. In recent years I've developed a fondness for the isle of Mallorca and, in particular, the limestone mountains of the Sierra de Tramuntana. But an invitation to visit a mountain area of mainland Spain, the Sierra de Aitana, tempted me to become a snowbird and migrate to the sun every winter. Dream on...

The radio news had been giving out gale warnings and the possibility of local flooding. It was already cold, wet and windy as I made the short sprint from the airport car park to the departure terminal. It was the weekend in late October when we put our clocks back, the mechanical equinox that heralds the winter blues.

I suspect I suffer from Seasonal Affective Disorder, the mind's way of retreating into itself when the days become short and sunshine is limited to television's National Geographic channels. As sure as autumn follows summer, the onset of November's grey days inevitably brings on a darkening of my mood and a corresponding depression that is only lifted by exposure to sunshine, even a glint of sunshine...

For some years, in a King Canute-like attempt at holding the dark season at bay for at least a week, I've grasped the opportunity to flee from the encroaching dark season and, like a migrating bird, head south to the south of France, the foothills of the Pyrenees or the scented island of Mallorca. Indeed Mallorca has also become a regular destination at the fag-end of winter when the sun-kissed limestone mountains of the Sierra de Tramuntana, the orange and lemon groves and the blue sparkling seas have proved the ideal tonic for a spirit starved of light. This time I was fleeing to the sierras of southern Spain where I had been promised the sun would shine and my spirits would be lifted. I wasn't disappointed.

Just over three hours later I sat outside a harbour bar in Alicante in Valencia, eating fresh panfried whitebait with garlic, and drinking San Miguel beer. The evening temperature was 22° and locals and visitors alike were wandering around in shorts and T-shirts. My host, local climber Jose Miguel Garcia, was laying out plans for the week ahead and suggested I should buy some sunscreen!

Next morning, just over 12 hours after my arrival in Spain, Jose and I set off on what was to be the first sun-kissed, wind-free day of the seven I was to enjoy in Spain, climbing the second highest mountain in the area. From the summit wide views extended out across the sparkling Mediterranean and, inland, over the limestone landscape of the little-known Sierra de Aitana.

Puig Campana, 4,612ft/1,406m, is a magnificent double-topped mountain which seems to rise sheer from the back door of a burgeoning Benidorm conurbation. The mountain's western top looks as though a square hole has been kicked out of the summit ridge and Jose told me that an ancient giant by the name of Roldan had this gap in the cliff gouged out. It had been prophesied that his wife would die when the sun went down behind the Puig Campana summit, so by creating a great notch in the mountain he could enable her to live just a little bit longer. Logical really!

Just as Roldan tried to tame the natural cycle of the day, so thousands of rock climbers have been coming here in recent years to try to squeeze a few more weeks out of their summer, or prelude the notoriously unstable weather of the British spring with some precious sun-blessed weeks in March and April.

We climbed the Puig Campana from Jose's climbers' refugio, a delightful hut set deep amid soaring crags and shining rock faces near the village of Sella. Rock climbers from various countries shared the basic amenities. Several tents were scattered in the woods. The atmosphere was relaxed and friendly and we drank thick Spanish coffee as we planned our route on the map.

An ancient footpath meandered up the valley from the refuge, tracing its way through olive groves and fields of almond trees. Scents of thyme and rosemary filled the air as we passed long-abandoned fincas, old farmhouses, and the sun shone from the blue Mediterranean sky. It was the last day of October and it was hot. I didn't dare think what the weather was like at home...

After an hour or so of easy walking we left the olive terraces behind and climbed up into another world, to a rough scree-girt col between Campana and its northern neighbour, the crag-bound Monte Ponoch. A short descent, another climb to another col then a long scree scramble led towards the summit slopes, an arduous toil that had us sweating in buckets, hands on thighs, making slow but steady uphill progress. It was good to eventually leave the limestone scree and feel the solid reassurance of the grass-covered summit slopes. Released now from the narrow gully we were rewarded with contrasting views on either side of the summit ridge; and what a contrast it was.

Below us lay the mini-Manhattan outline of Benidorm and the neighbouring holiday resorts of the Costa Blanca – the tentacles of package tourism spreading ever closer to the foothills of the mountains. Jose told me of plans for a new multi-million pound theme park; of the problems of water shortages caused by providing showers and bathing facilities for millions of tourists; and his fears that the powerful hotel corporations would soon turn inland and lift their eyes to the hills. Already there are modern hotel blocks in the nearby Valle de Guadalest and 4x4 vehicle safaris, with anything up to 20 vehicles at a time, regularly rut and tear at the lower mountain tracks, the high octane recreation of the mass holiday market.

But it was to the north and west that our gaze lingered, over a beautiful and rugged landscape corrugated by long valleys that rise from the coast and run inland, parallel to each other, separated by mountain massifs with rocky ridges and fronted by crags of immense proportions. Tiny, picturesque villages clung to the spectacular crags, others were tucked away in wooded ravines. Forests of cork-oaks covered valley floors where large fincas shone white in the sun. Elsewhere smallholdings were scattered on the lower slopes, their olive groves strung out in long terraces. Here was the old Valencia, where the ancient pulse of rural Spanish life beats slowly, old rhythms still dominated by the seasons, the holy festivals and the leisurely evening paseo...

Immediately below us I could retrace the route of our ascent from the beautiful valley of the Barranco del Arc which runs down to the old hillside village of Sella. Great leaning upthrusts of shining white limestone, like sharks' fins, vie with each other for prominence, rising sheer from the greens and yellow and reds of the autumn-hued maquis. Between the Barranco and Puig Campana a horseshoe-shaped ridge rises in small sharp-topped wedges, gradually growing into vertiginous spires, towers and buttresses. This is the curved ridge of Monte Castellets and Jose told me that an expedition along the entire ridge would take about three days, with several pitches of severe rock climbing and a lot of rappelling involved. I mentally postponed that trip for another time...

The south-west ridge of Puig Campana itself boasts a number of long and serious rock climbing routes and with literally hundreds of virgin crags in the valleys it's no wonder this area has become a Mecca for rock jocks.

Paradoxically, few walkers have heard of the Sierra de Aitana, this range of mountains and isolated valleys that forms the hinterland of Benidorm and this part of the Costa Blanca. Every years tens of thousands of sun worshippers gaze up at these high mountains from their beach resorts before turning their attention back to the sea, sand

and sangria, and long may they do so. It's only 30 minutes or so by car from Benidorm to the unspoilt mountain villages of Sella, Benimantell, Confrides or Castell de Castells, 30 minutes in which you leave one world behind and enter an older, gentler world where simple values are cherished and the pace of life is more relaxed.

Curiously, these highlands of the Costa Blanca have strong parallels with many of the upland areas of the UK. Both suffer from unemployment, traditional industries like small-scale farming are being run down and both are relying more and more on green tourism. And while the big hotel consortiums lift their eyes to the hills from the Costa Blanca coastal fringe and calculate what scope the mountains have for their swelling number of tourists, there is a growing body of opinion in Valencia that believes another kind of tourism would better benefit these mountain areas – eco-tourism.

The Valencians have recognised that the island of Mallorca has long been a popular winter destination for sun-seeking British walkers, and now the people of this tiny area of mainland Spain are keen to lure winter visitors to their sun-kissed mountains, visitors who won't demand large scale developments but prefer the more traditional casas, pensiones and fondas.

My friend Jose Miguel Garcia and his business partner, Jeroni Garcimartin, have won an award for promoting the rural economy of the Sierra de Aitana area. The competition, run by Ceder Aitana, the region's rural development agency, spurned the large-scale development proposals of the large holiday corporations in favour of this small two-man operation called Terra Ferma.

Jeroni and Jose began their walking and climbing holiday company because they wanted, in some small way, to offer a green solution to the area's economic problems. They also wanted to work in the mountains, not an unreasonable desire for two keen climbers since the hills and valleys of the Sierra de Aitana are among the most unspoiled and ruggedly beautiful landscapes of Spain.

Rising to almost 5,000ft (1,525m) from the olive and almond terraces, the limestone mountains of Aitana offer a variety of expeditions ranging from the technical multi-day scrambling routes over the incredible pinnacles of the Monte Castellets ridge, a technically easier but still demanding scramble over the Cuillin-like Bernia ridge which looks down over Calpe and the Mediterranean Sea, or a straightforward hill-bash up Puig Campana, at 4,612ft/1,406m the highest mountain in the area that is free of access.

The highest mountain, (5,1134ft/1,559m) Aitana itself, has a military installation on the summit and is closed to visitors.

Ancient Mozarabic trails, dating from the early centuries of the Islamic occupation of southern Spain, criss-cross the area and, like the old stalkers' paths of the Scottish Highlands, stand testament to the skills of those who built them. Using such trails, Terra Ferma has developed a number of multi-day walking tours visiting remote mountain summits, sensational ridges, hill-top castles and tranquil, high-mountain meadows with nightly accommodation in small hotels in the mountain villages. Vehicles transport your luggage from hotel to hotel and all you have to carry is your lunch, some water and in the unlikely event of rain, waterproofs.

And when they're not guiding walkers and climbers around the mountains, Jose and Jeroni busy themselves with archaeological detective work: rediscovering the ancient trails that have been lost in time and rebuilding and maintaining them for the travellers of our new leisure generation.

These Mozarabic trails zig-zag into the most unlikely places: down into deep barrancos, up through narrow gaps in the crags, ranging along below enormous crags and across endless miles of maquis-covered plateau – places that would be unattainable if these cobbled stone highways had not been created by the master craftsmen of yesteryear. The best of them are apparently to be found in the Val de Laguart where the Camino de Juvias drops down the steep walls of the wonderfully-named Barranco del Infierno before climbing out of the valley on the opposite side towards the Val d'Ebo.

Jose and Jeroni's love of this rugged landscape was evident as they showed me some of the natural wonders of their area. We queried the antiquity of prehistoric cave paintings, visited natural rock arches, crawled through limestone caves, teetered along narrow ridges, searched for the area's neveras (deep snow pits once used to make ice from snow, the original fridges), sang operatic arias as our voices bounced back at us from vast overhanging limestone cliffs, and enjoyed the hospitality of generous mountain folk. Every day the sun shone from a blue sky and the only firework we saw on Guy Fawkes night was the odd shooting star falling from a cloudless, black sky.

There is an alluring attraction in swapping thermals and ice axes for shorts, T-shirts and lightweight boots at this time of the year, even if only to give us the strength to face the long dark months of another northern winter at home. The Sierra de Aitana's healing powers certainly worked their magic on me.

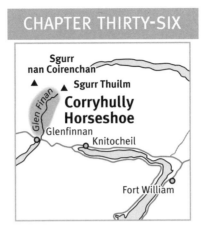

CHAPTER THIRTY-SIX

Sgurr
nan Coirenchan
▲ ▲ Sgurr Thuilm
Corryhully
Horseshoe
Glenfinnan
Knitocheil

Glen Finan

Fort William

THE CORRYHULLY

HORSESHOE

Some folk call it the Glenfinnan Horseshoe, others call it the Corryhully Horseshoe, but the name doesn't really matter. The two hills involved, Sgurr Thuilm (try *hoolim*) and Sgurr nan Coireachan always feel deliciously remote from tartan-clad Glenfinnan and its associated tourist trail. The Raising of the Standard was the genesis of a sad, some would say ill-conceived episode in Scotland's history but the legend of Bonnie Prince Charlie shows that the Braveheart syndrome was alive and well in Glenfinnan long before Mel Gibson put on his woad and waggled his bare bum!

The West Highland Railway viaduct forms a massive gateway between this tartanland and the long approach to what is some of the roughest hill country in Scotland. Sgurr Thuilm and Sgurr nan Coireachan could almost be refuges from a neighbouring landscape, for in terms of their rough and craggy slopes, their air of remoteness and views to the west, they are really Rough Bounds of Knoydart-hills misplaced.

Just past the National Trust for Scotland visitor centre and coach park there's a smaller car park just off the A830, on the western side of the

River Finnan. This car park lies in the shadow of the 21-span Glenfinnan railway viaduct which has been named, with some justification, as one of the great sights of the Western Highlands – man-made sights that is. Even this great work of man is dwarfed by the mountains that surround it.

Built in 1897 the viaduct was the world's first significant mass-concrete structure. Isn't it ironic that such a structure, built in one of the finest landscapes in the Highlands, should be made of concrete, that metaphor for urban decay, an unyielding, unforgiving material whose very name evokes the resonance of 60s inner city architecture? It seems that concrete was preferred in the building of the viaduct because the local rock was so hard and difficult to dress. The builder, Robert McAlpine, he of the eponymous fusiliers, was apparently very enthusiastic about concrete, pointing out to anyone who would listen that it did not rust, nor need painting. Observant chap; he probably richly deserved his nickname of 'Concrete Bob'!

There exists an apocryphal story about a horse and cart having apparently fallen into one of the hollow piers of the viaduct but a recent survey of the structure revealed no trace of the unfortunate beast. However, it does seem that engineers have found some evidence to suggest that old Dobbin didn't fall into the Glenfinnan viaduct supports but those of the Loch nan Uamh viaduct several miles further west.

A track below the viaduct runs north, principally to service Glen Finnan Lodge, but turns into a footpath short of the Corryhully bothy, an idyllically-positioned doss near the stream which drains the massive Coire Thollaidh and Coire a' Bheithe. Nearby the track skirts a wonderful rock pool where I've enjoyed more than one skinny dip after a sweaty descent from Sgurr nan Coireachan.

Higher up you leave the track and the cascading stream behind for an obvious spur which leads on to a long ridge called Druim Coire a' Bheithe – this is where the hard work begins. Grass-covered slopes lead to a small subsidiary top and then north up stony slopes to the summit of Sgurr Thuilm itself, at 3,159ft (963m), the peak of the round hillock. To the north-west, the hills of Knoydart fill the horizon beyond the silver slash of lonely Loch Morar. Further east another silver slash, Loch Arkaig, gives way to the Loch Quoich hills.

Below your feet to the north lie some rough and wild corries which overlook the narrow pass of Glen Pean where the existence of the Pean bothy will no doubt tempt many into attempting these two hills from the comforts of a dry base. The approach from the Pean side is infinitely rougher than the southern approach I've described and in times of spate it is well-nigh impossible to cross the River Pean. In such conditions it's best to cross the river by the footbridge at the bottom of Gleann a' Chaorainn and tackle Sgurr Thuilm by its steep north-east ridge.

But it's to the west we look now, where our next Munro summit, Sgurr nan Coireachan (3,136ft/956m), demands attention. A wide, knobbly ridge, dotted with lochans and adorned by a line of old fence posts which runs over the spine of the intermediate tops of Beinn Garbh and Meall an Tarmachain, creates a superb rocky highway in the clouds, an easy and comfortable ridge before it begins to narrow and steepen as it rises to its summit.

Sgurr nan Coireachan might be slightly lower than Sgurr Thuilm but is aesthetically a much finer summit, the apex of a number of remote corrie ridges, craggy and wild. The final ridge to the summit cairn is narrow and rocky, with the depths of Coire Thollaidh dropping away on one side and the steep flanks of Glen Pean on the other. Rocky slopes tumble from the summit towards the head of Loch Morar and its wild, secretive country; to your left the hill's south-east ridge becomes steep and rocky as it abuts on to the vertiginous cliffs which drop into Coire Thollaidh, a craggy place of stunning character. The ridge continues, in form and interest, across the minor top of Sgurr a' Choire Riabhaich and soon begins to drop down towards the River Finnan again. Eventually you'll see a good stalkers' path below so break off east from the ridge to reach it. The path skirts the foot of the main crags to link up with the main track again. If it's been a good day but the thought of the long walk back to Glenfinnan is a drudge, remember the little pool I mentioned earlier. A dip in the clear, cold waters might be just the revitalisation you need and, with toes tingling, the return past Corryhully Bothy and back to Glenfinnan could be a lot better than you could have hoped for.

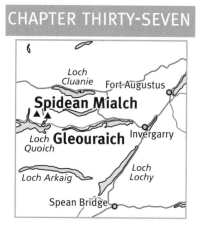

CHAPTER THIRTY-SEVEN

THE LEGACY OF THE
SHINING LEVELS

In a land notorious for its high rainfall, the area around Loch Quoich, just west of Glen Garry, has the distinction of having an exceptionally high rainfall. One particularly memorable day in December 1954 saw 10 inches of rain fall in a 22 hour period and the annual average is in the region of 135 inches. It's not surprising, then, that the North of Scotland Hydro Board has harnessed the waters of Loch Quoich for hydro-electric purposes and in so doing changed what was a seven-mile natural loch into a 10-mile-long reservoir. By raising the waters by some 100ft they drowned the small village of Kinlochquoich and doubled the maximum breadth of the loch.

Such loss of human habitation has given the area a wilderness feel, despite the presence of the single track road that runs along the north shore of the loch between Glen Garry and Kinloch Hourn and, for all its wetness, the Loch Quoich area remains a great favourite among hill-bashers. Where would the world be, once bereft, of wet and of wildness, asked the poet Gerard Manley Hopkins? Where indeed? Wetness and wild, the two conditions go hand-in-hand in Scotland, and if we can't cope with the wet, we'll never appreciate the wild.

But despite its high rainfall sometimes, just sometimes, the sun does shine on this land of mountain and flood. When the hills are swathed in snow two hills in particular just beg to be climbed. Gleouraich, 3,396ft/1,035m, and Spidean Mialach, 3,268ft/996m, stand on the north side of Loch Quoich, their summits the culminating points of an undulating two-mile ridge.

Gleouraich lies at the western end of the ridge and overlooks the lower part of Loch Quoich. Half a mile from the summit is the east top of Gleouraich, beyond which the main ridge drops down steeply to the Fiar Bhealaich (2,433ft/742m) and then rises to the summit of Spidean Mialach. Both hills have several great corries biting into the steep flanks on their north side, particularly Garbh Choire Mor and Garbh Choire Beag which fall between the two tops of Gleouraich, and the walker, traversing both hills, can admire them from best advantage. Snow cornices overhang the topmost slopes into the early summer and the views north to the Glen Shiel hills and beyond, on a clear day, display a jumble of hills and mountains that seem to roll on indefinitely.

Gleouraich and Spidean Mialach might be difficult to pronounce (try *Glaw-reech* and *Speetyan Mee-a-lach*) but as mountains go they're straightforward enough to climb and well-worth a visit. They must be among the most accessible of all the hills in the western Highlands, making their seven-mile traverse an ideal outing for a short January day.

A small cairn on the west side of the Allt Coire Peitireach, close to the road, indicates the start of what soon turns out to be one of those magnificent footpaths of old which seems to elevate you from the lower slopes to the summit in no time at all. The stalkers of yesteryear certainly knew how to build hill paths. Wide zig-zags efficiently ascend a grassy spur before the path works its way uphill and along the steep, airy edge of Gleouraich's south-west ridge. Ice and snow gave an adventurous feel to this ridge when John, Phil and I climbed it a couple of Januarys ago, and we were glad of our ice axes as we gazed down on an arm of Loch Quoich glistening a couple of thousand of feet below us.

Crossing the ridge we cast our eyes to the west, along the length of the main part of the loch. The view was majestic, with the big hills of

Knoydart, Sgurr na Ciche, Luinne Bheinn, Meall Buidhe and Ben Aden all clearly visible. With the stalker's path now only a slight indentation in the snow we continued to the top of the ridge, then headed sharply up to the summit, the hill of uproar, at 3,396ft/1,035m above sea level. There was certainly little uproar on this day and with some soft warmth touching us from the weak winter sun it was a great excuse to sit by the cairn and simply fester for half an hour, sipping whisky-laced coffee and drinking in the tremendous views around us.

To the south Ben Nevis stood out defiantly against the pale blue sky, its white shroud bright and shining. Creag Meagaidh, or at least the backside of Creag Meagaidh, was equally plastered with early snow and to the north the hills of the south Glen Shiel ridge and the mountains of Affric were clear and spotlessly white.

From the summit the ridge flows on east. It drops and then rises again to ascend an intermediate top, Creag Coire Fiar Bhealaich, beyond which a steep drop to another excellent stalkers' path takes you to the Fiar Bhealaich. From this pass you climb on to yet another subsidiary top from which a broad ridge sweeps majestically round the top of the corries to the cairn on Spidean Mialach, the peak of wild animals.

From the summit of Spidean Mialach it's best to drop in a south-east direction for a while before descending an obvious spur towards Loch Fearna. From the small saddle above the loch you can make your way across the open acres of Coire Mheil to pick up another stalkers' path on the west side of the burn, a path which can then be followed back to the road near the starting point.

It was still early as we dropped down the slopes back to the road, and we had time to linger. The sun was sinking into the jumble of peaks that make up the Rough Bounds of Knoydart, casting long shadows from the west and turning the hills to silhouettes. Lochs and lochans lay like pools of mercury, the shining levels that are the legacy of this wet and wondrous landscape, a landscape that had blessed us abundantly with gifts the likes of which money just can't buy. It was a January day to remember.

CHAPTER THIRTY-EIGHT

SHADOWS OF REALITY IN THE ANCIENT STONES

Our upland areas are full of historical resonance and even the remote and isolated areas of the Scottish Highlands still define their ancient links to man's passage and settlement. The ruckle of stones that betray the whereabouts of old shielings or the lichen-tinged drystone walls that still run along a mountain ridge remind us that our modern wilderness is a land emptied and abandoned. Yet, by spending time there we can still experience a sense of history, we can still encounter a distinct spirit of place...

Consider if you will those far-off days when our hills and mountains were regarded as wild areas of desolation and abomination rather than arenas of recreation. Closely associated with such landscapes were Celts and Fingalians, Iron Age traders and Roman soldiers, Redcoats and Jacobites, road builders and clansmen, poets and artists. Robbers, poachers, illicit distillers and even political adversaries would take refuge in the remoteness, hiding from the authorities of the day, and spiritual men often found sanctuary here, withdrawing from society to create a peaceful haven in which they could find fellowship with their god.

It's intriguing to stand on a mountain top and look around at the empty lands that lie below. It's a fanciful thought, but one I'm sure that most hill-goers are familiar with, that we could be the first person ever to stand there. It's even more overwhelming to realise that man has been climbing our hills and criss-crossing those areas we would consider as wilderness since time immemorial – which makes a mockery of any suggestion that such land is private and we have no right to be there. Tell that to the ghosts of yesterday, to the holy men, to the Pictish warriors, to the cattle drovers and the navvy soldiers, the artists and the poets and the writers, the precursors of the hill-walkers and the climbers and the skiers and the ornithologists. The tradition of access is inviolate, inextricably tied up in the comings and going of centuries of human movement and settlement.

But in many of these emptied lands I believe we can still discern the winds and whispers of former times; in the place names that commemorate people, battles, legends and deeds, in the ruins that lie abandoned in secret corners of silent glens and in the crumbling drystone walls which still mark out the in-byes, tilting up steep slopes on the boundaries of ancient steadings.

But is it only our imaginations that occasionally suggest a distant peel of laughter, or a wail of sorrow blowing on the breeze? Is it mere fancy that suggests the amorphous shadows of things that have long passed; sounds, perceptions, emotions that still faintly stir us? Is there something peculiar to those places, often physically derelict, that haunts us with a spirit of place? Is it conceivable that a manifestation of such a spirit could possibly exist, given the right circumstances?

Some time ago my wife Gina and I had been backpacking on the Southern Upland Way and were making our way to St Mary's Loch and the historic Tibbie Shiel's Inn, an old watering-hole of Sir Walter Scott and James Hogg, the Ettrick shepherd. We had climbed over the pass from Ettrick off the east side of Peniestone Knowe and dropped down towards Riskinhope Hope, an old sheep farm of which only a few crumbling walls remain. 'Hope', in this part of Scotland, means a valley with a meandering burn and has nothing at all to do with expectation or optimism; indeed there was little that was optimistic about this place, the ubiquitous nettles clustered around the crooked portals of the old door, the only real evidence of occupation. The old in-bye walls were decayed and tumbled and even the old Scots pines which had once proudly protected the house from the westerly winds were now gaunt and bent, geriatrics with no progeny.

We stopped for a while, the gable end preventing the wind from chilling us and almost immediately I sensed something. Despite the rural dereliction I became aware of the past, the recognition of it took shape in my consciousness as a lonely little spot among the folds of the Border hills where people were born and died, laughed and cried, rejoiced and were saddened, worked and made love. Was there something of these human emotions and interactions forever bound up in the spirit of this place, something that my diminished 21st century senses were no longer capable of fully comprehending?

As I questioned my own senses I was aware that I'd experienced such sensations before, in deserted Himalayan villages close to the Tibetan border, in ancient settlements in Tunisia and Morocco and in countless ruins I'd visited throughout the world. Could it be that strong human emotions, like the grief of leaving a lovely spot like this, of allowing the house to fall into dereliction, could be channelled into something that is bound up forever in those ruins, in the land; a soul, a spirit that pervades the ether of the place for years, for centuries to come? A genuine spirit of place?

I'd first come across this term in the writings of Jim Perrin, our greatest landscape essayist. He named one of his collections of essays *Spirits of Place* and in that book he defined the phenomenon as a profound interplay of consciousness. This is what he says:

"On the coast of Llyn I know a set of steps cut once into the rock and smoothed by centuries of feet. They lead down to the wave margin and to a well. If you listen, the clamour of voices here, of wave-sound, tide race, the stilled pre-Cambrian magma – a drowned girl's scream, a pilgrim's prayer, slap of a launched coracle, the crack and hiss of cooling rock – are co-existent along the flicker of time. It happened here, and so much else besides. The distillation of these events is the spirit of the place."

I wonder if there is more to it than that? Could there be more than just a distillation of events, perhaps some quantum physics concept of the simultaneous nature of time – past, present and future – that we don't yet understand? The late Bruce Chatwin once described the link between the physical world that Australian aborigines inhabit and a parallel world from which they believe their physical world is derived. This other world is their 'dreamtime' and for them is as real as the physical world in which they live. The difference between the native Australians and modern urban man is that we've lost the use of many of our original senses. Even some of our basic senses – touch, smell, hearing, sight – have diminished through lack of use.

Could it be that we now have dormant senses, deeply submerged in our consciousness, that only come to the surface when certain conditions create the right mood or atmosphere? An awareness, indeed an enthusiasm, for what has gone before us is not an unusual sensation in those who love wild places, particularly when those wild places are speckled with the tumbled ruins of long-deserted fortifications.

Close to the village of Inverfarigaig on Loch Ness-side there is an exposed and rocky bluff. Below the bluff lie the silver waters of the long loch, steel blue more often than not reflecting the dour sky, stretching both east and west like some great sea.

Almost directly across the loch the remains of Urquhart Castle rise like some Disneyland fortress, dark and brooding on its promontory, surrounded it seems by the dark storm eddies which move across the water of the loch on the mild breath of the south-westerly breeze.

If there is a finer point from which to speculate on the mysteries of Loch Ness then I'm ignorant of it. Great stones lie around, the foundations of another ancient fort perhaps. The hill itself is cone-shaped, three sides of which form sheer precipices. At the foot of the hill the River Farigaig takes a tumultuous course down to the lochside, a Highland river of crashing foam, intermingled with deep, peat-stained pools. Birches whisper in the breeze and the small stones of the scree-covered path crunch beneath your feet.

This place is Dun Dearduil, or the Fort of Deirdre. The bitter-sweet legend of Deirdre and the Three Sons of Uisneach is one of the finest and best-loved of all the Celtic folk tales. A tale of romance and treachery, Deirdre came to Scotland from Ireland, fleeing from a jealous High King of Ulster to whom she had been unwillingly betrothed. She fled in the company of the Three Sons of Uisneach, the eldest son being Naoise, her lover. It's always been believed that they came to Loch Etiveside in Argyll but local tradition has it that they also spent time on Loch Ness-side. Indeed, some would claim that Ness is a derivation of Naoise.

You can climb to Dun Dearduil from close to Inverfarigaig by taking the hill's south-east slopes. It's not a difficult climb. Very little is left of the fort but the ancient stones of what might have been the foundations are still plain to see, exuding their air of mystery and timelessness. If you have any imagination at all you can easily visualise a stronghold here, high above that long stretch of water that even then mystified people, locals and visitors alike. It was St Columba, in 565AD, some time after the period in which Deirdre would have lived, who first recorded a sighting of a monster in Loch Ness. Is it possible to find a more unimpeachable witness than Columba? But there are other mysteries in the area, perhaps only believable by those who have the ability to discern the past...

Not far from Inverfarigaig lies the lonely Loch Duntelchaig. It is close to here, in May, soon after dawn, that a ghostly battle apparently takes place. Cairns mark the ancient graves of long dead warriors, and it's close to them that the fighting takes place. Some claim the battle was a mirage of the fighting in France in the 1870s but the ghost-like battle has been seen since that time. On one occasion a man was cycling to Inverness when he saw three horsemen on the road in front of him. He followed them but, on rounding a bend, he astonished himself by running into, and through them. So surprised was he that he fell off his bike, only to see two phantom armies approach, one of infantry to one cavalry. He didn't wait to find out who won. Could this man have experienced a spirit of place?

It wasn't unusual for early Christian monks to recognise such places and more often than not they'd set up their churches on traditional pagan sites, as though the goodness and light they were bringing to the people would dispel what they believed to be the darker forces. It must have been an amazing time. The years following the settlement of Columba's church on Iona saw his followers sent out to win a nation. Many of us are familiar with the names of some of those men: St Ninian, St Cuthbert, St Adamnan, Columba's first biographer. But there were many, many more.

St Kenneth settled in Badenoch, in the area we now know as Kinloch Laggan. Indeed the area was once known in full as St Kenneth's Lagain (hollow). It would be wrong to think of men like Kenneth as purely priests; they were invariably men of some learning, skilled in herbal medicine, well-practised in agriculture and fishing. Not only did they bring the Gospel to these remote places but a sense of care, community and peace and it's little wonder that the principles of Christianity that they taught brought people together into large settlements. Indeed, it could be that Kenneth's followers created a place of learning, perhaps an early theological college, in Glen Banchor near Newtonmore.

From the 7th century on St Kenneth's cell was considered to be a holy burial place second only to Iona and, as a result, according to the Rev Thomas Sinton, writing in 1906: "St Kenneth's occupied a central situation for a wide surrounding district including the vale of the Pattack and Strathmashie, the whole range of Loch Laggan and beyond, and Glenshiaro in the valley of the Spey past Loch Crunnachan."

According to Sinton, many ancient tracks converge on St Kenneth's at Kinloch Laggan and these were mainly burial tracks, or coffin routes. They were roads from out-of-the-way settlements to churches and churchyards. Many were very long indeed and the poor coffin bearers would have needed a fair amount of strength. Many hill-walkers follow these ancient routes today, often unfamiliar with their original purpose. The Macgregors, for example, would walk from Glen Lyon to Dalmally to their clan burial ground at the foot of Glen Orchy. Another funeral party once crossed the broad ridge of Ben Ledi in the Trossachs. They had left Glen Kinglass and were bound for St Bride's Chapel in the Pass of Leny. It was the middle of winter and the members of the cortege perished when they fell through the ice of a frozen lochan; even today the name of the loch commemorates the grisly march, Lochan nan Corp, the lochan of the corpse.

The Scottish Rights of Way Society book *Scottish Hill Tracks* recalls the writings of Osgood Mackenzie, the botanist who planted Inverewe Gardens. When Lady Mackenzie died in 1830, 500 men, taking turns, carried her coffin 60 miles from Gairloch to Beauly. When the bearers took a rest, everyone added a stone to a cairn on the spot, a custom that was responsible for many of the cairns which even today mark some of these historical routes.

The Rev Thomas Sinton tell us: "In the absence of proper roads, bodies were always carried shoulder high to their last resting place. They were often enclosed in cases of wicker-work or perhaps, merely surrounded by long saplings placed side by side and withe-bound. Thus having been borne hither young men and maidens in the bloom of youth, parents followed by their weeping children, infants taken from their mother's arms, husbands and wives separated by death; soldiers, who had fought for their country in foreign lands; churchmen, who had dispensed the sacraments within that ruined shrine; chief men and peasants; bards, whose quips and cracks, and jests and jibes, were silenced forever; unknown strangers who had perished on the mountains. Huge companies of people from the Braes of Badenoch and the Braes of Lochaber, who had journeyed to St Kenneth's, carrying thither their dead with the wail of pibroch and cry of coronach, and who thronged yonder burial ground in summer's sun and winter's blast, have themselves, long since, paid the last dept to nature and come to dust."

Not so very far from the old St Kenneth's graveyard lies the remains of an ancient burial stone, a simple and nondescript artefact which nevertheless is resonant with this spirit of place. The Highlands are speckled with such artefacts, many of which are the only living reminders of the events that they commemorate. Most of the tales have been lost in the mists of time, but many, such as the Curse of Cluny, survive to this day.

In the 16th century, Cluny, chief of the Clan MacPherson, betrothed his eldest daughter to one of the great High Kings of Ulster. This gentleman made his way across the Moyle, the ancient name for that stretch of water between Scotland and Ireland, to Badenoch with a huge entourage of knights and nobles. One of them, apparently of lesser rank than most of the others, was a young warrior by the name of Cathalon.

While the wedding feast was in full swing, Cathalon fell in love with the bride's younger sister. The young couple, passionately in love by all accounts, believed that Cluny would never offer the hand of his youngest daughter to any other man than an independent chief, so they decided to elope. The time being unsuitable, Cathalon said he would return to Ulster with the wedding party but would come back to Badenoch on his own just as soon as he possibly could.

True to his word, Cathalon returned in early winter and the young lovers set off towards the wilds of Corrieyairack, their plan being to flee to the west coast of Scotland by the Great Glen, where they could catch a boat across the Moyle to the Antrim coast.

Sadly, the young lady couldn't travel very fast as by this time she had become heavy with Cathalon's child. Nightfall caught them only a few miles up the glen and they sheltered in a cave, known even today as Creag-a-Cathalain.

Meanwhile, Cluny had discovered what had happened and ordered his ghillies to give chase and return with the heart of this Ulsterman who had been rash enough to run off with his younger daughter.

Unfortunately the weather deteriorated during the night and by morning the glen was swathed in a blanket of fresh snow. This made the job of tracking the young lovers a lot easier and about two miles from the cave the couple were overtaken and, despite a brave fight, Cathalon was overcome. He was put to the sword and his heart cruelly carved from his body to be taken back to Cluny as a trophy. As they buried the body the ghillies discovered some papers in the young man's pouch which showed that young Cathalon was in fact no mere 'duine uasal', or simple laird. He was the rightful heir to the High King of Ulster, a true and legitimate thane. To this day no-one knows why he had kept this fact secret, although it's thought that he wanted to find someone who loved him for his own character and personality, and not because he was of royal lineage.

When Cluny was told of Cathalon's death he expressed great sorrow but was secretly delighted that his youngest daughter hadn't been carried off by a commoner, but by a true prince. He ordered a giant standing stone to be placed over the burial place in due respect of Cathalon's rank.

It's good to pass time leaning against that stone on its level stretch of ground close to the River Spey near Melgarve, recalling its antiquity and purpose. There isn't much left of it but it remains as a reminder of the consequences of hasty vengeance, the swift retribution that for many years was known as the Curse of Cluny.

Such a sense of antiquity can be stimulating and can often provide the *raison d'etre* for a long walk, linking up ancient sites and taking time to consider their purpose and function, allowing the resonances of their ancient connections to help us somehow understand more of their meaning. I enjoyed such a walk a few years ago along the western seaboard of the Isle of Lewis.

It had been a good walk. Early in the day I had been dumped at Shawbost and had slowly traversed the indentations of the Lewis coastline near Tiumpan Head. The Isle of Lewis tends to be disregarded by many walkers in favour of the mountainous landscape of neighbouring Harris. Lewis is generally low and flat, a great peaty moorland with a magnificent rocky coastline, while Harris is gloriously rocky, and home to the highest of the hills, culminating in the highest of them all, Clisham, 2,621ft/799m above sea level.

However, Lewis has more subtle attractions and all day I had been struck by a real sense of the past. Ancient stone dykes still lined the in-fields and the ruins of old cots and black houses littered the otherwise empty landscape. The relentless toil against the vagaries of the Atlantic and the rough, rocky ground, which obviously served well-enough in the past, are obviously not for the modern Hebridean. There are apparently still more than 3,000 crofts on the Isle of Lewis but many are too small for economic viability. The current state of the agricultural industry obviously doesn't help. Apart from growing the year's supply of potatoes and raising a few hens most modern crofters prefer to run the croft on a part-time basis, the main job in Stornoway or in the fishing or tweed industry offering a better return. As a result, the more exposed parts of this Hebridean coastline have been left to the wheeling gulls and the ghosts of yesterday.

I had wandered the cliff tops in an aura of absolute peace. The Atlantic pulsed against the cliffs and the azure sea and warm sun were a constant temptation to stop and linger, but I wanted to reach Carloway and its broch, one of the best surviving examples of a circular defensive tower of the Iron Age.

I wasn't disappointed. The dry stone wall is almost perfectly circular, ten-feet-thick at the base and rising to a height of some 30ft. Who were the people who built this fort, and why? Was it to offer protection from an enemy? Only a small, low doorway offers entry. The broch builders – and there are about 500 brochs left in Scotland – were most likely to have been the Picts but did they create these structures as defensive forts, or offensives? Archaeologists cast little light on the matter. If they were defensive structures who was the enemy? The Iron Age in Scotland is reckoned to have been around 450BC to 400AD which would seem to rule the Norsemen out as enemies; indeed there wasn't even an organised civilisation in Norway in such far-off days. Having said that, rock carvings of 1000BC and earlier have been found in Norway and Sweden, carvings that depict longships. Is it possible that bands of Vikings sailed the northern seas in expeditions of plunder long before the establishment of a kingdom in Scandinavia? The early Vikings were illiterate and kept no records but history nevertheless points the finger at those seafaring explorers as the enemy of the broch people.

A few miles south of Carloway stands the village of Callanish and, close by, on a headland overlooking Loch Roag, the Callanish stone circle. The stone circle at Stonehenge might be bigger than its Hebridean counterpart, and indeed its surroundings might be more manicured, but the Callanish circle is infinitely more atmospheric. It positively exudes drama and mystery and I wanted to spend a night there.

Local folk call the place 'Tursachan' which loosely translated means the place of pilgrimage, a name that throws little light on the reasons the stones are there. The circle is believed to have been built some 3,500 years ago; 53 massive slabs of Lewis gneiss, each apparently positioned with mathematical accuracy, and no doubt immense labour. What made the people of the day take on such a task?

Equipped with a stove, some extra clothes and a bivvy bag, and with a forecast of clear skies and a good moon, I wanted to consider some of the theories that have been put forward as to Tursachan's origin, hoping that perhaps the circle's spirit of place would invoke in me some sense of purpose, a hint of its distant origins. I wasn't altogether hopeful…

Some people were still wandering around the stones when I arrived, so not wanting people to know what I was up to I wandered down to the shore where the low moon gave a hint of a silvery light across the loch, silhouetting a couple of small boats. By their very nature the Hebridean islanders have an affinity with the sea, and the ancient lore of the tides is as deep and mysterious as the stone circles, the dolmens and the brochs.

In the Outer Isles there was a belief that the soul of man leaves his body when the ocean tide is ebbing. Similarly, when the tide is in flood, life will be given. Ebb and flow, the cycles of nature, rhythmic, unceasing, timeless. But the tides of the sea are not all the same. There are the greater tides, the spring tides, which arrive every 14 days. These come at the times of the full moon and the new moon. For several days the spring tides sweep through the Minch and are succeeded by an equal period of lesser tides, the neap tides, when the ocean is quieter and the ebb and flow less impetuous.

Ancient man held the natural things of the world in great importance, hence the legends of the tides, or of the rising moon. Perhaps it's not unrealistic to consider that these great stones of Callanish were used for astronomical observations? If that is the case why is there a chambered cairn among the stones where, last century, archaeologists found the remains of charred human bones? Were human sacrifice, worship and astronomical observation linked in some ancient ritual? It seems likely.

Modern theorists have credited the Lewis builders with the ability to measure the major positions of the sun and moon in the same way as their counterparts on Salisbury Plain. It's even believed they could calculate an accurate calendar and predict solar and lunar eclipses, so it's possible that the stone circles were used both as some form of ancient calculator and as a temple – a place of worship, learning and sacrifice. It's good to think of Callanish standing as a tribute to a people whose lives were closely interwoven with the natural world.

I made my way back to the stones in the darkness, stumbling on the uneven turf. Only the ceaseless wash of the surf broke the silence and I found myself walking stealthily, unsure and uncertain. The dark shadows were heavy with threat and the chambered cairn looked distinctly intimidating. Earlier, in the confident clarity of daylight, I had planned to bivvy down in the centre of the circle, to lie within the temple of the ancients and look out at the stars and the moon as they must have done, to sense something of the spirit of place of Callanish, to allow the stones themselves to teach me something of their purpose.

Now, on my own and in the still darkness of the night I discovered I couldn't. Picking up my gear and vaguely embarrassed by the childhood bogeys that were threatening to engulf me, I retired quietly to the shore again, feeling rather foolish, but there the life-pulse of the sea and the sounds of the occasional sea-bird were soothingly tangible.

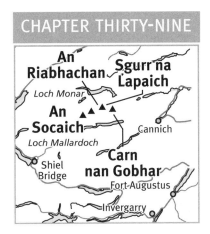

CHAPTER THIRTY-NINE

THE MUNROS OF LOCH MULLARDOCH

It's always good to drive past the wonderfully-named Crask of Aigas, for beyond it lie three of the finest glens in Scotland. The road follows the course of the River Beauly, a winding approach to the delights of Glen Affric, Glen Cannich and Strathfarrar and, just as the Crask of Aigas forms the gateway to the roadless glens of the west, so the golden woodlands of Glen Cannich form the portals to Loch Mullardoch and its Munros.

Rising on the north side of the loch, Carn nan Gobhar (3,255ft/992m), Sgurr na Lapaich (3,772ft/1,150m), An Riabhachan (3,704ft/1,129m), and An Socach (3,507ft/1,069m), form a ten-mile, corrie-bitten and wind-scoured ridge between Glen Cannich and Glen Strathfarrar, a remote group of hills that require a long walk-in along the northern shore of Loch Mullardoch if you want to climb them in one long 20-mile day. But you don't have to make a marathon of it.

Consider treating yourself to a two-day visit, either trekking along the lochside to the lower reaches of Coire Mhaim, camping and tackling the ridge in its entirety next day, or basing yourself at Cannich (hotel, bunkhouse and youth hostel), taking two days to climb the four Munros. From the Mullardoch dam at the Cannich end of the loch you can make a shorter circuit of the two easternmost hills, Carn nan Gobhar and Sgurr na Lapaich, returning by the south ridge of the latter. The other two hills of the group, An Riabhachan and An Socach, can be climbed from the west end of Loch Mullardoch after the lochside walk-in. Alternatively, you could cycle in to Iron Lodge in Glen Elchaig in the west and climb them from there but, Munro-baggers being what they are, I suspect most will want to climb all four in one expedition.

Munro; how that name has changed attitudes and perceptions in the hill game over the past ten or so years. It's not long since Munro-baggers were looked down on by climbers and mountaineers as some lower form of life, often referred to as 'dirty' Munro-baggers. But it would appear that Munro-bagging has become acceptable, even trendy. Fashionable young things who would never have been seen dead in a pair of stout boots and a woolly bobble-hat can be see on any weekend sweating their way up some 3,000-footer, and enjoying themselves into the bargain. And it's not only young things who have been bitten by the Munro bug. I know a number of folk who have taken up Munro-bagging as a retirement hobby, indeed at least one couple has 'compleated' the Munros, having climbed all 284 peaks in their retirement years. I know of many others who have taken early retirement to give them more time to climb the Munros, then the Corbetts, then the Grahams...

Well over 2,000 people have now registered with the Scottish Mountaineering Club as having climbed all of the 3,000-footers – so what's the attraction?

I suspect most people like to have some form of framework on which they can hang their odd and curious passions, and the Munros offer such a hook. They also bring a methodology, a purpose to the rather aimless (but nonetheless fine) occupation of stravaiging, just wandering the hills. One thing is certain: in the course of climbing all 284 Munros you not only collect ticks in a guidebook but a breadth of rich experience, considerable experience of mountaineering skills and a knowledge of Highland Scotland that would be difficult to gain by random wandering. I've often written that by the time someone has climbed all the Munros they have become an experienced and skilled mountaineer, in the widest sense of the word.

It's also refreshing to discover a game that is distinctly lacking in standard rules and regulation. There is no competition at stake, no laurel wreaths or five-figure cheques – essentially the Munros don't really matter a damn. It's being out there that matters, on the hills, simply enjoying the uplift, the beauty, the essence of the green world. If Munro-bagging introduces people to those gifts, then it has to be worthwhile. The only warning I would give is that it shouldn't be taken too seriously but I know from experience that such a warning will fall on deaf ears. Once the bug bites, it's well nigh impossible to shake it off.

Mullardoch's lochside footpath is somewhat sketchy in its middle parts but runs along the north shore of the loch for about five miles to the estate buildings at the outflow of the Allt Coire a' Mhaim. From there, easy slopes climb north-west out of the peat bog-ridden Coire Mhaim and lift you on to the curved south ridge of An Socach, not named on some of the older OS maps.

From the summit trig pillar a grassy ridge runs east, where a hefty descent of some 1,500ft (460m) drops you into a narrow bealach before the climb up on to the sweeping, twisting ridge of An Riabhachan, the brindled, greyish one. There are two main parts to this ridge: the north-west section which is tight and exposed and connects the west and south-west tops; and the main ridge, a long, broad and level affair which gently climbs to the summit cairn and a little beyond, before dropping to the bealach above Loch Mor, the Bealach Toll an Lochain.

From this pass a 1,200ft (370m) climb up steep grassy slopes takes you to the south ridge of Sgurr na Lapaich, only a short distance from the rocky summit. A narrow and rocky rib forms the beginning of Sgurr na Lapaich's south-east ridge, a narrow and rocky crest which makes for much scrambling and slow progress. Better to stay slightly south of the crest where screes and then grassy slopes lead down above Loch Tuill Bhearnach to the next col. Beyond it, boulder-covered slopes gradually steepen and narrow before reaching the broad summit of Carn nan Gobhar, the cairn of the goats, the last top of the round.

CHAPTER FORTY

Achnasheen

Sgurr a'Choire

R Orrin

Sgurr Fhuar-thuill ▲

Sgurr na Ruaidhe ▲ ▲

Loch Monar

Carn na Gobhar ▲

Cannich

THE STRATHFARRAR
FOUR

Glen Strathfarrar is curiously misnamed, perhaps a cop-out by the Ordnance Survey to avoid the argument of differentiation between glen and strath. At least Strathfarrar locals don't have to suffer the ignominy of Farrar Valley, unlike those who live in Strathspey.

Access to Strathfarrar is by Struy which lies at the north end of Strathglass and the road which runs up the glen to the dam at Loch Monar is closed to cars; if you want to drive in you can make arrangements with the local Scottish Natural Heritage warden who conveniently lives beside the locked gate. There is a small nature reserve in the glen.

I suspect that restriction of cars actually benefits Strathfarrar and at the risk of sounding elitist there's a real joy in being able to ramble along the single-track road without having to step aside to let traffic past. Indeed, there's a real sense of peace here, although it wasn't always like that. Two hundred years ago the residents of the glen were savagely cleared, the native Caledonian pine forest, which once sheltered the black kye in winter, was burned down to make grazings for sheep and more recently hydro-electric workings have left their scars. Despite that, Glen

Strathfarrar is still worthy of a visit, and the jewel in this lovely Strathfarrar crown has to be the long ridge that makes up its northern boundary wall. Four Munros, Sgurr na Ruaidhe, Carn nan Gobhar, Sgurr a' Choire Ghlais and Sgurr Fhuar-Thuill offer a long and airy traverse of about 14 miles with views west to some of the emptiest landscape in Scotland.

The hills are fairly easily accessible from the road but no matter how you tackle them you're inevitably left with a long walk on the road at the end of the day. Unless, that is, you tackle the five-mile road section between the start and finish of the traverse first. Alternatively, you might want to compromise, by parking mid-way between the start of the ridge and the end. Two or three miles of road walking warms you up for the day ahead and a couple of miles isn't too bad at the end. For those who prefer to leave their car at Struy, a mountain bike makes the best compromise.

A stalkers' path leaves the road beside the tumbling Allt Coire Mhuillidh and on a glorious autumn morning my friend Bob Telfer, taking a break from running his Newtonmore outdoor centre, and I followed it up into a radiant corrie. The sun hadn't yet appeared over the southern hills but its luminescence was already burnishing the hills in front of us in a warm orange glow. Early overnight snows had decorated the tops, marking the change of seasons.

The eastern hills of this ridge are well-rounded and offer easy walking; Sgurr na Ruaidhe and Carn nan Gobhar, the peak of redness and the cairn of the goats, were easily climbed from the roadside. Wide open slopes from Coire Mhuillidh gave way to the flat, bald summit of Sgurr na Ruaidhe (3,259ft/993m), and an easy descent of some 700ft (210m) to the north-west dropped us on to the Bealach nan Bogan, where a broad, curving ridge lifted us on to the scree-covered wastes of Carn nan Gobhar, (3,255ft/992m). A slight covering of snow made the boulder-hopping awkward but highlighted the northern hills against a slate-grey sky. Like wee children we were excited by the snow. Bobby is a keen skier and over the years we had enjoyed a number of ski touring trips on the Scottish hills. These first snows of the year were enough to get our adrenaline running in anticipation of a good winter.

Sgurr a' Choire Ghlais, our third Munro of the day, came and went; the summit boasts two large cairns and a trig point, the highest position being a little to the south-south-east of the main ridge on a broad platform which gazes down a broad sweep into the depths of Strathfarrar. An orange haze shimmered on the southern horizon, masking the distant hills into curious shades of yellow and grey. To the west, where the air appeared clearer, the ridge rolled on towards the wild, empty quarter near the head of Loch Monar, an area dominated by two of the loneliest Munros in the land, Lurg Mhor and Maoile Lunndaidh.

From Sgurr a' Choire Ghlais the ridge dropped again and narrowed appreciably before rising over the top of Creag Gorm a' Bhealach, the crag of the blue pass and its continuation to Sgurr Fuar-Thuill. Although this is the final Munro of the day it was well-worth wandering on to the top of Sgurr na Fearstaig, the peak of the sea-pinks, for the view along the length of Loch Monar and its clutter of hills, now fading below a darkening sky. It was time for us to leave the high places for another day, dropping south along the ridge towards Sgurr na Muice for a few hundred yards until an easy descent down a scree gully carried us to the stalkers' path below.

Our delight at reaching such a good descent path was short-lived, for it disappeared for a short section just before we reached Loch Toll a' Mhuic below the steep crags of Sgurr na Muice, but almost magically it re-appeared, a real work of art which hugged the contours and followed natural lines, a joy to walk on and a fine example for modern footpath builders. It seemed like no time before we reached the road, ready for the tarmac plod back to the waiting car. The dimmed velvety sky accentuated the snow-covered peak of Sgurr na Lapaich behind us, an important mountain in this part of the Highlands. Sgurr na Lapaich is to the Frasers of Strathfarrar what Ben Venue is to the Macgregors of the Trossachs or Craigellachie is to the Grants of Rothiemurchus. These were ancient places, rich in history, resonant in memory. This Strathfarrar has its own resonances, a majestic place, a lonely place, a place of sadness and a place of immense natural beauty. It's also a place of delight for anyone who enjoys Scotland in the raw.

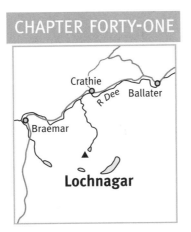

CHAPTER FORTY-ONE

THE SUBLIMITY AND BLACKNESS OF DARK LOCHNAGAR

Mountains and wilderness, like shoes or hats, often fall prey to the dictates of fashion, so Byron's description of the steep, frowning glories of Dark Lochnagar might well have been influenced by the dramatic writing style of the great English romantic poet John Ruskin.

Much of Ruskin's work characterised an era that saw mountains and wild places as gloomy and frowning, dark and dangerous and yet curiously attractive. There was a sublimity in any natural feature that was unusually high, deep or steep, a perceived vulcanism in the violence of a thunder and lightning storm or in fiery, angry sunsets. John Muir described the trend as "made up of alternate strips and bars of evil and good". Others have described it as all "sublimity and blackness", a fusion, as Ruskin perhaps intended, of science and aesthetics. The science might have been emotive but the blackness can be overwhelming and, like John Muir, I'm uncomfortable with the fearful element portrayed in that particular art form. I love mountains and wild places, but while love makes for a bringing together, fear only drives apart.

Having said that, I suspect that, subliminally at least, my initial perceptions of Lochnagar were a tad Ruskinian. Work had moved me to Aberdeen from the west of Scotland and I found the city to be dour and gloomy. I was homesick for Glencoe and the Ben, I preferred the pointy peaks of the west to the broad, rounded tops of the east and I badly missed the western seaboard and its cultures. To escape my homesickness I tried to flee to the nearest mountains but initially found Lochnagar, like the granite city, to be dour, grey and unwelcoming.

But like most mountains, Lochnagar is rich in healing qualities and in time, as I grew to love the mountain, I also overcame my west of Scotland prejudice and recognised that there was, indeed, a sparkle in the grey granite. I eventually became extremely fond of Aberdeen and my youngest son was born there, putting a personal seal on a longstanding relationship with the city and its mountain. Indeed, I've never left the Cairngorms and for the past 25 years have lived in Badenoch, in the very shadow of these hills. The hills of the west still exert a strong pull but the Cairngorms are the hills of home now.

There are a number of routes to the summit of Lochnagar and many would suggest the finest approach is from the Invercauld Bridge through the Ballochbuie Forest, the oldest stand of ancient Caledonian Pines in Scotland, and The Stuic. Some prefer the route from the north via the estate cottage and adjacent hut at Gelder Shiel, while a much longer route takes the footpath from Glen Callater via the stalker's path up Carn an t-Sagairt Mor.

In many ways this is my favourite route to Lochnagar. Just south of Braemar a long glen slashes its way on to the vast Lochnagar/Glenshee plateau. The name Callater comes from 'caladair', which means hard water. The loch itself is just less than a mile in length and has an average depth of about 10ft although it does become deeper in parts.

Glen Callater was at one time known as the 'miracle glen', following the deeds of a local clergyman who was known as Patrick, or Peter the Priest. The story goes that the whole Braemar area was suffering from intensely cold weather which went on well into the spring. Eventually a holy well near Lochcallater Lodge froze up leaving the people without any water at all. Peter the Priest was summoned and he decided the only thing he could do was pray – and his prayers were miraculously answered. As he knelt before the holy well the ice began to melt and great clouds gathered over Carn an t-Sagairt. Within moments the frost began to loosen its grip and a thaw had set in. A large stone commemorates the site of Peter's Well, close to Lochcallater Lodge on the east side of the loch.

From close by the lodge a good path climbs steadily round the side of Carn an t-Sagairt Mor and across the plateau of the White Mounth to skirt the edge of Coire Loch nan Eun before rising steadily to Cac Carn Mor of Lochnagar, then north to the summit of the mountain, Cac Carn Beag.

The most popular route, without doubt, is from the Spittal of Glenmuick at the end of the public road which runs up Glen Muick from Ballater.

A track runs in a north-east direction from the Spittal of Glenmuick visitor centre through the pines to Allt-na-giubhsaich. Beyond the houses, a track climbs steadily for about three kilometres to a broad bealach east of Meikle Pap where the track continues downhill on its way towards Gelder Shiel and Deeside. From the bealach, a maintained footpath climbs west past the Fox Well Cairn to a col between Meikle Pap and the Cuidhe Crom, a good viewpoint for glimpsing the dark bowels of Lochnagar with its black lochan reflecting its cirque of granite cliffs. Just before you reach the col, the path bears left and begins to weave its way fairly steeply to reach the plateau above.

The route now follows the corrie rim towards Cac Carn Mor, where the path divides. Keep going north at this point, past the deep gully known as the Black Spout, to the summit of the mountain, Cac Carn Beag, at 3,789ft (1,155m). The cairn sits in a commanding position on top of a great granite tor.

Return across the plateau to the path divergence and turn left. Follow this path for a short distance before dropping south-east, by the waters of the Glas Allt. Lower down you'll pass a fine waterfall before some zig-zags ease you down to the woods of Glas-allt-Shiel and the Victorian shooting lodge where the road along the north shore of Loch Muick returns you to Allt-na-giubhsaich and the track back to the car park.

CHAPTER FORTY-TWO

LAND USE LESSONS
IN KNOYDART

One of the great hopes of a new Scottish parliament was that land reform would be high on the political agenda. While the young parliament has indeed addressed many of the problems relating to land reform, it did not go far enough to solve some age-old problems. But despite that, some good things have happened in recent years, changes in social structures that have seen crofting communities buying their own land in places like Assynt, Eigg, Valtos on Skye and, most notably, Knoydart...

Less than a month after the Knoydart Foundation turned down entrepreneur Sir Cameron Macintosh's offer to buy the 17,000 acre Knoydart Estate and lease it to them on a peppercorn rent, the foundation, a partnership of the local community, the John Muir Trust, the Christopher Brasher Trust and the Highland Council successfully purchased the estate for a knock-down price of £750,000. A few weeks later missives were formally concluded with receivers appointed by the

Bank of Scotland, the secured creditor of Knoydart Peninsula Ltd, thus ending the first stage of a hard-fought campaign by both residents and those who love and cherish this very special place.

It had been a long drawn-out saga of epic proportions, fit to take its place in the treasure-trove of Celtic legend. A bitter-sweet tale of suffering, feudal injustice and dashed hopes, the Knoydart story epitomises the reasons why land reform in the Highlands has been so necessary. Now, the 70-strong community of Knoydart follows in the footsteps of those other land reform pioneers from Assynt, Eigg and Valtos, and has to face up to the responsibilities of land ownership. It's a challenge it is well-prepared for.

"The people of Knoydart are now free from the threat of suffering and injustice, which was once so brutally inflicted by its owners during the clearances of 1853 and at the times of the land raiders in 1948. This is a time for cautious celebration," said Bernie Evemy, Knoydart's sub-postmaster and a director of the Knoydart Foundation after their successful bid. "We have won the first stage, but our struggle must continue if we are to once again establish Knoydart as a thriving community."

It had been a long time since Knoydart could be described as a thriving community. The area's struggles began soon after the failure of the 1745 rebellion when a long drawn-out period of emigration began. A succession of potato blights and the failure of migrating herring shoals brought famine and poverty to the area. Following the death, in 1852, of Aenas of Glengarry, a largely benevolent clan chief and landowner, his widow Jospehine Macdonnell ordered her factor Alexander Grant to clear the remaining tenants to make way for sheep. Four hundred people were evicted, their homes torn down around them, and they were hounded like animals on to the *Sillary*, the transport ship supplied by the British government.

A contemporary report from *The Times* described the scene: "So long as there was hope of being left with a covering over their heads, the cottars were comparatively quiet, but now that they were homeless many of them became frantic with grief, and were driven to seek shelter in some of the neighbouring quarries, where some are now living, and others among the caves of the rocks with which this wild district of the highlands abounds."

The report's conclusion was cruelly prophetic: "It is thus clear that the highlands will all become sheepwalks and shooting grounds before long."

Less than 100 years later seven local Knoydart men, recently returned from serving their country in the second world war, were angered at the changes forced on them by an uncaring landlord. Rather than simply accept what was happening they decided to fight for what they saw as justice. They passionately believed they had a moral right to farm crofts and work land that was deliberately being allowed to go to waste, asserting that they were the subject of 20th century clearances, this time to clear the land to make way for well-off sportsmen and deer instead of sheep. Estates of 20, 30 and 40-thousand acres were cleared of tenants so that a privileged few could enjoy the sport of stalking and killing red deer stags. Great deserts of Highland landscape were created, a few stalkers were employed and the 'sporting estate' was born.

The Seven Men of Knoydart, as they became known, had chosen a formidable opponent, a millionaire brewer by the name of Arthur Ronald Nall-Cain, later to become Lord Brocket. An old Etonian and a graduate of Oxford he had spent some years as a barrister in London before becoming a Conservative MP, but his politics weren't purely confined to Britain. A staunch member of the Anglo-German fellowship he was a close friend of Ribbentrop, had met Adolf Hitler and was apparently known to be a Nazi sympathiser.

Brocket wanted to keep Knoydart for himself and his sporting (a modern metaphor for 'hunting') friends. He discouraged visitors and made many of the estate's older employees redundant, forcing them from their homes. He also refused to keep up the maintenance of the estate. The scourge of Knoydart depopulation began all over again.

Resorting to the tactics pioneered in the days of the old Highland Land League, the Seven Men of Knoydart staged a land raid, clearing small areas of land, marking them out and claiming them as their own.

Their case was doomed to failure. Brocket had powerful friends and even the socialist government of the time singularly failed to help the men. After a lengthy legal battle they had to give up the land they had seized. Today, their efforts are commemorated by a small memorial plaque in Inverie that states:

"Justice! In 1948, near this cairn, the Seven Men of Knoydart staked claims to secure a place to live and work. For more than a century Highlanders had been forced to use land raids to gain a foothold where their forebears lived. Their struggle should inspire new generations of Scots to gain such rights by just laws. History will judge harshly the oppressive laws that have led to the virtual extinction of a unique culture from this beautiful place."

Bold words, but the mis-management of Knoydart continued. In 1982 the Ministry of Defence showed an interest in buying the whole 55,000 acre Knoydart peninsula for a training area. Appalled at the thought of war games taking place in such a wonderful landscape and the resultant loss of access, there was widespread protest from mountain-user groups and conservationists. The MoD eventually capitulated only for the estate to be sold to a south of England-based property speculator who broke the entire peninsula into smaller parcels of land and sold them piecemeal. The rest is history, and the residents of the comparatively small Knoydart Estate continued to suffer at the hands of poor and insensitive land ownership.

Meanwhile, some families and several individuals moved to the area and created businesses, primarily in the tourism sector. One such family was the Robinsons of Doune.

Alan and Mary Robinson first saw the Knoydart coastline when they were enjoying a sailing holiday. In particular, they had come across a wonderfully-situated bay at the western extremity of the peninsula that overlooked the Sound of Sleat. Beyond the pebble beach was a semi-derelict cottage and, beyond it, the open hillside. No roads served the bay, nor man-made tracks. The only access was by sea. The views from the cottage thrilled them – out across the sound to the coast of the Sleat Peninsula of Skye and rising beyond the lower hills the jagged, almost improbable outline of the Cuillin. They were bewitched.

The couple made enquiries, and eventually made an offer for the cottage and surrounding land. It was the ideal location to begin building their dreamed-of marina, offering accommodation for sailors, divers and indeed anyone who wanted to divorce themselves from civilisation for a while. With the help of their two sons, Jamie and Toby, they quickly rebuilt the cottage, created a new pier and began offering holidays.

It was about this time that I first visited Doune Marine, ostensibly to test some walking boots with Chris Brasher, the one-time Olympic steeplechase champion and now boss of the Brasher Boot Company. Chris is a passionate lover of wild places – a climber, backpacker, hill-runner and conservationist – and has become a good friend over the years. Chris and I were met at Mallaig pier by Alan Robinson and his boat, the Mary Doune, and taken over the waters of Loch Nevis to the nascent Doune Marine. After a wonderful dinner (Mary is a divine cook and utilises local produce the way it should be) I discovered Alan was something of a folk-singer. As Chris and I settled in to make some sense of a 20-year-old Laophroig, Alan disappeared to his attic to search of his old guitar. When he found it, and tuned it, Chris and I were ready for a song or two. It was the first of many delightful folk-singing sessions I've enjoyed at Doune over the years and the first of many bottles of malt whisky to be enjoyed in such delectable surroundings.

Since that first memorable visit I've been back many times, most notably to help Brasher celebrate his 70th birthday in 1998. Just as I've noticed the development and growing success of Doune Marine, I've seen the development of a strong, growing community, with the Robinsons, and particularly Toby, very much at its centre. This community spirit was a critical factor in the negotiations for control of Knoydart Estate.

Chris Brasher has been a staunch supporter of the local community since the early 80s when he campaigned effectively against the possible MoD ownership. His Christopher Brasher Trust (largely made up of royalties from the sale of Brasher boots) contributed £200,000 to the Knoydart Foundation. "Since 1982 I have watched the decline of Knoydart with a growing anxiety – a decline caused by the neglect of the entire fabric of the estate. As that physical decline has deepened so the spirit and will of the community strengthened. The community buy-out has only happened because the people of Knoydart have been united in their desire to be masters of their own future," he said.

But despite its undoubted determination, the community of Knoydart couldn't have done it on its own. A neighbouring landowner, the John Muir Trust, added £250,000 to Brasher's contribution, and another neighbour, Sir Cameron Macintosh returned to the fray after an earlier withdrawal. Because of various legal considerations, which prevented him from simply giving the land to the community, Sir Cameron offered to buy the Knoydart Estate and rent it to the community at a peppercorn rent, but was turned down. The community wanted a buy-out, nothing less. This time Sir Cameron promised to match any contribution by the Government. Late, but nevertheless welcome, the Government eventually did contribute £75,000, through Highlands and Islands Enterprise, and that was topped up by £50,000 from Scottish Natural Heritage and a £100,000 anonymous donation from, according to Chris Brasher, a "half-Welsh/half-English lover of mountains and wild country who has never set foot on Knoydart".

Such conservation partnerships are at the sharp end of land reform in Scotland. Nigel Hawkins, director of the John Muir Trust, told me: "Many people talk about partnerships but here in Knoydart we are at the sharp end in delivering a partnership which is very much in tune with the times and which offers the very best hope for one of the most wild and beautiful places in the country to its local community. Bringing together community and conservation interests in ownership and management of areas like Knoydart is the best possible way of securing their long-term future."

But the John Muir Trust and the other members of the partnership pointed out that the purchase of the estate was only the first round in the battle to save it. The directors of the foundation were anxious to renew their public appeal to raise funds to allow them to implement their draft business plan and make the estate viable. They launched a new appeal to raise £30,000 and Highland Council's development company, Highland Prospects, came up with a loan facility towards working capital.

The business plan was very much geared towards a programme of initiatives that encompassed social, economic and environmental aspects of the Knoydart Estate, particularly in redressing the neglect that the area has suffered over many years. Their key objective was to make Knoydart self-sustaining within five years through the implementation of a number of projects including the recruitment of an estate manager to administer and oversee projects on a day-to-day basis, the upgrading of local infrastructure like the dam and hydro-electric generator, the repair of property, the encouragement of new business initiatives and implementation of the forestry project.

Crucially, the foundation saw the encouragement of green tourism as a primary part of its long-term strategy. Maintenance of access to the hills was paramount, as was the upgrading of footpaths, the establishment of a visitor information facility and the implementation of conservation initiatives. Deer stalking was to be run in harmony with other land uses and it was hoped that people with business flair and skills, from outside Knoydart, could be encouraged to move to the area and join the community.

It was significant that the deal should be concluded so soon after the 50th anniversary of the Seven Men of Knoydart's celebrated land raid. One of those men, Archie MacDougall, in his book *Knoydart – The Last Scottish Land Raid*, suggested that the depopulation of the Highlands would continue until there was legislation to have a compulsory land register and to stop the purchase of undeveloped areas of land by speculators. The successful purchase of the Knoydart Estate, at the time, highlighted a united will from the local community, its conservationist partners and, at long last, an apparently sympathetic government. The future of the Highlands was looking brighter than it had done for many a long year.

But I wonder how many more local communities will get the chance to follow in the steps of those land-reform pioneers from Assynt, Eigg, Valtos and Knoydart.

As Scotland regained its own parliament after 300 years of Westminster rule, there was a growing optimism that the new parliament's proposed Land Reform Bill would change the face of land ownership in Scotland. While the bill did address the problems of feudal reform and while the new legislation made it easier for local

Mount Ritter from Thousand Island Lake, Ansel Adams Wilderness, Sierra Nevada.

The Ridge of the Kincardine Hills from Meall a'Bhuachaille.

Descending on to the Moine Mhor, the great moss, from Braeriach.

Timeless hills – Baosbheinn and Beinn Dearg in the Flowerdale Forest.

Approaching the hydro-dam on Loch Tummel, the key to the Heart of Scotland route.

The remains of Bynack sheiling in upper Glen Tilt.

Marmots: you can hear 'em – but you can't always see 'em.

The curved ridge of Monte Castellets in the Sierra Aitana of Southern Spain.

Limestone crags on the eastern fringes of the Sierra de Aitana.

The Glenfinnan hills beyond the houses at Strathan.

Lochan nam Breac, one of the real jewels of the rough bounds of Knoydart.

Sgurr a'Choire Ghlais, one of the Munros on the wonderful Strathfarrar ridge.

The serrated ridge of the Cuillin, Isle of Skye. Are the mountains worth
£10 million or are they simply priceless?

communities to be given first refusal when estates came on the market, it didn't go as far as Archie MacDougall had hoped. There was no legislation for a land register and nothing to stop prime areas of heritage land being sold to speculators.

The issue was of course highlighted when, in early 2000, John Macleod of Macleod, chief of the Clan Macleod, put the Cuillin of Skye on the market at an asking price of £10 million, the proposed sale of which created much-needed debate on the whole question of land ownership in Scotland, and particularly land ownership in the Highlands. Most notably, the Scottish parliament's new legislation for land reform was found wanting.

While it was proposed that local communities should always have the first right to buy such areas of land that come on the market it was soon realised that such a proposal isn't always practical. It might have worked well in Assynt, or on Eigg, and even on Knoydart, with the help of other conservation interests, where the local community knew the land intimately. But to make this a point of law, that whoever happens to live on an area of land should have a statutory right to buy it, is potentially very problematic and actually misses a greater point.

I'm sure many of us can think of groups of individuals who live in what we could describe as being 'important national heritage areas' who should never be allowed to buy that land and run it as an estate, sporting or otherwise. But more importantly, the new legislation gives such people a legal preference over any potential bids from organisations which would want to buy the land for the nation; for example, the National Trust for Scotland or the John Muir Trust.

The Cuillin situation was an interesting one because there wasn't a local crofting community living and working on the estate and the immediate neighbours in Sligachan and Carbost were unlikely to be interested in buying the estate. Most commentators agreed that Macleod's asking price of £10 million was grossly over the top and many suggested that the Scottish Parliament should use its compulsory purchase powers to buy the Cuillin for the nation.

Whatever eventually happens to the Cuillin and any other mountain heritage areas that might come on the market, I believe we badly need a new approach to land ownership and management in Scotland. We've seen the good, the bad and the ugly of both private ownership and ownership by national conservation bodies. Surely we should be seeking a brand new agenda by which communities can take charge of the future of areas like the Cuillin and, with the support of recreational and conservation bodies, ensure they are managed for the public good.

I'm reminded of an ugly-looking monument in the tiny hamlet of Lochbuie on the Ross of Mull. It commemorates a former laird, 'Lochbuie and his Highlanders', and his loyalty to king and queen. It's dated 1902, 50 years or so after the same family cleared the lands of people to make way for sheep. Later, more families were evicted to help create the huge deer forests of Laggan and Carsaig.

There is a post office at Lochbuie, a tiny wooden building run by a pleasant lass, the mother of two small children who play outside when the weather is warm. A shadow crosses her face when you talk of privatisation of the Post Office and it's clear that this last community stronghold is under threat. Outside the tourist season, there just aren't enough people to keep it viable. It's ironic that the post office and the monument, a pyramid of cemented stone that would look more at home in Milton Keynes, should stand cheek-by-jowl. One symbolises the essence of community life, the other is an epitaph to a system of land use that has emptied, and continues to seriously damage, the very fabric of the land.

We've had the sheep, we've had the sporting estates. The sheep only now survive because of huge subsidies – it costs every one of us £30 a year in tax to keep the industry alive, and the sporting estates are rapidly falling into the hands of foreigners, the majority of them extremely wealthy, who have little commitment to local communities other than keeping on one or two stalkers' jobs. Is it not curious that if you wanted to buy a 10 acre croft you would be confronted by bureaucracy of nightmare proportions, but if you wanted to buy a 30,000-acre sporting estate all you have to do is hand over the cheque? No questions asked.

Of greater concern is that the sheep, and to an even greater extent the deer, are destroying the very landscape that we hold precious, the landscape that is the future saving grace of this country, the landscape of green tourism, the landscape that attracts walkers and climbers to the tune of hundreds of millions of pounds a year.

Recreation is now the major land use over the mountain areas of Scotland and, according to a report commissioned by the Highlands and Islands Enterprise, climbers and hill-walkers who go above 2,000ft/600m (the report doesn't take into account ramblers, lowland walkers or long distance backpackers) contribute almost £200 million to the HIE area economy. And yet such recreation does not enjoy the kind of priority in land use planning and policy that it so clearly deserves. It's apparent that Scottish Natural Heritage, the government's countryside watchdog in Scotland, doesn't recognise the importance of recreational use either for there is no representative of any of the recreational user groups on its main board, or area boards. This is, at least, a short-sighted policy. At its worst it's an indictment of an organisation that bases its decisions solely on economic or scientific grounds, at the expense of philosophic, aesthetic or recreational grounds.

Politically, we still value land in the UK more or less solely on economic grounds, an attitude that falls in line with our anthropocentric Judaeo-Christian heritage that claims man has been given dominance over all the beasts of the land, the fish of the sea and every living thing. How much more rewarding it is to consider the root of that word 'dominion' as *dominus*, which literally means a caretaker in the house, or a steward of the land. Only then might we be able to understand the wisdom of the ecologist Aldo Leopold who wrote: "We abuse the land because we regard it as a commodity belonging to us. When we see the land as a community to which we belong, we may begin to use it with love and respect."

That statement lays the foundation for Leopold's Land Ethic and I would suggest that here in the UK we desperately need to develop a similar land ethic of our own. We need a national mind-set change, a paradigm shift, that turns the role of Homo Sapien from the conqueror and owner of the land-community to an ordinary member and citizen of it. Such a land ethic simply enlarges the boundaries of, say, the Knoydart community to include the soils, waters, plants and animals as well. Put collectively, the community incorporates the land.

A Land Ethic reflects the existence of an ecological conscience and this in turn reflects an awareness of individual responsibility for the health of the land, that health being the capacity of the land for self-renewal. Conservation could then be defined as our efforts to understand and preserve this capacity.

But it seems to be that here in the UK we are still a million miles from being able to comprehend such an ethic, never mind adopt it, and the reason is simple. We continue to value land almost purely on economic grounds. Very few of us value land in an aesthetic or philosophical sense. The familiar argument is that people come first. After their problems have been sorted out we can perhaps enjoy the natural environment as some form of luxury goods. If that indeed is the answer, then the wrong question was asked. You see, when we ignore the aesthetic and philosophical value of land, or the spiritual value of land, we end up with the kind of situation that occurred on Skye when Macleod decided to sell the Cuillin.

A sense of belonging, a sense of kinship, rather than a sense of outright ownership is, I suspect, one that can be identified among many of us who walk or climb in areas like the Cuillin, or Knoydart, or one of the other wild areas of Scotland.

I remember the first time I sweated up the Great Stone Shoot from Coire Lagan, up to that narrow stance between Sgurr Mhic Choinnich and Sgurr Alasdair and then up to Alasdair itself. I remember trembling with the exertion and with excitement. I felt I had undergone a kind of rite of passage that had earned me my kinship with this marvellous mountain range.

The emotion was greater than ownership, deeper than ownership. I felt I had become accepted as part of the fabric of the mountains, of the land, part of that community that's made up from rock and light and air. And if we insist on defining such mountains by outright ownership then surely, by right of usage, by habitual resort, by unchallenged possession, by moral justification, if these mountains of the Cuillin belong to anyone, they belong to the mountaineering fraternity of the world.

But by the same token, the indigenous Gaelic population of Skye can make a similar claim to moral ownership. Didn't their bard, Sorley

Maclean, describe these Cuillin crags as "the mother-breasts of the world, erect with the universe's concupiscence"?

Here lies the very heart of Gaeldom, "white felicity of the high-towered mountains", beckoning the Gaels to their homeland.

I have to confess that from my narrow mountaineering and hill-walking perspective I was ignorant of such a cultural claim on the Cuillin until I spent a week walking through these mountains with Donnie Munro, the former lead singer of the folk-rock band Runrig, now rector of the Highlands and Islands University. Donnie is also an accomplished artist, a bold supporter of the Gaelic language and a prospective politician. He grew up with this landscape. As a youngster going to school he watched the Cuillin in all her moods and sometimes would be late because he just stood and stared at the wonder of it.

Donnie told me that that enduring image of the Cuillin landscape strengthened his love of the Gaelic language and was a foundation for his interest in the music and culture of the Western Highlands, indeed for his love of the landscape. They're all inextricably tied and I know that Donnie, like many others, finds it difficult to comprehend how one person can lay claim to a legal ownership of such an iconic monument as the Cuillin.

There are those privileged few in Scotland who would lay hereditary claims to such as the Cuillin as their ancient birthright but, in a modern Scotland, in a new visionary Scotland, don't we all share such a birthright: the mountaineers whose claim is in their habitual resort, the Gaels of Skye whose claim is in their culture and the spiritual qualities of their very being, and those who come, looking, looking and are uplifted and inspired by the splendour of such natural heritage?

But back to Mull. Even on this island of extravagant natural woodland the trees are in decline. I've often wandered through magnificent stands of pine, oak, ash and birch and one thing is noticeable by its absence – the growth of young saplings. I've also seen the ubiquitous deer fencing all over the place, bordering off squares and oblongs where everything within survives and everything without gets eaten. What sort of landscape will that produce in the future? I'll tell you. The same blocks and serried ranks as the conifers and the lodgepole pine that are so despised.

And yet paradoxically, at SNH's own reserve at Creag Meagaidh we already see the first fruits of a ten-year-old vision. Instead of building fences round the woodland areas the deer numbers have been drastically cut and now the woods are looking healthy, the undergrowth is rich, regeneration is assured and the deer that remain are bigger and healthier than their neighbours. Every landowner in Scotland should visit that reserve and learn its lessons.

But they won't. Old habits die hard and short-termism still rules. We continue to perpetuate the myth that the anachronistic sporting estates provide the life blood to our small rural communities and without them the Highlands will die. Tell that to the young postmistress at Lochbuie on the Ross of Mull.

Abbey, Edward, *Desert Solitaire*, McGraw-Hill, 1968: probably the best of Ed Abbey's books in which he captures the very essence of desert life during three seasons as a park ranger in south-east Utah. It's the anguished cry of a man challenging the growing exploitation of wilderness.

Barcott, Bruce, *The Measure of a Mountain,* Sasquatch Books, 1997: a superb celebration of Mount Rainier in the Pacific North-West of the USA. A lyrical account of one man's ambitions to stand on the summit of this, Seattle's own mountain.

Bartlett, Phil, *The Undiscovered Country*, The Ernest Press, 1993: a bold and fascinating attempt to look beyond the dreams and aspirations of mountain lovers to ask the simple question 'what is the attraction of hills and mountains and why should we want to climb them?'

Brown, Hamish, *Hamish's Mountain Walk*, Gollancz, 1978, republished with *Climbing the Corbetts,* by Bâton Wicks, 1997: the much-loved narrative of the first non-stop round of Scotland's Munros. The original Munrobaggers' guide.

Brown, Hamish, *The Last Hundred,* Mainstream, 1994: a series of essays on the hills of Scotland which ask some intriguing questions about how we look after our wild places.

Charlesworth, Edward, and Nathan, Ronald, *Stress Management,* Souvenir Press, 1982: the authors believe if you can identify the cause of your stress you can channel the tension into a positive source of energy.

Chatwin, Bruce, *The Songlines*, Picador, 1987: an amazing account of travelling with the native people of Australia, by one of our finest travel writers.

Cooper, Adrian, *Sacred Mountains*, Floris Books, 1997: another book that asks the eternal question 'why do we climb mountains?' Cooper looks specifically at the sacred in mountain experiences, where many have met a spiritual dimension that has often changed their lives

Craig, David, *Landmarks*, Jonathan Cape, 1995: David Craig is a man with a heart for the land. This book examines the significance of great rocks, cliffs and outcrops and the influence they have over those who climb them or live near them.

Crumley, Jim, *A High and Lonely Place*, Jonathan Cape, 1991: a radical look at the Cairngorms and how we have failed to protect this, the most important environmental site in the UK.

Csikszentmihalyi, Mihaly, *Flow, The Psychology of Optimal Experience,* Harper and Row, 1990: an amazing investigation into how we can focus our concentration so much we become completely absorbed in the activity. The author calls this state of consciousness 'flow'.

Drummond, Peter, *Scottish Hill and Mountain Names*, Scottish Mountaineering Trust, 1991: a must for anyone interested in the mountain names of Scotland. A fascinating piece of research that also includes phonetic pronunciations of all the Gaelic names.

Emerson, Raph Waldo, *Nature,* Beacon Press, first published 1836: an illuminating essay on the natural world by one of America's foremost philosophers.

Firsoff, V A, *On Foot in the Cairngorms*, Chambers, 1965: a delightful and evocative celebration of the Cairngorms with some excellent descriptions of wildlife, geology and flora.

Fletcher, Colin, *The Complete Walker,* Knopf, 1984: the most amusing, instructive and sensible how-to-do-it book on backpacking I've ever read.

Fletcher, Colin, *The Man Who Walked Through Time,* Knopf, 1968: an account of the first foot traverse along the length of the Grand Canyon. Packed with wisdom and inspiration. The finest outdoor book I have read.

Fletcher, Colin, *River*, Knopf, 1997: Fletcher's latest offering takes to the water of the Colorado River as he follows it from source to mouth, first by backpacking to the source then, when the water became deep enough, by inflatable raft to the sea.

Fletcher, Colin, *The Thousand Mile Summer,* Knopf, 1964: everything by Fletcher is good. An account of a summer walking the length of California through desert heat and mountain cold.

Gifford, Terry (ed), *John Muir – The Eight Wilderness-Discovery Books*, Bâton Wicks, 1992: everyone should read Muir. It should be taught in schools and politicians should be regularly tested on Muir's prophetic acclamations.

Gifford, Terry (ed), *John Muir – His Life and Letters and Other Writings*, Bâton Wicks, 1996: fascinating insights into the character of this Scot who became the father figure of modern ecology.

Good, Cherry, *On The Trail of John Muir*, Luath Press, 2000: a useful *potpourri* of Muir's life. Some original and fascinating observations.

Gordon, Seton, *Highways and Byways in the West Highlands*, 1935, republished by Birlinn, 1995: a classic work. Gordon is one of the great outdoor writers of the 20th century. A walker, naturalist and piper he straddles the worlds of the recreational hill-goer and the professional naturalist.

Hepworth, James R, and McNamee, Gregory (ed), *Resist Much, Obey Little – Remembering Edward Abbey*, Sierra Club Books, 1996: Edward Abbey seen through the eyes of his friends, colleagues and fans. The title is a good summation of the man's attitude to life.

Jardine, Ray, *Beyond Backpacking*, Adventure Lore Press, 1999: the seminal work on ultra-lightweight backpacking by a modern day guru of the art.

Leopold, Aldo, *A Sand County Almanac*, Oxford University Press, 1949: the book in which Leopold sets out his ideals for a land ethic. Should be read by every student of landscape.

Lopez, Barry, *Arctic Dreams*, Picador, 1987: a poetic and visionary account of several trips to the Arctic regions by one of America's finest outdoor essayists.

MacGill, Patrick, *Children of the Dead End*, 1914, republished Birlinn, 1999: a classic account of life on the road in the early part of last century and in particular the gruelling descriptions of what life was like during the creation of the Blackwater Reservoir near Kinlochleven.

McOwan, Rennie, *Magic Mountains*, Mainstream, 1996: a superbly-researched collection of tales of odd happenings in the hills. Not a book to be read when solo backpacking on long, dark, winter nights.

Mayne, Michael, *This Sunrise of Wonder*, Harper Collins, 1995: a deeply moving account of how the author came to unify his outer and inner worlds, the ordinariness and yet the extra-ordinariness of everything. Passionate and overflowing with wisdom.

Murray, William H, *Mountaineering in Scotland* and *Undiscovered Scotland*, J M Dent and Sons, 1947 and 1951, republished in collected form by Diadem, in 1979: the books which launched several thousand mountaineering careers. Classic accounts of pre-war mountaineering and hill-walking expeditions in Scotland written by Scotland's most articulate mountain writer.

Nash, Roderick, *Wilderness and the American Mind*, Yale University Press, 1967: what does wilderness mean to the American nation? According to this fascinating book it's meant different things at different times. A wonderful history of wild land protection in a country that probably does it better than anywhere else.

Perrin, Jim, *Spirits of Place*, Gomer, 1997: a powerful collection of essays, mostly on Wales, that describe the spirit of the people and the places held dear by the author, Britain's finest outdoor writer – by far.

Reid, Robert Leonard, *The Great Blue Dream*, Hutchinson, 1992: what's the affinity between the mountaineer and the mystic? This book confronts the question head-on.

Reynolds, Kev, *The Walkers' Haute Route*, Cicerone Press, 1997: guide book to the Chamonix to Zermatt route, written with a joy and passion that is infectious.

Schaffer, Jeffrey P, *Yosemite National Park*, Wilderness Press, 1995: full of facts, full of information. A must for any visitor to this incredible landscape.

Selye, Dr Hans, *Stress Without Distress*, Hodder and Stoughton, 1974: how we can turn stress into a positive factor in our lives.

Shepherd, Nan, *The Living Mountain*, Aberdeen University Press, 1977: a hard-to-find celebration of the Cairngorms that contains some of the most insightful observations on these mountains I've ever read.

Snyder, Gary, *Mountains and Rivers Without End*, Counterpoint, 1996: Snyder is probably the poet laureate of the American ecology movement. This epic poem was initially inspired by East Asian landscape painting and the author's experience within "a chaotic universe where everything is in place".

Snyder, Gary, *The Practice of the Wild*, North Point Press, 1990: a collection of essays which form a far-sighted articulation of what wildness and grace mean, using outdoor lessons to teach us how to live.

Thoreau, Henry David, *Walden*, first published by Ticknor and Fields, 1854: Thoreau's account of back-to-basics living. A wise, well-loved classic.

Thoreau, Henry David, *Walking*, Beacon Press, first published 1862: Thoreau's endearment to the world was 'simplify, simplify'. We can do that by walking…

Townsend, Chris, *The Backpackers Handbook*, McGraw Hill, 1991: a modern how-to-do-it manual by Britain's most knowledgeable and prolific long distance backpacker.

Townsend, Chris, *The Munros and Tops*, Mainstream, 1997: an account of the first continuous traverse of all Scotland's Munros and Tops.

Watson, Adam, *The Cairngorms*, Scottish Mountaineering Trust, 1982: the best of all the Scottish Mountaineering Club District Guides, written by the country's foremost authority on the area.

Watson, Adam, and Thompson, Desmond Nethersole, *The Cairngorms*, Collins, 1974: wonderfully authoritative work on the Cairngorms, landforms, flora, fauna and birds.

Weir, Tom, *The Scottish Lochs*, Constable, 1970: a superbly-researched description of Scotland's major lochs and many of the hills that rise beside them.

Weir, Tom, *Weir's World*, Canongate, 1994: the autobiography of one of Scotland's best-loved and much respected mountaineers.

White, Graham (ed), *Sacred Summits: John Muir's Greatest Climbs*, Canongate Books, 1999: was John Muir the greatest mountaineer of his day? This collection of essays would suggest he was, and more besides.

Wilson, E O, *Biophilia*, Harvard University Press, 1984: an eloquent statement of the conservation ethic. Wilson claims biophilia is the essence of our humanity, a state that binds us to all living species.